Rhetorics of the Americas

Rhetorics of the Americas

3114 BCE to 2012 CE

Edited by
Damián Baca
and
Victor Villanueva

palgrave
macmillan

First published in 2010 by
PALGRAVE MACMILLAN®
in the United States—a division of St. Martin's Press LLC,
175 Fifth Avenue, New York, NY 10010.

Where this book is distributed in the UK, Europe and the rest of the world,
this is by Palgrave Macmillan, a division of Macmillan Publishers Limited,
registered in England, company number 785998, of Houndmills,
Basingstoke, Hampshire RG21 6XS.

Palgrave Macmillan is the global academic imprint of the above companies
and has companies and representatives throughout the world.

Palgrave® and Macmillan® are registered trademarks in the United States,
the United Kingdom, Europe and other countries.

ISBN: 978–0–230–61903–6

Library of Congress Cataloging-in-Publication Data

Rhetorics of the Americas : 3114 BCE to 2012 CE / [edited by]
Damián Baca and Victor Villanueva.
    p. cm.
Includes bibliographical references and index.
ISBN 0–230–61903–7
    1. Rhetoric—History. 2. Persuasion (Rhetoric)—Political aspects.
3. Persuasion (Rhetoric)—Social aspects. 4. Persuasion (Rhetoric) in
literature. 5. Language and culture—History. 6. Indians of Central
America—Languages—Discourse analysis. 7. Indians of North America—
Languages—Discourse analysis. 8. Indians of South America—
Languages—Discourse analysis. I. Baca, Damián, 1975– II. Villanueva,
Victor, 1948–

P301.R4726 2010
808'.0097—dc22   2009023412

A catalogue record of the book is available from the British Library.

Design by Newgen Imaging Systems (P) Ltd., Chennai, India.

First edition: January 2010

10 9 8 7 6 5 4 3 2 1

Printed in the United States of America.

Transferred to Digital Printing in 2010

We have dreamt our past and we remember our future.

Cumbre Continental de Pueblos y Nacionalidades
Indígenas de Abya Yala. Iximché, Guatemala

Nuestro indio vive todavía: en lo físico, los sentimientos de nuestra gente, la bondad, y la toponomía.

Our Indian still lives: in the physical, the feelings of our people, the kindness, and in the toponymic.

Rafael González Muñiz, in a speech delivered
at Roberto Clemente Middle School,
New Haven (Trans. V. Villanueva)

CONTENTS

PREFACE

. . . we must interlace a number of colors without them becoming grotesque or antagonistic, and we must give them brightness and a superior quality, just the way our weavers weave. A "guipil" shirt brilliantly composed, a gift to humanity.

—Rigoberta Menchú Tum

This book is the first work to begin to fill a gap: an understanding of discourse aimed to persuade, rhetoric, within the Pre-Columbian Americas; that is, in presenting the rhetoric that coincided with but was not influenced by Greco-Roman inventions. *Rhetorics of the Americas* provides glimpses into what those indigenous rhetorics might have looked like and, of equal importance, how their influences remain. In his 1999 keynote address to the primary organization for the study of rhetoric and writing in the United States, the Conference on College Composition and Communication, Victor Villanueva pointed to the need for rhetoricians, scholars of the history of literacy, and teachers of writing to examine rhetorical productions indigenous to the Americas, noting the distinctions and overlaps of the study of language use recorded by the Spanish missionaries who had accompanied the Conquistadors and the canonical understanding of rhetoric developed by ancient Athenians and Romans. Since that address, younger scholars have taken the call. Yet to date these ventures into an understanding of rhetorical practice before Conquest have remain scattered. America—in the continental sense—is hardly featured on the map of Rhetoric and Composition studies. This book provides the first collection of original research and scholarship on uniquely Western Hemispheric rhetorics. Such a study should cause readers—students and academics alike—to recognize "the invention of the Americas," providing other ways of seeing the consequences of racialization, occupation, and colonization, providing historicized perspectives of the West and of the "Discovered West," telling us a great deal about material life prior to contemporary capitalism, telling us about the global from long ago to current global capitalism. Bringing together scholars from Rhetoric and Composition studies, American Indian studies, Mesoamerican and Latin American studies, Ethnic studies, and Comparative Spanish Literatures, among other disciplines, this book is the drop that will ripple, creating all new lines of inquiry into understanding language use within the Americas and those uses' ties to genocide, conquest, and cultural survivance.

Damián Baca

Threaded
Project
— All projects
rely on
each other

ACKNOWLEDGMENTS

We are indebted to all Indigenous peoples of Americas and the land upon which our contributors' universities and colleges are built: Anishinaabe, Coeur d'Alene, Hawai'i Maoli, Haudenosaunee, Huron Potawatomi, Illiniwek, Ottawa, Pascua Yaqui, Saginaw Chippewa, Tohono O'odham, Wintun, and Ysleta del Sur Pueblo.

The editors would also like to thank those who have offered support and inspiration for the scholarship in this collection: Linda Martín Alcoff, Joyce Rain Anderson, Loyola Bird, Resa Crane Bizzaro, Rosario Carillo, Ginny Carney, CCCC/NCTE American Indian and Latina/o Caucuses, Lucha Corpi, Ellen Cushman, René Agustín De los Santos and the Latin American Rhetoric Society/Sociedad Latinoamerican de Retórica, Enrique Dussel, Larry Evers, Cheryl Glenn, Patrisia Gonzales, Lewis Gordon, P. Jane Hafen, Gordon Henry, Ku'ualoha Ho'omanawanui, LeAnne Howe, Ronald Jackson, Susan Jaratt, Rhea Lathan, Aurora Levins Morales, Adela Licona, Carol Lipson, Andrea Lunsford, Scott Lyons, E.A. Mares, Demetria Martinez, Walter Mignolo, Devon Abbott Mihesuah, Terese Guinsatao Monberg, the Native American Literature Symposium, Susana Nuccetelli, Estevan Rael-Gálvez and the National Hispanic Cultural Center Foundation, Debbie Reese, Elaine Richardson, Roberto Rodriguez, Jacqueline Jones Royster, Geneva Smitherman, C. Jan Swearingen, Luci Tapahonso, Silvio Torres-Saillant, Morris Young, Ofelia Zepeda, and former NCTE employee Dr. Sandra Gibbs.

CHAPTER ONE

te-ixtli: *The "Other Face" of the Americas*

DAMIÁN BACA

Are uxeʻ ojer tzij
waral Kʻicheʻ ubʻiʻ.
Waral
xchiqatzʻibʻaj wi,
xchiqatikibʻaʻ wi ojer tzij,
utikaribʻal
uxeʻnabʻal puch rnojel xbʻan pa
ramaqʻ Kʻicheʻ winaq.

This is the root of the ancient word
of this place called Quiché.
Here
we shall write,
we shall plant the ancient word,
the origin
the beginning of all what has been done in the
land of our people.
                                   —*Popol Vuh*, Chapter 1

The Americas continue to contain the legacy of classical colonialism and remain tied to the economic dependencies of neocolonialism, so that the "post" of postcolonialism reflects more of a wish than a reality for too many of the Western Hemisphere. Since the time of Columbus, colonial agendas and policies have engendered their own rhetorics of justification and explanation. European modernity presumed a universal hegemony over political ideology, cultural meanings, and historical narrative. This legacy can be heard today in the discourses of "advanced/primitive," "development/underdevelopment," "modern/premodern," or "citizen/alien," terms that organize geopolitical locations by their purported relationship to the vanguard narrative of Occidentalism. But rhetorical traditions of the Americas and the Caribbean evidence a rich discourse of critique of Anglo- and Eurocentric ideologies. In a real sense, modernity begins with the encounter of the "New World" and the creation of a new "Other Within," so that rhetorical practices of the Americas stand in a unique position vis-à-vis the development of that modernity—and its concomitants of colonialism, of racialized subjectivities, of the crisis of European reason, and of late global capitalism. Argentine liberation philosopher Enrique Dussel points out that the more recent metanarratives of Western thought—postmodernism, transnationalism, and globalization—are themselves still mired in an Occidental teleology that imagines European and Anglo-American cultures to be the sources of historical advance, theoretical transformation, and literary vision.[1] Conversations in Rhetoric and Composition Studies that engage in these topics need to take notice and understand this critique.

Intellectuals of the Americas from various arenas of social life—from community coalitions, to academic critique, to religion, to art and culture—have resisted the hegemonic power of colonial discourses in the aftermath of 1492. But what is effective resistance? How is resistance intertwined with modification and accommodation? What are the strategies of adaptation without assimilation? Is it effective to try to "prove" the humanity and rationality of colonized peoples? Can procolonial forces be convinced by rational argumentation? When might a "defense" of indigenous cultures become exoticism? Can effective forms of resistance be propagated from commercialized cultural productions (e.g., poetry and popular art)? Given that no indigenous community is today free from Euro-American influence, what kind of autonomy or self-determination is possible? To the extent that diasporic and other new forms of identity are the product of colonialism, what are the "identity politics" of decolonial resistance? If the claims of universalism made on behalf of Occidental macro-narratives are bankrupt, are we left only with "local histories" and particularist politics? In an era of late global capitalism, when colonial power and market fundamentalism are inseparable, what counts as effective rhetoric? Writers of this book consider such questions, exploring new and old rhetorical strategies of cultural resistance to colonial power.

In addition to these guiding questions, we must also consider the predicament of academics presuming to speak for indigenous communities. Who might be authorized to do so? From whom should Rhetoric and Composition scholars learn? Historian Devon Abbott Mihesuah advises, "Non-Natives must take care that the voice they hear actually is Native. Within the academy, numerous 'wannabees' and 'marginal' Natives with little connection to their tribes publish with the claim of writing from an 'Indian perspective.' "[2] Documented incidents of ethnic fraud and identity theft are serious matters. Grants, fellowships, conference travel awards, and even faculty positions, for example, are given to individuals with no connection or contact with the indigenous communities of which they claim affiliation. In place of restricting our attention to individual claims of indigeneity, perhaps we might consider a much larger collective of voices: which indigenous nations and communities recognize and claim these scholars as their own? We look forward to further interrogation of these pressing concerns.[3]

Ultimately, accounting for historically grounded voices and communicative practices promotes a more inclusive and historically sound theory of how rhetoric is and has been practiced across regions, cultures, and migrations unique to the Americas and the Caribbean. Accounting for such practices, further, provides more accurate understandings of how indigenous artists and writers have responded and continue to respond to imperialist teleology and Western expansion. Urging scholars away from sources that reinforce Eurocentric perspectives of Pre-Columbian history, this collection advances a revision of colonial images of the Americas that have continued over the last 500 years. Focusing on rhetoric outside of the dominant and virtually exclusive Greco-Latin canon, our contributors look to the practices and traditions unique to Mesoamerica, México, Guatemala, Peru, Boriquén, Hawai'i, and the U.S./México borderlands, among other places within the Western Hemisphere.

The timeline referenced in this book's title follows the Epi-Olmec/ Maya calendar, thereby evoking indigenous chronologies and cosmologies that our contributors engage. While the ancient 5,000 year calendrical cycle concludes in 2012 CE, the Epi-Olmec/Maya formation of time known as the Long Count certainly continues, just as temporal patterns and cosmovisions of indigenous world cultures continue to speak actively to the past and simultaneously to the present. Indigenous temporal patterns can have advantages over linear conceptions of Western history. The discipline's myopic rhetorical history marches across the planet from East to West, from ancient Athens to the present-day United States. But chronologies and knowledges emerging from the Americas potentially enact "new" possibilities. Grounding ourselves in the soil and soul[4] of our own continent invites dialogic situations for thinking between co-evolutionary and parallel cultural traditions, without the baggage of Western teleologies.

I imagine a hermeneutical shift that would locate the colonization of rhetorical production at the center of disciplinary and postdisciplinary thought. Moreover, to comprehend a plurality of rhetorical practices, I advance this book collection as a theoretical paradigm through which competing yet interwoven histories and theories of rhetoric are fore-grounded. This book is a textual site where divergent rationalities and memories converge, thereby inviting new ways to understand and per-form rhetoric, history, and subjectivity. These admixtures provide a new vantage point to theorize complex cultural legacies of rhetorical practice—especially those rhetorical ancestries that have been excluded and denied by the colonial imaginary of Rhetoric and Composition Studies.

In Nahuatl, a common language throughout the Valley of Mexico and beyond, *te-ixtli* means "other face."[5] During the aftermath of the first European Conquests in the mid-sixteenth century, Nahuatl speakers began using this expression to give voice to themselves, to the newly emerging hemispheric legacy of becoming the "Other Within" Western civilization. As the transnational colonial transfer of civilizing missions attempted to eliminate all Pre-Columbian ways of life, such expressions began to materialize. *Nepantla*, another Nahuatl concept, refers to the interspace of feeling in between,[6] the unique epistemolog-ical and textual spaces created between Indigenous, Iberian, and neo-African traditions. This book looks to the "other face," the alterity of the Americas, the underside of Western Hemisphere, and the survivors of global colonialism.

Despite well-established Western feminist, neo-Marxist, and post-modern critiques of the Greco-Latin canon, Rhetoric and Composition scholarship has yet to engage in sustained investigations of communi-cation practices among cultures unique to the Americas. For Athenian and Roman rhetoricians such as Aristotle, Cicero, and Quintilian, rhetoric was confined to speech acts aimed at persuading in political, forensic, or ceremonial environments. This edited collection, however, recognizes that every communicative act is tied to rhetorical produc-tion, and as such works to influence specific audiences to some action whether material or epistemological. Expanding the Greek-specific *Rhetorike* to include Pre- and Post-Columbian cultures of the Americas poses numerous methodological obstacles. In *Mestiz@ Scripts, Digital Migrations, and the Territories of Writing* I address this very concern. The Pre-Columbian Americas cannot be conceived as having Athenian *Rhetorike*, yet conceptualizing the Americas as having lowercase "alternative rhetoric" presents a colonial negation. This is the problem with the concept of *Rhetorike* once we move across cultural borders. On the one hand, *Rhetorike* supposedly belongs to the West; on the other hand, lowercase and pluralized "rhetorics" are something that the Americas might have as objects to be studied under Western eyes. In either case, Western categories work to predetermine and fossilize the terms of debate.[7]

If the culturally provincial concept of *Rhetorike* is indeed the historically unavoidable point of origin, I propose the enactment of "thinking between" multiple means of identification, between the colonizing West and *te-ixtli*, the "other face" of the Americas. Crossing between comparative and conflicting communicative strategies creates symbolic spaces beyond the mere coming together of two halves. The strategy implied here involves thinking between the hierarchical tensions of Western and American traditions to embrace different ways of knowing and communicating, where individual and collective expressions merge.[8] I have no investment in naïve attempts to reconstruct "authentic" Pre-Columbian epistemologies, and thus I cautiously defend the application of the term "rhetoric" while remaining attentive to potential colonial dangers in doing so, dangers that speak directly to current debates on globalization, empire, and assimilation. Contemporary problems related to scenarios of neoliberalism, transnationalism, migration, social movements, and cultural hybridity, moreover, cannot be appropriately analyzed without an understanding of the Americas. In this spirit, I now offer a brief chapter overview.

In "Rhetoric of the First 'Indians': The Tainos of the Second Voyage of Columbus," Victor Villanueva opens the collection by looking to the first indigenous peoples of the Western Hemisphere that Columbus met, the ones he renamed "Indians," the Taínos of the West Indies. The Taínos of the Greater Antilles thus became the first colonized people of the Western Hemisphere, with Puerto Rico remaining a colony to this day, perhaps the world's oldest continual colony (although serving several colonizers: the Island-Carib people of the Lesser Antilles, the Spanish, and the U.S. Americans). Yet because of a widely held belief dating to 1540 CE that the Taínos of Puerto Rico (Boriquén) had been exterminated, nothing is known of the rhetorical ways of the original habitants of the island of Puerto Rico. But Villanueva asserts that there are ways of coming to understand these rhetorics. With the second expedition to the "New World," Columbus was accompanied by Dr. Diego Alavarez Chanca, the physician to Isabela and Fernando, and for this trip, the physician to "the Admiral" (Columbus). Dr. Alvarez recorded his eyewitness account of the ways of life of the inhabitants of Boriquén. These accounts were then supplemented by the writing of the well-known Fray Bartolomé de las Casas, whose father had also been on Columbus's second voyage. Eight years after the second voyage, Columbus commissioned Fray Ramón Pané to return to Boriquén (whose name had been changed to la Isla de San Juan Bautista). Fray Ramón's charge had been to record the language of the indigenous of the island. It was not until 1508, with the arrival of Ponce deLeón, that the island was occupied by the Europeans, thereby beginning the radical change in the language and rhetorics of the Taíno (with the renaming, yet again, of the island to Puerto Rico in 1521). Using the work of linguists whose studies of the language and language roots of the Taínos go only as far back as 1965 and the detailed notes of the first linguist, Fray Ramón, and the first ethnographers, Dr. Alavarez Chanca and Fray Bartolomé, Villanueva provides a first glimpse into the rhetorics of the original inhabitants of the world's oldest colony and the Western Hemisphere's first named "Indians."

Following Villanueva, Erika Gisela Abad Merced shifts our attention to the ways in which rhetorics of nineteenth- and twentieth-century Puerto Rican nationalist leaders imitate the ongoing legacies of imperialism. Abad argues, specifically, that narratives of Puerto Rican national origin and origin stories of nation imitate the Judeo-Christian creation story. The propertied males imitate repressive authority figures while placing blame on secondary citizens, often women, for the nation's limitations. A focus on key nineteenth-century leaders and ideologies demonstrates the essentialist gendered supremacy within dominant narratives of nationalism. Abad questions how these rhetorics fail to address the psychological effects of oppression because of the dissident narratives that are silenced.

"Spanish Scripts Colonize the Image: Inca Visual Rhetorics" examines how sixteenth-century chronicles written by native Andean authors such as Guamán Poma de Ayala uncover systems of record-keeping and communication in the early colonial Andes that combine alphabetic writing and Andean *visual rhetorics*. Studying texts produced by early native authors of the Americas, Rocío Quispe-Agnoli explains how native authors were able to assimilate the European alphabet rapidly and to develop new textualizations of their cultures *vis-à-vis* a rich, sophisticated, and ongoing development of visual arts in the pre- and post-Hispanic Andean world. These chronicles lead Quispe-Agnoli to an exploration of the relationships between verbal and iconic textualizations found in the dialectics between Western practices such as alphabetic script, painting, sculpture, engravings, and maps and native Andean systems of information such as *quipus* and *tocapus*. Considering the dialectical nature of alphabetic script and Andean *visual literacies*, Quispe-Agnoli reviews two aspects of the rhetorical colonization of Andean societies: (1) the invasion of alphabetic writing in iconic images that depict the early colonial Andes by native authors and (2) the visual nature of alphabetic writing that is revealed in its contact with indigenous systems of communications from the Americas. In the early sixteenth century, European and Andean systems of communications made contact, opening spaces for hybrid textualizations. Examples of these spaces may be found in colonial Andean textiles, ceramics, coats of arms, public signs, and paper/ink. In addition, looking at the alphabetic script as a visual system of signs makes it equivalent to the Andean systems of communication and record-keeping. This approach to visual and verbal textualizations directly challenges the colonial myth that the Incas were a great but incomplete civilization because of their apparent lack of letters.

In "Translating Nahua Rhetoric: Sahagún's Nahua Subjects in Colonial Mexico," Cristián Roa de la Carrera examines fray Bernardino de Sahagún's compiling, collating, and translating of indigenous speeches as samples of Nahua moral philosophy within processes of cultural translation of indigenous rhetorical practices. These speeches came later to inform the development of classical Nahuatl employed by missionaries in sermons and devotional texts for purposes of evangelization. Roa de la Carrera explores the political implications that this study of indigenous rhetoric has within his larger encyclopedic project to produce an all-encompassing source on Nahua life and language and its application to the production of Judeo-Christian texts in Nahuatl. Readers are urged to consider the impact that cultural translation, and more particularly European appropriations of indigenous rhetoric and speech, had in the development of what scholars have termed Nahua Christianity, that is, Christian practice informed by Nahua subjectivity and cultural categories. Roa de la Carrera focuses on the displacements involved in the changing loci of enunciation between Nahua and Christian rhetorical performances to interrogate how cultural categories, beliefs, or forms of rhetorical entitlement are transformed through the process of appropriation and reinscription of linguistic and rhetorical practices. This work opens possibilities for rethinking how cultural translations of rhetorical practice might enable or foreclose various forms of agency and subjectivity, as well as how we are to assess the political and cultural implications behind such processes.

"Practicing Methods in Ancient Cultural Rhetorics: Uncovering Rhetorical Action in Moche Burial Rituals" asserts that when studying nonverbal cultural artifacts from beyond the Greco-Roman rhetorical traditions, scholars must listen to the embodied discourse in the ancient practices themselves to uncover the rhetorical actions of those very practices. Extending W. J. T. Mitchell's theory that images have a meta-language of their own, Laurie Gries contends that we can hear those artifacts speak to us if we listen close enough and that in the hearing we are able to render the terms with which we can begin to uncover rhetorical actions contained within the meta-language. To illustrate, Gries turns to ancient royal tombs of Moche elite rulers, tombs constructed on the northern coast of Peru between 100 and 800 CE. She describes the ritual symbolic construction of the burial chambers evident in the intentional placement of certain artifacts, such as human bodies, earthenware, and gold and silver ornaments. Gries argues that the tombs comprise a rhetorical genre containing tropes of *duality, concealment,* and *inversion.* The chapter ends with a caution on the degree to which rhetoricians can appropriate the purposes and meanings of these ancient rhetorical traditions, asking that we move slowly and carefully so as to let those traditions reveal their rhetorical function.

In "Rhetoric and Resistance in Hawai'i: How Silenced Voices Speak Out in Colonial Contexts" Georganne Nordstrom asserts that in a colonized locations such as Hawai'i, rhetorical strategies not easily identifiable in "classical" rhetorical frames have been employed as acts of resistance to dominant Euro-American discourse. While indigenous peoples have been most obviously oppressed and disenfranchised in Hawai'i, immigrant settlers brought in to work on the plantations also experienced marginalization. Thus Nordstrom examines the ways in which the three authors writing at different periods over the last 150 years in Hawai'i have consciously employed particular rhetorical strategies to disrupt colonial narratives of the dominant culture. Looking to *The Queen's Songbook* by Queen Lili'uokalani, the last reigning monarch of Hawai'i, Nordstrom points to the traditional Hawaiian rhetorical strategy of *kaona* in songs written during the last four decades of the nineteenth century to send messages of resistance to her people before and after the overthrow of the monarchy. Next, Nordstrom provides an analysis of Milton Murayama's *All I Asking for Is My Body*, written in 1959, which establishes a particular ethos by using Pidgin English—Hawai'i's creolized English—to affirm the experiences and identity of plantation-era immigrant workers in Hawai'i. This is followed by a discussion of Hawaiian scholar Noenoe Silva's 2004 *Aloha Betrayed: Native Hawaiian Resistance to American Colonialism*, which demonstrates how her book works rhetorically to resist the dominant discourse in both content and form—both her analysis of the ways Hawaiians used Hawaiian literary traditions to resist the encroachment by Western settlers as well as her own act of writing about these forms of protest as resistance. Particularly in colonized locations, the kinds of resistance recognized in Western epistemological frames, the essay or physical protest for example, can be impossible either because of the fear of physical violent repercussions or because cultures operating within ideological frames other than the dominant traditionally negotiate resistance differently.

Damián Baca's "Rhetoric, Interrupted: La Malinche and *Nepantlisma*" proposes decolonial possibilities of La Malinche, Hernan Cortés' sexual slave and translator. La Malinche, more accurately known as Malinalli and Malintzin Tenepal, has become a dominant historical figure of sexual betrayal and Christian assimilation, placed at the center of the defeat of the Aztec empire. Baca builds upon Chicana and Chicano scholars who have reinvented Malinche as an empowering symbol of agency and resistance. In this context, Malinche's rhetorical exchanges of intermediacy and border crossing may be intertwined with *Nepantlisma*, the Nahuatl articulation of being torn between ways and the space between two oceans. Baca synthesizes key movements and symbols that are enacted within colonial structures of power with attention to resistance and revisions of the hierarchical logic of imperial Christendom. Specifically, he examines how Malinche strategically employs both Aztec and Roman Catholic cosmologies, thereby signifying adaptation and survival—not betrayal—of Mesoamerican cultures. Presenting Malinche's *Nepantlisma* as rhetorical strategy provides a revised account not only of the practices at the time of the conquest, and before, but also of the evolution of mestizaje, a "gradual and cautious syncretism" that has been practiced ever since. This revised history reads both the differences and similarities that exist between Mesoamerican and European worlds.

There are but a few surviving examples of the Mesoamerican books of fate, the graphic texts that diviners used to understand time and the world of the supernatural entities that controlled it. The books of fate were deemed a threat to the religious aims of the Spanish friars, and they were among the first books to be burned. Unlike those that accounted for historical events, these books spoke of the "invisible world," or the world of "cosmic and spirit forces" (Hill Boone). The word *invisible* is central to the following chapter, "In Search of the Invisible World: Uncovering Mesoamerican Rhetoric in Contemporary Mexico," insofar as contemporary rhetorics of Mesoamerican cosmologies seek to make the invisible visible. The works Tracy Brandenburg discusses include the painting of the Martyrs of Cojonos, a portrait of two Zapotec martyrs who were beatified by Pope John Paul II in 2002. This portrait, which is currently displayed in the cathedral in Oaxaca City, appears to be a straightforward representation of the two men: they wear humble clothing and each carries a cross, illustrating their allegiance to the Catholic Church. The artist of this work, however, serves as a modern-day diviner, revealing layers of rhetorical meaning, including a reading that views the two martyrs as the deities Tezcatlipoca and Quetzalcoatl, each represented respectively by a small black and red circle in the center of each of their crosses. Much like the books of fate that illustrated the forces of the cosmos with rhetorics that concealed meaning, the Oaxacan artist obscures meaning as well. Brandenburg traces the painting from its commission to its reconfiguration for mass-consumption, where we find that the image has been altered so that the red and the black (a Mesoamerican metaphor for rhetoric) are replaced with a Spanish cross. The chapter illustrates how the struggle for symbols, souls, and writing systems persists, and that some books are still dangerous.

Building upon Brandenburg's chapter, Dylan A. T. Miner's "'When They Awaken': Indigeneity, Miscegenation, and Anticolonial Visuality" investigates the way in which visual practices of indigenous projects are always entwined in multiple discursive fields. Therefore, aboriginal visual rhetorics transgress the limitations of disciplinary knowledge and the coloniality of biological racism through a particular visual language. By focusing on visual rhetoric, Miner provides a critical analysis of the discourses of *mestizaje* (*métissage* in the Francophonie) and indigeneity, while critically looking at the efficacy of using racializing discourses to discuss cultural practices. Although migrating throughout the environs of Turtle Island (or Ixachilan in the Nahua), Miner pays particular attention to the rhetorical practices of the Chicana/o and Métis (Mixed-blood Canadian) communities. He approaches contemporary visual rhetorics among detribalized aboriginal populations and demonstrates the manner that the rhetorical arts function as an anticolonial device. Evoking the seminal texts of Frantz Fanon as well as Howard Adams and Taiaiake Alfred, Miner discusses the rhetorical strategies apparent in these objects and practices. Using indigenous methodologies and epistemologies, the chapter is divided into six sections based on the cardinal directions (east, west, north, south, underworld, and skyworld). Overall, Miner provides an investigation of contemporary indigenous visual rhetoric as a dialectic and dialogic site where colonialism may be confronted, disavowed, and overcome.

Laura E. Pérez' "Spirit Glyphs: Reimagining Art and Artist in the Work of Chicana Tlamatinime" advances an extensive discussion of Post-Columbian "hybrid spiritualities" and their decolonizing politics and aesthetics. Providing a rich interpretive framework, Pérez describes how indigenous Chicana artists invoke a culturally hybrid spirituality to challenge present-day forces of racism, bigotry, and misogyny. Such decolonial spiritualities make use of, and often radically rework, pre-Columbian Mesoamerican and other non-Western notions of writing/art/art-making, and they struggle to create liberating versions of familiar iconography such as the Virgin of Guadalupe and the Sacred Heart. Filled with representations of spirituality and allusions to non-Western visual and cultural traditions, Pérez shows how the work of these Chicana artists is a vital contribution to a more inclusive canon of rhetorical arts across the Americas.

Drawing from the U.S.-Mexico border of El Paso, Texas, and Juarez, Mexico, John Scenters-Zapico shares the results of a four-year study of the social, economic, cultural, and political factors that have shaped the ways 118 participants born between 1920 and 2001 have learned to use technology. The rhetorical notions of sponsors—those who teach, grant, and restrict access to an education involving technology—and gateways—the actual sites where people have access and learn technology—become critical in understanding how an array of exigencies influences who becomes electronically literate and where.

From U.S.-Mexico stories and data on literacy, literacy access, and border education gathered over the last four years by surveying and interviewing some of the 118 Latino/a participants, two important issues came to the forefront: gateways and sponsors are complex variables that shape how people here learn to become electronically literate. In addition, traditional formulations of gateway and sponsor are not as clear-cut as we may assume and are in need of expansion. Scenters-Zapico begins to shed light on how these Latino/as born between 1920 and 2001 learned and had access—or not—to electronic literacy sponsors and gateways over the last 79 years both in and around the Mexico-U.S. borderlands.

Finally, in the spirit of "in xochitl in cuicatl," the Nahuatl phrase for poetics, Rafael Jesús González closes this book collection with "Las Cobijas/The Blankets," a bilingual narrative that illustrates a wise humility that is at once matrilineal and material, born of a cuencentenary of difficult survival. Collectively, these chapters make the case that rhetorics of the Americas significantly challenge the vanguard narrative of Occidentalism. Beyond European modernity, a plurality of rhetorical strategies and points of origin are possible. Yet neocolonial powers continue to de-authorize the Americas within a largely unquestioned intellectual dichotomy in higher education: that of "high" and "low" theory. For example, "high" theories that inform "Classical Rhetoric" and "Modern Rhetorical Theory" hold an institutional and historical ethos that is denied to those of the Americas. Likewise, in rhetoric curricula at every level, the Americas hold little academic importance when placed next to modes of Athenian and Roman argumentation. Rhetoric and Composition's macro-narrative "from Ancient Greece to Modern America" continues to imagine the origins of rational thought and communication in the minds of Western thinkers. This foundational myth signifies a colonial supremacy that is incompatible with the very possibility of achieving cultural pluralities. At the same time, a mere inclusion of the scholarship in this book would only add to the content of an Occidentalist narrative and not reform the construction of the narrative itself. Even the very concepts of "alternative rhetorics" and "rhetorics of difference" are already embedded in the Anglo- and Euro-centered idea of modernity. Therefore, moves toward decolonizing the field's horizons, toward moving beyond its cultural and epistemological flaws, require rhetorical mediations that operate out of Western reason, mediations that originate from *te-ixtli*, from the voices, testimonies, communicative strategies, and perspectives of the colonized. These strategic moves not only affirm our own ideologies, cultural meanings, and historical narratives; but they also assert that the colonial foundations of the West and its presumptions of universal hegemony must be rethought and retold. These are the activities that may bring us toward "new" rhetorics and rhetorical inquiries across the Americas, the Caribbean, and beyond.

The *Popul Vuh*, possibly the oldest "book" in the Americas and the one that many understand as part of their collective ancestry, records that the Maya feared a scarcity of fire. A mid-sixteenth-century Quiché interpretation of the ancient text was more recently given an English translation:

And they did not have fire. Only the people of Tohil had it. He was the god of tribes which first created fire..."Ah, we have no fire yet! We shall die of cold," they said. Then Tohil said to them: "Do not worry! Yours shall be the lost fire that is talked of. Yours shall be what is spoken of as lost fire," Tohil said to them.[9]

Our often concealed, slow burn; *te-ixtli*, the "other face" of the Americas, will not perish.

Notes

1. See Dussel.
2. Mihesuah, 7.
3. We are naturally attentive to the lived experiences and perspectives of scholars with tribal enrollment and affiliation. See the Association of American Indian and Alaska Native Professors, Ellen Cushman, P. Jane Hafen, Gordon Henry, and Devon Abbott Mihesuah.
4. See Anzaldúa.
5. León-Portilla, 13.
6. See Anzaldúa, Baca, and León-Portilla.
7. Baca, Chapter 1.
8. Baca, Chapter 2.
9. Tedlock, 153.

Bibliography

Anzaldúa, Gloria. *Borderlands/La Frontera: The New Mestiza*. 3rd ed. San Francisco: Aunt Lute Books, 2007.

Association of American Indian and Alaska Native Professors. "AIANP Statement on Ethnic Fraud." Native Professor's Conference: Decolonization Redux. April 21–23. University of Wisconsin-Milwaukee. 2005. Available from: University of Wisconsin-Milwaukee, http://www.uwm.edu/~michael/nativeprofs/fraud.htm. (accessed April 16, 2009).

Baca, Damián. *Mestiz@ Scripts, Digital Migrations, and the Territories of Writing*. New York: Palgrave Macmillan, 2008.

Cushman, Ellen. "Toward a Rhetoric of Self-Representation: Identity Politics in Indian Country and Rhetoric and Composition." *College Composition and Communication*. 60.2: 2008.

Dussel, Enrique. *The Invention of the Americas: Eclipse of the "Other" and the Myth of Modernity*. Trans. Michael Barber. New York: Continuum, 1995.

Henry, Gordon. *The Failure of Certain Charms*. London: Salt Publishing, 2008.

León-Portilla, Miguel. *Aztec Thought and Culture: A Study of the Ancient Nahuatl Mind*. Norman: University of Oklahoma Press, 1990.

Mihesuah, Devon Abbott. *American Indigenous Women: Decolonization, Empowerment, Activism*. Lincoln: University of Nebraska Press, 2003.

Tedlock, Dennis, ed. *Popul Vuh: The Mayan Book of the Dawn of Life*. Trans. Dennis Tedlock. New York: Simon and Schuster, 1996.

CHAPTER TWO

Rhetoric of the First "Indians": The Taínos of the Second Voyage of Columbus

VICTOR VILLANUEVA

This isn't an essay, not a full-blown chapter. It is an opening, Introduction-Part-Two. It tells very little of the rhetoric of the first "Indians." We cannot know it, really. But this opening tells of the language, the memory that lives on, the people lost and nearly forgotten but for the language, and the people who call each other ¡Boricua!, memory of an Island's first name. And even in exile, victims of diasporic disappearance, we hold on to this identity. Some have said that we have a common language heritage with the Chican Ostionoid, the ancestors of the Chicanos; some say we have a common language with the Hopi and the people of the U.S. Southwest.[1] Maybe. But the language of Americans is tied to the language of the Taínos. We are—all of us of the globe these days—tied to the Taíno in our language. And as we enter into the influences of the peoples of this hemisphere, we must remember the first the Europeans met, kidnapped, enslaved, and announced as dead. These are my people.

The first indigenous peoples of the Western Hemisphere that Columbus met, the ones he named "Indians" were the Taínos of the West Indies, those of Hispaniola (which the Taínos named Haiti) in the first voyage, and those of Puerto Rico (Boriquén) during the second.[2] Columbus' second trip was a huge affair, with 17 ships and 1200 all-male passengers. Among those passengers was Dr. Diego Alvarez Chanca, the physician to Isabela and Fernando, and for this trip, the physician to "the Admiral" (Columbus).

Dr. Alvarez recorded his eyewitness account of the ways of life of the inhabitants of Boriquén. These accounts were then supplemented by the writing of Fray Bartolomé de las Casas, whose father had also been on Columbus's second voyage. Eight years after the second voyage, Columbus commissioned Fray Ramón Pané to return to Boriquén (whose name had been changed to la Isla de San Juan Bautista, in contemporary Spanish—Sanct Juan Baptista in the Spanish of the time). Fray Ramón's charge had been to record the language of the indigenous of the island. What follows relies on these documents.

What follows, then, is a brief story. It is drawn from research that traces the Taínos from their linguistic birthplace in the Amazons, where a proto-Arawakan language first appears, up through the continent now called South America, to the Northeast corner of South America, into the Antilles. There, several linguistic and cultural groups form: The Island-Caribs, the Eastern Taíno, the Classic Taíno, Western Taíno, and the Guanahatabey of Western Cuba. The Classic Taíno occupied the greater windward area of Cuba, all of Hispaniola, and Puerto Rico.

The stories are told of the people from what would be Florida escaping to the islands of their East. And that story appears true. Deep within the ground of the Greater Antilles are the remains of the Northern People and the remains of people of Africa. It is a commonplace that Columbus knew of African presence in the "New World." The Americans of the Southeast portion of what is now the United States and of Africans before the slave trade are a part of a story of this hemisphere. But it is not the story of the Taíno.

The language roots of the Taíno tell of a people of the Amazon basin. Biological remains tell also of features in common with the Taíno. The people who believe they were born of Sun and the Moon in a cave on the island of Hispaniola carried a word, *Shingu*,[3] which refers to the Amazon River. So a people of the Amazon ventured by the Río Negro, through the Casiquiare Canal, down the Orinoco River, eventually coming to the northeasterly tip of the continent, to a string of islands that Columbus would name The Eleven Thousand Virgins. The language of these people would be Arawak, and later, Lokono, the language of today's Guyana and Trinidad. Yet some would not stop there. They built boats of hollowed trees, *kanoa* in Taíno, took them up the islands, pass the Islands of the Virgins to Puerto Rico, Hispaniola, and Cuba, with a few venturing up to the Bahamas. And these people's language broke from the Arawak/Lakona and became Taíno, about the time of the break from BCE to CE, the time Europe marks as the birth of Jesus.

The people, Taíno, created a culture. There was an origin story: how the people were born in a cave, and how the guard of the cave fell asleep, failing to mark the dawn, and the sun took him away, and how others who left the cave to fish would be turned into trees, and the treeless place they called *sabána*, acquired trees, *jobos*, the fruit of the Island still, the ambarella in English. And there was a god, an immortal, invisible, whose name is Yúcahu Vagua Maorocotí. He was of no beginning and no end but who had a mother, Atabey. And Man is the first human creation; and some of the men tied Inriri to their bodies, birds that bore holes in tree trunks, so that their "branch" might be whittled and thereby become women. And since man and woman were fundamentally the same, both ruled, so that there was patriarchy and matriarchy, depending on who rose to *cacique* from the *nitaíno*, leader from those of the ruling class, a ruler of the group, some groups amounting to approximately 3,000 people on Boriquén. And heredity was marked by the line of women—sometimes matriarchal; always matrilineal. Men and women kept their hair long in back with bangs in front, and the men would wear a short skirt, as would the women after they married, and they'd decorate themselves with *cibas*, beads made of stone, tied to their arms and necks, and wear *guanines*, a golden crest worn by the cicique or smaller golden ornaments hanging from earlobes, the ears pierced when young.

The Taíno lived on fish and fruit and tubers and birds and lizards. And they grew squash and pineapple and peppers and cashews and especially, after yucca, *batata*, sweet potatoes. They would cook such things over a fire they called *barbacoa*. And on religious occasions, they would inhale *tabaco*, also called *cogioba*, and worship the god Yúcahu and Atabey, the god of the cassava and his mother.

They lived in organized communities called *yucayeques*. Round houses that would accommodate from fifteen to thirty of the common folk. The insides were decorated and contained alters to the gods, and their beds, made of cotton and hemp and palm, strung between poles. The beds were called *hamaca*. The cicique and his or her family were distinguished in having a rectangular home that opened into the town plaza—an open field, most often round, used for religious ceremonies, cultural events, and especially the game they called *batey*, played with a stick and a rubber ball. And when there would come the Center of Wind, the *huraca'n*, people would seek the caves, then return to rebuild and to continue.

And there were occasional wars, mainly against the Island Caribs, who would raid the Taíno, mainly to take their women, so that the language that had been Arawak becomes Igneri, a creole combining the language of the mainland and of the Taíno. But otherwise, the Taíno were a peaceful people. Their name, *taíno*, translating to The Good.

But Fray Ramón, recorder of the first Contact, tells that a cicique, consulting his *cemi*, his lesser god, had heard that the Good would be overrun and enslaved. And each time the Europeans came, they came by the hundreds, all of them men. And so we all became mestizo, and when the slaves died or moved inland and the African slaves were brought to the Island and the islands, we all became mulato. We are mulato, mestizo, Taíno.

First contact. From the diary of Dr. Diego Alvarez Chanca, 1493, as revised by Fray Bartolomé de las Casas, 1527:

On Thursday, the 14th of November, the Admiral stopped at another island which he called Sancta Cruz [St. Croix, today]; and he sent men ashore to capture some natives, and thus learn their language. They seized four women and two children, and, as they were returning in the rowboat, they encountered a canoe, which contained four Indians and an Indian woman; when the Indians realized that they could not flee, they, including the woman, began to defend themselves; they began to fire arrows, and they wounded two Christians, and the woman even pierced a shield with her arrow; the sailors crashed their boat into the canoe and overturned it; one of the Indians, who had not lost his bow, swam and fired his arrows with almost the same vigor as if he had been ashore. They saw that one of the Indians had his generative instrument cut off; the Christians believed it was so that he could grow fatter, like a capon, then the Caribs would eat him.... [F]rom there, he reached another large island, which he called Sant Juan Baptista, which we now call Sant Juan, and which, as we mentioned before, was called Boriquén by the Indians, in a bay of the island toward the west, where all the ships caught many kinds of fish....

Several Christians went ashore and walked to some houses that were very artfully made, although all were of straw and wood; and there was a plaza, with a road reaching from it to the sea, very clean and straight, made like a street; and the walls were of crossed or woven cane; and above, beautiful gardens, as if they were vineyards or orchards of orange or citron trees, such as there are in Valencia or in Barcelona; and next to the sea there was a high watchtower, where ten or twelve people could fit, also well made; it was probably the pleasure house of the lord of that island, or of that part of the island. The Admiral does not mention having seen any people there; they must have fled in fright when they saw the ships.[4]

And so myth is born out of ethnocentric anthropology: the good doctor and the loving priest interpreting a watchtower, a lookout for the *huraca'n* or the Carib invader, as a pleasure dome, unable to fathom a strong woman or a transgendered warrior, conferring the name of the ruthless on the region, the Caribs who were not cannibals of the sort that would castrate to fatten a meal, but who consumed the desired attributes of enemies—the heart of the courageous, the arm of the great marksman or markswoman. The region named after a small group of the ruthless when the region had been dominated by The Good.

And insofar as Taíno literacy was confined to the petroglyphic, we can know very little of their rhetoric. We can know that good was paramount—Taíno; that nobility was worshipped, *Boriquén* meaning land of the valiant and noble. We can know that their religion was not greatly different from Christian in important ways—an Adam, an immortal son of a virgin mother, woman born of man. We can know that they loved art and play and understood agriculture and horticulture. And we can know that their language lives—the yucca, tobacco, the hurricane, the canoe, the hammock, the potato, even baseball, likely. It is strange that we think of the baseball and the potato as English and Irish. But we know. The memory cannot be killed, even when the people are.

So Carol laughs the laugh of joy and not derision and says that even as I have the face of a European I have the body of a South American Indian. I used to get offended at that; somehow, the David or the Hercules my ideal; we are so much the victim of hegemony and internal colonialism. And then I discover the archeological, anthropological, and the linguistic record, and maybe she's right.

We are going to discover, in the pages that follow, the ways with words of those whom the Europeans "discovered." But this book, like this history, opens here, in the West Indies. In the home of my ancestors.

Notes

1. Rouse, 27–30.
2. All that is written here finds its sources in two collections: *The Puerto Ricans: A Documentary History* and *The Taínos: Rise and Decline of the People Who Greeted Columbus*.

3. There now exists two dictionaries of Taíno terms, one in English and one in Spanish. They are complementary, insofar as terms translated into English are not contained in the Spanish version, and vice versa. Words translated here, come either from the voyage records of Alvarez Chanca (through Fray Bartolomé), Frey Ramón, or the Dictionary. See "The Dictionary of the Spoken Taino Language."

4. Waggenheim and Jiménez de Waggenheim, 3–4.

Bibliography

Dictionary of the Spoken Taino Language, http://www.taino-tribe.org/tedict.html, accessed April 13–15, 2009.

Rouse, Irving. *The Tainos: Rse and Decline of the People Who Greeted Columbus.* New Haven, CT: Yale University Press, 1992.

Waggenheim, Karl and Olga Jiménez de Waggenheim, eds. *The Puerto Ricans: A Documentary History.* Princeton, NJ: Markus Wiener, 2006.

CHAPTER THREE

Imperialist Rhetorics in Puerto Rican Nationalist Narratives

Erika Gisela Abad Merced

In the Beginning

The Spanish arrived in the Americas looking for gold, looking to serve God, and seeking glory. Their mission had also been, in part, to maintain Catholicism's hegemonic stronghold in the New World. Catholicism remains one of the strongest bits of residue remaining from Spanish colonialism of the Americas. Although other forms of spirituality, religion, and Christianity are gaining numbers in Puerto Rico and among Puerto Ricans, there is the strong influence of Catholicism, its philosophy and ideologies that permeate throughout the rhetorics of political and cultural Puerto Rican nationalism. Part of what I will argue here is that rhetorics of nationalism for Puerto Rico are tied to the myths of Catholicism, in keeping with Barthes' conflation of the terms *ideology, myth,* and *rhetoric.*

Barthes argues that myth "has the task of giving an historical intention a natural justification and making contingency appear eternal" (142). In Kenneth Burke's terms, ideology can be conceived as "[a]n inverted genealogy of culture, that makes for 'illusion' and 'mystification' by treating ideas as *primary* where they should have been treated as *derivitive*" (104). Or, for the Athenian rhetoricians—delivering *nomos* as *physis.* Or—myth is ideological. In *Image-Music-Text* Barthes defines rhetoric as that part of ideology that signifies. In other words, ideologies, myths, and rhetorics enjoy symbiotic relations; they might even be synonymous. The myths of Catholicism, then, blend with the ideologies of imperialism to give rise to Puerto Rico's peculiar rhetoric of nationalism.

So this discussion of Puerto Rican nationalisms must begin in the beginning: the creation myth. The tree of knowledge has dual representations. For the Creator, it is the prohibition from which human creation, two first "citizens," cannot consume. For the serpent, it is the fruit that would bring a consciousness equal to that of the Creator. That is the myth. In the ideology (now tied to the natural, to the greatest of all Authority in the Spanish world) the Creator would be the colonizer, who arrives in what he perceives to be untouched territory, there to create the extension of his empire. The serpent would represent those who would attempt to resist the power of the creator/colonizer. From the perspective of the colonizer, the serpent would be the terrorist, the dissident, the noncitizen attempting to obtain rights.

The tree of knowledge and its implications in understandings of colonialism are significant precisely because of who/what has control of knowledge production, distribution, and the material realities that inform the possibilities/opportunities for contribution. In the introduction to *Third World Women and the Politics of Feminism,* Chandra Mohanty writes of the necessity to disrupt dominant histories. Attempts at rewriting history need to address "the significance of producing knowledge for our communities" (11). The relationship between the forbidden fruit, on the one side, and Eve, Adam, and the serpent on the other is important to consider in that the relation parallels the colonial relationship between the state, the Criollo elite, and the colonies' working class. The temptation, framed as the serpent's seduction that Eve and Adam could be equal to the Creator, can first be seen in the process of rewriting the narrative of a colonized group. The significance in rewriting is that the process rejects the cultural political status imposed on the colonized by the state. The rhetoric created in the creation myth and its parallel to colonialism deflects the argument that the colonized are inferior. They are blessed, the creation. The dichotomy constructed between the serpent's seduction and the Creator's unexplained ambiguous limitation is a reflection of extremities that are construed as the struggle between good (equated with the status quo) and evil (deviance from/resistance to the hegemonic). Such a construction at first comes off as almost absolute security and freedom: the edenic possibilities of intervention (and, later, industrialization), set against the desire for power. In nation-building projects, resistance to coloniality

is at times understood as a rhetoric of benevolence set against a rhetoric of banishment from the Garden. In the case of Puerto Rico, the
"choice" of continued dependence versus independence is framed by
the common topic of "example." Puerto Ricans are asked to look at
comparable territories, their neighboring Caribbean nation-states, and
to note those states' impoverishment and neocolonial condition. This,
for some scholars and political leaders in Puerto Rican history, explains
the unwillingness thus far to take of the tree. Puerto Rican political
status is linked to its material.[1] Globally and regionally, neighboring
Carib nations' banishment from the false security of colonial protection
acts as a politico-economic indicator of Puerto Rico's greater political
economic condition. It remains under the protection of a benevolent
Creator.

Factions of Puerto Ricans in Puerto Rico and U.S. diasporas still seek
the ideological possibilities of cultural separation.[2] Cultural nationalist
projects rewrite some aspects of the Puerto Rican narrative to demonstrate an idealized separate history, all the while taking the divergent
stands on the issue of Puerto Rico's status. In a reconfigured history,
independence does not mean "taking of the fruit"; rather, it marks an
appreciation for the access to luxury, material needs, military protection, democratic and capitalist rights that a relationship with the United
States appears to guarantee.[3] In short, accepting the status quo can be
equated with being conscious of the tree without performing the dissidence of an alternative consciousness the tree's fruit could provide.

In colonialism, the colonial state positions itself as the Creator. The
state defines and names in conquest; it writes a narrative that caters to
centering itself as a point of origin for civilization. Its creation serves
the purpose of extension without imitation. But the tree of knowledge
bears the fruit of dissent. The colonial state, in its conquered territory,
sets to create an extension of itself that will neither equal the power
nor the magnitude of the state. This new colony, however, caters to
the material and empire-building needs of the colonizer/creator. Any
attempt from the colonial territory to identify itself as equal to its colonizer is shunned.

The conqueror is the mediator between both territories and, in con-
quering and defining, is the carnal representation of the "perfection"
of the originator. He plays the role of an Adam in being the first to
name, define, and enjoy dominion (not an accidental term: Dominus
is Lord) over the new territory. In the generations to follow, however,
it is apparent that the criollo is not equal to the peninsular citizen.
This incites the need for separate nation-states among various colonies.[4]

Territories large enough and with sufficient economic resources fought and won wars for independence. Puerto Rican political leaders, however, sought only greater autonomy from Spain, seeing Spain as being able to provide Puerto Rico's sugar and coffee hacendados greater access to the world market.[5]

Then there is Eve within the rhetorics of power and nationalism. The linearity of the creation narrative—God's prohibition to the serpent and Eve's and then Adam's defiance of that prohibition—carries political economic implications, paralleling the historical narratives of sexual subordination and nation. While the first man, the first citizen, the criollo modeled after the colonizer, has the majority of kinds of rights afforded his creator, it is through the resistance of lesser bodies that he possesses and or emulates the desire for liberation, for a consciousness outside of what the colonizer created for him. It can also be seen in the attempt of nineteenth-century intellectuals to rewrite the indigenous into the Puerto Rican narrative.[6] It is the male who rewrites the narrative of a people because it is precisely the Christian model of linear creation that is imitated in the creation of a nation.

The Nation Thrives on Gossip

> Everybody talked about it...Most people...would have never known who Pedro Albizu Campos was.
>
> —Ramos-Zayas

Pedro Albizu Campos was arrested for sedition, a rhetorical crime, because of twelve speeches he delivered, because of the knowledge disseminated from his discourse (Villanueva). A man of color who gained legitimacy from his white father while Albizu was in his late teens, he had every opportunity to assimilate. He received his education from some of the best East Coast universities—the University of Vermont and Harvard. He served in the military and had achieved a certain level of socioeconomic mobility. It was not enough for him, however, to consent to what other Puerto Ricans had constructed as a "paradise": a codependent relationship with the United States.

Albizu is important in the conversation of knowledge production and distribution precisely because of who frames him and to what extent. He is also important because of the gendered and racialized continuity of knowledge production and distribution regarding the construction of the Puerto Rican nation. He fought for freedom for Puerto Ricans, a hybrid, mixed race people. He did so, however, by looking to Spain as a model, as the better example of a country to emulate than Puerto Rico's current colonizer. The hybridity he called for was a discursive one, a move that had started in nineteenth-century intellectual and political practices to call for a more autonomous relationship with Spain.

Discussions and debates on Albizu Campos, what he represents and what he has or has not contributed to Puerto Rican history, demonstrate the complexity of what one figure can represent. His iconicity and infamy also represent the significance of why discussions, gossip, and more specifically what Puerto Ricans understand as *bochinche* contributes to the dissemination of information and critical consciousness. A mentor had recently advised that I not pay attention to "bochinche." Bochinche, loosely translated, can mean either the act of or the message of gossip, which also includes scandals. Bochinche can have damaging effects. Its degraded, invalid social reputation, much like that of the serpent's speech to Eve, stems from the value placed on oral knowledge distribution. It also stems from the primary form of knowledge production and distribution that is based on such an exchange. The epigraph to this subsection is indicative of the greater significance Pedro Albizu Campos has as a nationalist icon among Chicago Diasporic Puerto Ricans. It also demonstrates the significance of conversation, gossip, and scandal in resurrecting a Puerto Rican pro-independence, successfully upwardly socially mobile, national prophet. Yet he remains tied to the rhetorics of Genesis, the Creator, the Colonizer, and the Subject/Colonized.

Albizu's narrative is important. His narrative reflects the American Dream as well as a personal necessity to resist lending consent to the very forces that had taken a toll on his community and on him. He also reflects that as much as a nation needs a collective literature, a unifying story, it needs icons that signify the story. He reflects the power of myth in that Barthian sense and how its evolution can inadvertently aid in the hegemony it seeks to challenge. Albizu might well have been a Hispanophile, complete with a disregard for race, the denial or at least silence concerning his apparent African ancestry, but that same rhetorical strategy—Puerto Rican unity by way of racelessness—lends itself to U.S. notions of white dominance. The denial of racialization and its hierarchy negates the anti-U.S. colonial rhetorics it seeks to produce. Racism is denied in the name of a Spanish Adam, Albizu-the-icon, but in the process, a white male dominance is maintained.

Frances Negrón-Muntaner, in "The Trauma of Literature, the Shame of Identity," discusses the significance of myth in Puerto Rican elite men's attempts to reconstruct the virility of the Puerto Rican citizen. Negrón-Muntaner argues that the trauma of colonialism is constructed by men who are at a loss, insofar as the dominion they once had having had been removed with the U.S. invasion. In constructing the same dominant narrative of a unified country, the men of 1898 were aiming to paint themselves as victims despite their continued repression of other bodies within the nation for which they were fighting. Schmidt-Nowara finds, using Scarano, that the masquerade of *jíbaro* status, of revolution from below, was an attempt to be more inclusive. Such representation, however, did little to challenge hierarchies of power concerning who made decisions regarding what independence from Spain would look like. Self-determination remained governed by an educated, land-owning elite.

The question of what comprised the Puerto Rican nation maintained the racialization and gender qualities of the nation. The nineteenth-century Puerto Rican educator and writer Eugenio María de Hostos stressed that a woman's education would be needed to better train men to be the leaders their respective nations needed. Women's education was not for women's autonomy or authority; rather, it would serve to maintain and reify male dominance. Although it can be said that Hostos was an advocate for women because he had said that women are more loyal and faithful to the nation, that they have greater capacity to reason, he was not, in the end, advocating for the possibilities of women's political leadership.

Albizu Campos's perception of women was more complex. He advocated for his wife to finish her professional career. He had women like Julia de Burgos and Lolita Lebron work alongside him in the New Progressive Party. Yet he would maintain that it was Puerto Rican motherhood that provided the "very insides" of nationality, circumscribing any diversity of roles for women in leading a new Puerto Rico. Elevation of women into significant roles remained framed within motherhood, women's sacredness paralleling the purity of a pre-Fall Eve. In Albizu's writings, women remained informed by repressive heterosexist forces, despite the active women leaders next to him who were advocating different treatment.

The iconicity of women such as Lola Rodriguez del Tio, Lolita Lebron, Maríana Bracetti, remains overshadowed by the narratives of men who have statues in their honor or large, pro-independence organizations and cultural centers named after them. This process of naming, of making place an effigy of man, writes a particular history that makes public figures on the condition of what the nation needs: the pure male who imitates key forces of power inherited by the male supremacy of colonialism.

Men[7] have a more vocal agency, so that their knowledge and testimonies are less likely to suffer the accusation of bochinche via the political protest for their preferred community. Their maleness grants them audience, pen, and paper. Their maleness assures that they will be remembered, resurrected, although it does not guarantee how or to what extent. It guarantees that their narrative, their immortality, will not be written in the shadow of their peers. Their histories may only be in the shadow of the originators from whom they inherited their ideology and practice. Like Adam and the male prophets of Christian text, their birth, emergence, and even their resurrections are imitations of the first man-as-ruler of the Christian origin story.

Puerto Rican elite male's attempt to write themselves as originator-figures and rulers has failed because the economic security that allows for writing, recording, and speaking is dictated by imperial forces. U.S. capital and the U.S. government control the subject's continued ability to negotiate with U.S. rule as well as negotiate how Puerto Rican men can imagine themselves as Adams. Albizu Campos was a veteran of the U.S. Armed Forces and a Harvard graduate. He could perform in the school system beyond the social limitations of his racial background and socioeconomic position. His ability to imitate the speech of the members of the dominant class granted him the ability to speak against them. Yet even as he spoke against them, he spoke with them, wanting similar Christian family values and its work ethic for his nation. The legitimacy of his argument mirrored the necessity for the legitimacy of his name, governed by a racialized class system that only afforded him recognition as a man. The family values he advocated as a man and leader were the family values that, as the son of a black woman, he himself had been denied. Denial of racial hierarchies speak specifically to the necessity to consent to how they informed his subject position as well as to the necessity to maintain the participation of those who longed for a greater connection to the valid imperial connection—Spain. Like men of color in the United States who currently seek assimilation, Albizu Campos had consented to a self-imposed racelessness in an attempt to celebrate humanity as "one race."

If one looks historically at whose narrative counts as Puerto Rican history, one will find that the Spaniards have always dominated discourse on its history. Puerto Rican history before U.S. intervention was the invention of peninsular and criollo elites. Part of the reason that any claim of indigenous history and or identity remains subject to negative critique stems from who has controlled the narrative and the proof of their existence. Indigenous intellectual and historical erasure inspires the romanticized and perfect image that is contemporarily constructed. Informal knowledge challenges ignorance of Puerto Ricans' reality as well as the dominant's educational disregard for localized histories.

Angel Rama, in the first chapter of *The Lettered City*, writes that the *letrado*, the intellectual, is slave and master to power (27). The intellectual of letters works in complacency even as he remains in control of systems of power and inequality. The intellectual of letters defines parameters and possibilities, all the while being defined by the state. Ironically, it is the intellectual who reproduces the state, Rama argues, because of the system in which he is educated and who pays for his labor. The intellectual outside of the walls of the lettered city, which during Spanish colonialism existed within centers of economic and political power, did not have agency. The way in which consciousness outside of that center was raised nevertheless relied on relationships with colonial and imperial centers. Puerto Rico and Puerto Ricans did not have a printing press until the nineteenth century. Nor did Spain ever establish a university system in Puerto Rico. Adam and Eve were to remain pure, not to be tainted by the tree of knowledge.

Tree of Knowledge: Root of Freedom?

The tree of knowledge and its repercussions must be measured against the role of gossip as a strategic form of knowledge distribution. Knowledge distribution would bring a consciousness to Adam and Eve that would endanger them. Yet the serpent stated that the eating of the fruit of the tree would make Adam and Eve as "knowing" as God. The state constructs consciousness in a similar vein: promoting ignorance as a form of freedom. Dissidence, questioning the discourse and work of a nation's head figure, is socially constructed as threatening one's own access to rights. Zayas's analysis of the multiple perceptions of Albizu Campos in *National Performances* demonstrates this. As much as it is understood that Albizu represents the American Dream and the possibilities of freedom, his dissent against the United States also constructs him as a criminal and a terrorist. This allows one to look at knowledge production and distribution as both the endangering and liberatory possibilities for a people. For Puerto Ricans, it is pending on how consciousness changes one's relationship with the nation(s) in question—both Puerto Rico and the United States.

Because Puerto Rico did not have a university, a center in which knowledge could be produced at its highest level, Puerto Rico's elite relied on other centers of education to obtain training. As much as intellect could be produced and polished within Puerto Rican borders, it remained to be validated outside of its territory. Much like Adam and Eve who ate from the tree of knowledge, Puerto Ricans had to leave to get their consciousness accredited. Then Puerto Rican criollo elite were able to return with that the knowledge attained as a form of power.

Colonial intellectuals, Rama's *letrados*, were slaves and masters of power. In serving the state and maintaining its hegemonic power, the intellectual elite were indebted to and dependant on the state to maintain their positions. Their dependency on the state for resources and validation, according to Rama, made the traditional intellectual a slave to power. In holding the ability to educate, and being able to produce and distribute the knowledge to be consumed, letrados also held a great deal of power, which makes them masters of power. Through documentary analysis and historiography, Rama examines the role of the intellectual center in maintaining social order for the Spanish empire. The development of the colonial intellectual has had various waves. Their development began with the formation of universities in larger Spanish colonial urban centers such as Mexico City, Lima, Bogota, Quito, or Cuzco Santo Domingo (Rama 29) and the continued migration back to colonizing center of empire capitals such as Madrid and Paris. The rise of capitalist markets, coupled with varied forms of knowledge and technology in the advent of nineteenth-century nationalism, informed how education and the state complemented each other. Remnants of technology and a more heavily institutionalized form of education, the university, influenced newly formed nations' international relations, relations which were interconnected to colonizers' capital investments within each colony. This power dynamic delegated the relative power that each new nation could wield. At the end of the nineteenth century and beginning of the twentieth, the intellectual elite/national bourgeoisie authorized who ruled and how. The traditional intellectual held a great deal of power; however, the growing dependence on technological advancement expanded the understanding of who could be considered an intellectual. This, in turn, slightly spread authority of who could define the parameters of state and social power.

The Lettered City succeeds in drawing out the linear formation of the intellectual as producer, laborer, and intermediary between the state and the people. The intellectual in obtaining education, also obtained state-legitimated tools to reproduce knowledge by way of rhetoric, philosophy, and other forms of discursive education. As laborers, the intellectuals' production value was based on the value others in his class placed on what he produced as well as the state's consent. As one who served the state as well as his students, the intellectual served as an intermediary between the state and the community, the area in which his lettered city existed. He also served as an intermediary between those who sought socioeconomic mobility through education, those who resisted the state, and the state itself.

The state, however, was not the only player or institution that controlled colonial power. Rama also discusses the relationship between the church's and the empire's state control. He alludes to the division of the two as counter forces through the development of both, with the intellectual being the key player in negotiations. The primary form of knowledge produced within the first lettered cities was that of Christian text. Catholic teachings and ideologies aided in the coercion and repression of Africans and the indigenous of the West. The written word, the ability to write, print and reprint, to distribute knowledge via education, law, scripture, lay with a select few who had to be perceived as good Christians to validate their existence within the lettered city. The lettered city connected the church and the state, the place in which both supported each other in their mutually beneficial projects. The Spanish monarchy, Rama explains, paid more "attention to higher education...Reading, as well as writing, was practically reserved to the letrados alone" (29).

Schmidt-Nowara, in *Conquest of History*, examines the decline of the Spanish empire through the legal and cultural formation of nation within the nineteenth century. Framing the decline of the Spanish empire through the nation-building projects of its colonies, Schmidt-Nowara's work fills the gap that Rama has left. Rama overlooked the Spanish Caribbean nationalist intellectual and political leader who sympathized with the legacy of Spanish colonialism. Schmidt-Nowara demonstrates that criollo elites used Bartolome de las Casas and Christopher Columbus to purify the legend of conquest reaffirming intervention and colonialism as positive elements to be celebrated. In response to Adam Smith's vision of empire, Schmidt-Nowara writes, "Spaniards responded vigorously by rejecting the emphasis on markets and profits and defending the putative civilizing mission of the Spanish Conquerors" (4). The heroes of colonialism, such as indigenous sympathizer Bartolome de las Casas and "visionary" Christopher Columbus, served simultaneously to maintain colonies' false connection to the empire as well as its disruption. The Spanish priest sympathetic to the Carib or Arawak people of Cuba and Puerto Rico, in contrast with the idealized vision of Columbus, poorly serves the inclusion of Cuba and Puerto Rico in Spain's national consciousness. Intellectuals on both islands sought to set themselves apart because of the limitations Spain had set on political representation and participation. They also worked to set themselves as culturally different from Spain—as Spain had denied criollos equal citizenship rights as those received by Peninsular Spaniards. The colony-based Spaniard, the criollo, stood outside of the cultural and political formation of Spanish identity. Spain grappled with self-definition in their attempt to establish themselves as better than the islands' inhabitants. They wanted to set themselves as perfection—like God—that islands' residents'—Adams and Eves— could never fully emulate.

Poomer to
Give in to
temptation of the
Flesh

Uncovering Origins

Puerto Rican intellectuals vary on their support of Spanish influences. According to Schmidt-Nowara, nineteenth-century intellectual Salvador Brau's historical writings on Puerto Rico praised certain aspects of Spanish colonization and the extermination of Boriquen's indigenous population. Brau marks the beginning of history with the beginning of conquest. How those on Boriquén perceived themselves and believed their origin to take shape did not matter to Brau. For him, history began with the European and continued under Euro-Hispano influences. The indigenous, and later the African, served to complement Eurocentrism.

Schmidt-Nowara examines how the "discovery" of artifacts served to rewrite the indigenous into the concept of the Puerto Rican narrative. Like Brau's perception, the criollo elite defined indigenous contributions according to what best served the praise of European conquest and Western modernity. Schmidt-Nowara focuses on a few specific archaeologists who "recover" the indigenous and the African. Physical artifacts would prove their influence and continued presence within the island's population.[8] Schmidt-Nowara's comparative analysis maps out the various ways Puerto Rico, among Spain's other last colonies, used its otherness to construct social definitions. He deconstructs the limitations of such definitions in seeking to claim an indigenous past, although he does not fully address how the supposed genocide of the islands' indigenous restricts the ability to claim a completely non-Spaniard self-definition.

Duany argues that the claim of the indigenous within Puerto Rican culture through artifacts was to understand more fully African influences on the Puerto Rican national imaginary. As much as archaeologists and other intellectuals sought to claim strategic parts of the past, Duany argues, their primary concern had been to create a hierarchy within the self-understanding of racial and ethnic mixing.[9] Within that hierarchy, Spanish influence was the most important, indigenous second, and African the least important. This demonstrates the racism that informed self-perception as well as the necessity to recognize that there was a type of mixing. In such reclaiming and redefining, there had been an attempt to write a history that not only forgave Spanish colonialism but also praised the possibilities provided by colonialism in allowing various groups and histories to mix. Colonialist rhetoric becomes credited for bettering the human race by creating "opportunities" of mixture and complementary influences. The recovery project was required to form a Eurocentric nationalism distinct and separate from Spain, while simultaneously creating a narrative that equated its rights, reason, and self-perception of civilization as equal to the colonial and imperial centers of Europe.

In the nineteenth century, and well into the twentieth, as modern capitalism began taking shape, cultural superiority defined the right to resources, to power, which required that crimes of the past be erased. It is important to speak of cultural superiority as it informed racial hierarchies. Nationalism in the Americas and the Spanish speaking Caribbean had been informed by the need to equate the criollo and the colonized with the colonizer. Although the national bourgeoisie wanted to possess the same social and political power as the colonizing elite, they did so within the frame of the difference imposed on them by the colonizer. The national bourgeoisie wanted to challenge coloniality's imposed inferiority by proving themselves as equally civilized as their colonizer, albeit within divergent understandings and representations. The national imaginary project of Puerto Rico needed to construct the criollo as equal to the peninsular to create categories of Puerto Rican social membership worthy of colonial centers' recognition. The peninsulares presumed superiority over the others, which continued to define political and economic relations. The indigenous of the Caribbean represented what Spain did not want to be, what those on the islands and within centers of power wanted to replace, so that their defeat through Spanish conquest could construct them as inferior. Inferiority, in turn, meant lack of agency, read as effeminacy, and codependency, which would ideologically impede the move toward autonomy.[10] Self-governance required capital, a strong self-definition, and a cohesive intellectual and political front. Puerto Rico fails, and the ambiguity and repression that the white peasant demonstrates hides and suppresses the diversity and complexity of the island's population. Schmidt-Nowara's analysis of the *jíbaro* draws on Scarano's work that looks at creoles' strategic use of the *jíbaro* language and image in print media to represent dissent, despite the privilege of the educated elite who co-opted the poor's suffering as their own. The representation of the worker, his particular history, the way he spoke, had been constructed by the criollo and white elite, as a strategy against Spain's influence. This construction is false because of the histories it excludes and its depiction of the worker as content and not exploited. The worker is also racialized strategically to serve as dissident or emblematic. Those who used the *jíbaro* failed to achieve their goals because of the contradictory understandings of the *jíbaro* as black or white. While the *jíbaro* was supposed to represent a difference that was equal, his lack of education spoke to the understood inferior humanity based on lesser whiteness imposed on the worker by criollos and peninsulares. These false constructions represented the base *jíbaro* class as degenerate and in need of Western influence. It demonized the workers instead of praising them.

The Dilemma of Eve

The *jíbaro*, much like Adam, is at the will of those who created him and who seek to provide him another existence. The imagining of nation building, much like the myth of creation, relies heavily on a heterotopic frame. The *jíbaro*, like Adam, needs a woman to provide not only the solution to survival but also a more subordinate body on whom to lay blame. It is Eve who is the one, who the serpent approaches, not Adam. The gendering of resistance to propriety speaks to the continued myth of woman as traitor. Latin American countries have developed multiple archetypes of the woman as traitor, as in Malitzin's story in Mexican folklore and Anacaona's story for Dominicans. Male violence against women and male's silencing of women are not examined in these stories; rather, it is the women's failure to live up to masculinist ideas of salvation and redemption, demonstrating the myth of woman as inferior.

Another way to approach the limitations of the *jíbaro* construction is by way of its masculinist underpinnings. A masculine *jíbaro* was used in the nineteenth century as a symbol of dissent. In the twentieth century, the Popular Democratic Party used the *jíbaro* to represent its ideals. The *jíbaro*'s representation and meaning changed over time, from dissident to ideal citizen. The nation's ideal citizen, in the imagining of Puerto Rico's distinction, is male, whether portrayed positively, negatively, or both. The citizen is the Adam working in the fields; he is working class— either the peasant, the urban proletarian, or the worker. The *jíbaro*'s image, as an extension of a first man like Adam varied in construction and representation. This highlights the disorganization that continues to pause the struggle to define an autonomous nation, all the while articulating the limitations of maleness within the nation. Schmidt-Nowara's historical analysis focuses on intellectual male constructions of nation, despite the presence of women poets and thinkers whose discourses carried their own weight.[11] The Puerto Rican woman, as secondary citizen, was supposed to maintain virtue and ideals; all the while she lay as culpable for any social wrongs that took place within the nuclear family. Women poets, political leaders, and civil advocates did work alongside men to define the nation within Puerto Rico. Negligence to their involvement remains a crucial limitation to Puerto Rican nationhood. Eve could not rule, and Adam was insufficient to rule.

Nationalism: The New God

Benedict Anderson's *Imagined Communities* historicizes the process of nation building. He finds that the language, the symbols, and the sacred script of a group or a network of groups were primary in the construction of community, writ large. Anderson argues that at the root of nationalism was the new secularism, a new deity that offered a belief system based on more concrete ideas than the metaphysics present in religious fervor. Yet nationalism complemented religious fundamentalism in that it banked on entitlement. Within nationalism, however, the territory replaced the hereafter. Nationalism answered the question: who had the right to govern physical, corporeal place? Developing nationalism during and after colonialism needs more than place and narrative, however; shared symbols do not guarantee complementary understandings. Struggle as one of the primary narratives on which nationalists center their discourse, remains universal, even as the particularities change. As Torres-Saillant's literary analysis demonstrates, how a nation's citizens develop the struggle assists the process of nation building. The colonial context of national and diasporic narratives, distorts the complexity of the story, insofar as language and symbolism had been inherited from the conqueror. As much as they are inherited, aspects of them are negotiated and resisted in an attempt to rewrite the history of a racial/ethnic mixing that centers the colonizer. Still, there exists a consistent divide on the construction of a dominant narrative as it is precisely the desire to hold power like the colonizer that at times prompts the narrative's constructions. It is important to the concept of the fruit of the tree of knowledge. Is the fruit a product of resistance for the sake of liberation or for the desire to be like one's creator—in this case, the colonizer?

Nationalism as an ideology functions similarly, because of its dependence on technology, not only for the dissemination of information, but also for the distribution of resources. Technology informed Cuba's ability to establish economic autonomy; whereas Puerto Rico, less exposed to Western technologies by virtue of its lack of a localized higher education system, grappled with it. Full dependencies keep weaker nations from full development into autonomous agents, if they are unable to understand the assets they have within the territory and or community.

Women, in this respect, have been introduced as the figurative representation of nation and ideal nationalism. In their bodies they carry the nation; they have the responsibility to extend the love of the fatherland; their superior moral guide may better perpetuate loyalty and reason, if women are properly educated. Still, as Zilkia Janer demonstrates, middle-class women remained concerned with maintaining their privilege more than the creation of the "greater nation." Ana Roque de Duprey, who named herself the founder of Puerto Rican feminism, for example, did not participate in class or antiracist struggles, limiting her work to suffrage and education. While important, a critical Puerto Rican nationalist feminism would need to address material needs and structural inequalities across lines; otherwise, rights remain in the hand of the few.

Creole elite men and women, speak of nationalism through Western frames and discourses, operating with one set of symbols instead of the multiple contradictory ones that represent the Puerto Rican nation.[12] Classed and raced as Other, pending on who is constructing the Othering, they replicate the othering onto other bodies, despite the contributions of working class and communities of color within Puerto

Rico. Creole elites negotiate their difference from the colonial center and the exploited proletariat. Their works both show how Creoles isolate themselves with the frame of those from whom they seek autonomy and from those who will occupy their nation. Their imagined community pulls from both groups they intend to reject, wherein lies the contradiction that continuously leads to their failure. Their nationalism fails, not because nationalism cannot be strategic, but because it is essentialist, selective, and self-repressive in its construction. It carries the United States, Spain, and its sacred scripts. In Benedict Anderson's line of thought, the transition to the secular that marked the beginning of nation states has not been realized.

For nationalism to be successful, intellectuals need to listen to—not speak for—or the marginalized. It remains vital to work through shame of subordination, to start the process of working through shame from below to disrupt hierarchy of inclusion. The dynamic of microgrouping continues to set narratives against each other, creating the premise of erased (limited) narrative, displacement, limited political/economic citizenship. Nationalism needs to be a stage to work through, and live in, but not live for. Fanon's case studies in *Wretched of the Earth* demonstrate that revolution needs more than ideas and more even than physical action. After the war, the dialectic of ideology building, talk about freedom needs to ask what freedom is going to look like, not just for the one person, the microgroup, but for all directly and indirectly involved.[13] How to address the psychological affects of oppression, violence used in resistance and the rebuilding of the nation, especially when, as in the case of Puerto Rico, there remains various layers of colonization and imperialism to work through? The question remains difficult to answer when taking into consideration the focus on an end instead of a process. The tree of knowledge, consciousness about good and evil, does not stop either from existing, or did it remove the Creator's power. While taking from it, while other countries and colonies resisted colonialism and gained some leverage, Puerto Ricans remain economically codependent on imperial states. Like Adam and Eve, they traded one form of repression for another. It is the way in which resistance operates as imitation or as dissidence against the necessity to choose between codependent projects that need to be considered.

Notes

1. Cesar Ayala and Rafael Bernabe outline the various points in Puerto Rico's history under Spain's and U.S. colonialism, that the plantation economy, followed by projects of

urbanization and industrialization informed the codependency Puerto Rico had on its colonial rulers.

2. Jorge Duany discusses this in *The Puerto Rican Nation on the Move Identities on the Island and in the United States*. Arlene Davila also touches on it in her text *Contested Identities Cultural Politics in Puerto Rico*. Both authors discuss the ways in which cultural distinction is important to manifest and construct and, in Davila's specific arguments, to consume.

3. Ramón Grosfoguel discusses this in *Colonial Subjects*. The majority of his intellectual work, while arguing against globalization and the affects of colonialism, continues to defend the necessity of Puerto Rico's greater inclusion in the United States. He explains that Puerto Rico and Puerto Ricans were able to obtain more rights and more protections with United States' intervention. He understands that those rights remain limited because Puerto Rico is not fully incorporated, which he also articulates in the text. He explains that the current status of globalization and other former colonized Caribbean islands that, in comparison to their poverty and neocolonial repression under the current model of globalization, sets Puerto Rico apart because the island and its people have greater access to and fluidity with the imperial center of the United States.

4. Christopher Schmidt-Nowara, throughout his text, *The Conquest of History Spanish Colonialism and National Histories in the Nineteenth Century* discusses the Philippines', Cuba's, and Puerto Rico's need to cultural separate themselves from Spain because of how, despite centuries of rule and intervention, Spain viewed them as lesser citizens and as such, limited their cultural and political rights. Cultural distinction, cultural nationalism framed nationalist and independence movements in the Philippines and Cuba. Although there were Puerto Rican intellectuals who called for independence, those numbers were in minority. Various Puerto Rican intellectual and political leaders who had called for cultural distinction, called for greater autonomy, primarily.

5. Schmidt-Nowara, Christopher. *The Conquest of History*; Ayala, Cesar, and Rafael Bernabe *Puerto Rico in the American Century: A History since 1898*.

6. Christopher Schmidt-Nowara, in Chapter three, "The Problem of Prehistory in Puerto Rico and Cuba," out of *The Conquest of History Spanish Colonialism and National Histories in the Nineteenth Century*, examines the ways in which anthropologists seek to include indigeneity in definitions of Puerto Ricanness. Found indigenous artifacts and the ambiguity regarding indigenous presence, despite colonial claims at their annihalation, make their inclusion difficult for precisely that reason.

7. Heterosexual, intellectual upper class, socially read as white and male men. Men who do not perform dominant masculinity or, who do not follow the Western Christian guidelines of masculinity, do not fall into this category.

8. Schmidt-Nowara in Chapter three "The Problem of Prehistory in Puerto Rico and Cuba" juxtaposes how historians, anthropologists participated in "the idealization of the Indian past [as a] response to the rapid social and economic changes that overtook the islands [of Puerto Rico and Cuba] in the first half of the nineteenth century," (97) against history that began according to historians such as Emilio Castelar and Francisco Pi y Margall with Spain's conquest (120–23).

9. Duany, Jorge, "Making Indians out of Blacks: The Revitalization of Taino Identity in Contemporary Puerto Rico," in *The Puerto Rican Nation on the Move: Identities on the Island and in the United States*, 261–80.

10. Negrón-Muntaner discusses this in "1898: The Trauma of Literature, the shame of Identity." Specifically, she discusses that dominant men wanted to challenge the weakness that U.S. intervention had represented because they perceived the unwillingness and inability to fight made them feminine. This demonstrates primary understandings of manhood being equated with militarism and or the ability to fight.

11. Janer, Zilkia *Puerto Rican Nation Building Literature: Impossible Romance;* in the second chapter of the text, "Creating a National Womanhood," Janer examines how women constructed

themselves within nationalist definitions (36–39). In the first chapter, "Colonization as Seduction," she examines how male novelists and poets construct heteronormative roles; citing Francine Masiello's analysis of women resisting male domination as a metaphor for dissidence against the state/empire rule in the case of Spanish colonies (24).

12. This argument stems from the overlapping arguments of Schmidt-Nowara, Rama, Anderson, that examine what goes into nation building discourses, narratives, and practice. Anderson in his introduction argues that images used in nation building literature, that a group of disconnected individuals can relate to, may lay strategic foundations to disrupting self-hate, but that the connection is imagined. Symbols' meanings vary depending on interpretation, on race, class, and gender, as well as region, and on the physical landscape of a nation.

13. Fanon, Frantz *Wretched of the Earth;* Memmi, Albert, *The Colonizer and the Colonized;* both Fanon and Memmi wrote their works inspired by the Algerian war, attempting to make sense of what should take place in Algeria once the people achieved its goal of getting rid of the French. Their work points to the reality that liberation is a continuous process, whose end cannot be measured.

Bibliography

Ayala, Cesar J., and Rafael Bernabe. *Puerto Rico in the American Century.* Chapel Hill: University of North Carolina Press, 2007.

Barthes, Roland. *Image-Music-Text.* Trans. Stephen Heath. New York: Hill and Wang, 1977.

———. *Mythologies.* Trans. Annette Lavers. New York: Hill and Wang, 1972.

Burke, Kenneth. *A Rhetoric of Motives.* Berkeley and Los Angeles: University of California Press, 1969.

Davila, Arlene. *Sponsored Identities: Cultural Politics in Puerto Rico.* Philadelphia: Temple University Press, 1997.

Duany, Jorge. *Puerto Rican Nation on the Move: Identities on the Island and in the United States.* Chapel Hill: University of North Carolina Press, 2002.

Fanon, Franz tran. Philcox, Richard. *The Wretched of the Earth .* New York: Grove Press, 2004.

Grosfoguel, Ramon. *Colonial Subjects: Puerto Ricans in a Global Perspective.* Berkeley and Los Angeles: University of California Press, 2003.

Janer, Zilkia. *Puerto Rican Nation Building Literature: Impossible Romance.* Gainesville: University Press of Florida, 2005.

María de Hostos, Eugenio. *Obras Completas edición conmemorativa del gobierno de Puerto Rico, 1839, 1939...*Habana, Cuba: Cultural, s.a., Obispo y Bernaza, 1939.

Memmi, Albert. *The Colonizer and the Colonized.* Boston: Beacon Press, 1965.

Mohanty, Chandra. "Cartographies of Struggle." In *Third World Women and the Politics of Feminism,* edited by Chandry Mohanty, Lourdes Torres and Anne Russo, 1–50. Bloomington: Indiana University Press, 1991.

Muntaner, Frances Negrón. *Boricua Pop Puerto Ricans and the Latinization of American Culture.* New York: New York University Press, 2004.

O'Gorman Anderson, Benedict Richard. *Imagined Communities Reflections on the Origins and Spread of Nationalism.* London: Verso Press, 1983.

Rama, Angel. *The Lettered City.* Trans. John Charles Chasteen. Durham: Duke University Press, 1996.

Sanchez, Juan. "Two Variants of Puerto Rican Nationalism." *Centro Journal* 17, no. 1 (2005): 26–45.

Scarano, Francisco. "The Jíbaro Masquerade and the Subaltern Politics of Creole Identity Formation in Puerto Rico 1745–1823." *The American Historical Review* (American Historical Association), December 1996: 1398–1431.

Schmidt-Nowara, Christopher. *The Conquest of History Spanish Colonialism and National Histories in the Nineteenth Century.* Pittsburgh, PA: University of Pittsburgh Press, 2006.

Torres-Saillant, Silvio. *Intellectual History of the Caribbean.* Imprint Basingstoke: Palgrave Macmillan, 2005.

Villanueva, Victor. "Colonial Memory and the Crime of Rhetoric: Pedro Albizu Campos." *College English* 71 (2009): 630–38.

CHAPTER FOUR

Spanish Scripts Colonize the Image: Inca Visual Rhetorics

ROCÍO QUISPE-AGNOLI

Para que la letra la tenga en los ojos
And so the letter will be in their eyes
—Guaman Poma de Ayala, 1613

During the late sixteenth and early seventeenth centuries, native authors of the Andean region such as Titu Cusi Yupanqui (1570), Inca Garcilaso de la Vega (1609), Joan de Santa Cruz Pachacuti Yamqui Salcamaygua (1613), and Felipe Guaman Poma de Ayala (1615), wrote chronicles that uncover systems of record keeping and communication, and combine alphabetic writing and visual texts. Studying texts produced by early native authors and artists of the Americas reveals how these native authors were able to assimilate rapidly the European alphabet and the official genre of the chronicle of Indies to develop new textualizations of their cultures keeping in sight a rich, sophisticated, and ongoing development of visual arts in the pre- and post-Hispanic Andean world. My study of these chronicles has led me to explore the relationships between verbal and iconic textualizations that may be found in the dialectics between Western practices such as the alphabetic script,[1] painting, sculpture, engravings, maps, and Andean systems of record keeping and communication such as *quipus* and *tocapus*. Considering the dialectical nature of alphabetic writing and Andean visual texts, I propose to review the ways in which Andean subjects respond to the rhetorical colonization of their society and utilize the elements brought by the *conquistadores* to build representations of early colonial Andes and themselves. In this review, I also want to point out the visual nature of alphabetic writing that is revealed in its contact with indigenous systems of communications from the Americas.

Hybrid Textualizations

In the late sixteenth century, European and Andean systems of communication made contact and opened new spaces for hybrid textualizations. Examples of these spaces may be found in colonial Andean textiles, ceramics, coats of arms, public signs, architecture, and paper/ink. Andean designs and images were integrated in the colonial Spanish-Andean society and these visual texts experienced transformations throughout the centuries. Likewise, the alphabetic script that was used to initiate those transformations was regarded by Andeans as a visual system of signs that could be equivalent to their visual systems of communication. In other words, the representation of the new other went in both directions: Spaniards put Quechua in alphabetic writing and contributed to the transformation of abstract designs into figurative ones, and Andeans learnt to read and write not only to communicate with Europeans and their descents, but also to use elements of the alphabetic script in their ways of communications.

According to Garcilaso de la Vega's description, a *quipu* is not only able to record historical events, but rather, also stories, poetry, and laws (1609, Book 6, Chapter 9).[2] Ascher and Ascher (1981, 75) considered it possible to register the oral tradition in the *quipus*. The numeric sequences that they discovered speaks to the continual repetition of verses, which is typical of oral tradition. Furthermore, it seems that the abundance of colors would also be a sign that they could be treated as a "text." This affirmation is questioned by modern authors because the analysis of a series of literary traditional texts of the chronicles during the colonial period resulted in writing of oral traditions. The expert in producing and decoding *quipus* was an important position in Inca times and was named *quipucamayoc*, the *quipu*-keeper and *quipu*-reader. We also observe that there is no Quechua word to refer to the expert who would produce and decode *tocapu*.

During the centuries, learned men and scholars have admired the sophisticated *quipus* and the colorful *tocapus* as carriers of information, but most intellectuals were unable to look at them as equivalent to alphabetic writing. *Quipus* and *tocapus*, as visual and tangible as they are, like their Western counterpart—the alphabetic script—were not recognized as an efficient system of communication simply because of its lack of (verbal) letters. Joseph de Acosta would conclude that the lack of letters implied lack of History, and this would make the Incas inferior to the European because they were unable to generate and keep, for the future generations, a historical discourse (1590, 363).[3] With this approach to visual and verbal textualizations, I hope to combat the general idea that the Incas were a great but incomplete civilization because of their apparent lack of letters and thus, their inability to record history.

Uncovering tangible systems of record-keeping and communication that are different from the alphabetic writing in the early colonial Andes brought me to look at the verbal and visual texts included in chronicles produced by native authors. Furthermore, one realizes that paper and ink became a new space of textual negotiations between Europeans and Andeans from the sixteenth century onward. As we know, alphabetic writing reproduces verbal utterances that range from oral speech acts to sophisticated written artifacts such as those recognized as literature. However this system, especially in contact with non-Western systems of communication that do not reproduce necessarily the phonological structure of a language, has been explored by the Andean people also in its visual materiality.

Visual Culture and Visual Subject

In 1971 the Russian formalist and linguist Roman Jakobson stated the privileged place of audiovisual senses to effectively transmit information in a social context: "it is evident that the most socialized, abundant, and pertinent sign systems in human society are based on the sight and the hearing" (701). More than 300 years before Jakobson's semiotic statement, René Descartes acknowledged the privileged role of sight in human knowledge: "The conduct of our life depends entirely of our senses, and since sight is the noblest and most comprehensive of the senses, inventions that serve to increase its power are undoubtedly among the most useful there can be" (cited by Mirzoeff 112).[4] Nevertheless the scientific, philosophical, political, and religious evidence of the power of visual communication in the West, the discussion on colonial visualities in Spanish America remain an area that is pending study.[5]

To frame my reflection on colonial visualities, I will summarize now what I understand for visual event, visual culture, and visual subject.[6] According to Nicholas Mirzoeff, the visual event takes places when the individual seeks information in his contact with visual technologies (5). The main characteristic of the visual event may be found in its condition of an effect on the individual's actions: "The event is the effect of a network in which subjects operate and which in turn conditions their freedom of action" (6). The definition proposed by Mirzoeff seems to imply a saussurean idea. In his *Cours de Linguistique Générale*, Ferdinand de Saussure proposed that the transmission of meaning is possible thanks to a network that restrict the linguistic utterances within the limits of any given language. However, Iris Rogoff explains that the power of visuality is found in its capacity to displace and relocate meanings:

> [The emergent field of "visual culture"] encompasses more than the study of images. At one level we focus on the centrality of vision and the visual world in producing meanings, establishing and maintaining aesthetic values, gender stereotypes and power relations within culture. At another level, opening up the field of vision as an arena in which cultural meanings get constituted, anchors to it an entire range of analyses and interpretations of the audio, the spatial, and of the psychic dynamics of spectatorship. Thus visual culture opens up an entire world of intertextuality in which images, sounds and spatial delineations are read on to and through one another, lending layers of meaning and of subjective responses to each encounter we might have with film, advertising, TV, art works, buildings or urban environments. (24)

Rogoff's definition of "visual culture" reveals the text as a space for visual and aural intertextuality. However, Rogoff's citation refers to the use of simultaneous sounds and images within the visual event that may not be the usual case in the colonial texts that I analyze in this chapter. Then I find it useful to keep in mind Roman Jakobson's distinction between visual and auditory signs. The Russian linguist observes that while time is the structural factor for auditory signs to be produced and transmitted, visual signs need space, which may be combined with time, although space remains as the structural factor for the constituency of visual texts.[7]

We can understand pre- and post-Hispanic systems of communication within the frame of this intertextual world "in which images, sounds and spatial delineations are read on to and through one another, lending layers of meaning and of subjective responses" (Rogoff). Pre-Hispanic Andean *quipus* and *tocapus*,[8] for example, are visual texts that convey information about Andean history and Andean temporal and spatial world. *Quipus* are colored knotted strings, usually made of wool, cotton, animal fiber (camelids) and, in rare occasions, human hair.[9] *Quipus* were used in the Andes for record-keeping, which included numerical information with statistical and accounting purposes, and records of historical events. Once Spaniards realized that they could not have full control of and access to the information recorded and transmitted by means of *quipus*, these devices were burnt at the bonfire during the early colonial viceroyalty of Francisco de Toledo (1569–1581), in a similar way books forbidden by the Spanish Inquisition were burnt. According to Gary Urton, there are approximately 600 quipus surviving in museums and private collections around the world.

Tocapus refer to rectangles decorated with geometric designs and highlighted by contrasting colors.[10] They are usually found woven in textiles (royal garments and dresses) and painted or engraved on ceramics, metal, or wooden vessels (*qero*) used for ritual purposes (Cummins 2002b, Arellano-Hoffmann 1999). Spaniards regarded the *tocapu* as ornaments within Inca textiles and although wearing them in their garments was allowed and somehow regulated by Spanish law, they were not destroyed as the *quipus*.[11]

Visual culture, as defined by Rogoff, provides the visual articulation for the move and displacement of meanings in visual texts, and an appropriate intellectual arena to look at the visual intertextualities that the 1492 encounters inaugurate: "The emergence of visual culture as a transdisciplinary and cross-methodological field of inquiry means...an opportunity to reconsider some of the present culture's thorniest problems from yet another angle" (26). In contemporary societies, as well as the Spanish American early societies, meanings circulate through oral, alphabetic, and visual ways. Visual images transmit information, providing pleasure or displeasure, and mediate power relations. We may find examples of these visual effects in the native chronicler Felipe Guaman Poma de Ayala's drawings that intend to rescue the Andean past and challenge its reader by denouncing the colonial violence.[12]

Rogoff adds another characteristic of visual events that is useful to the intertextual analysis: our exposure to visual texts gives us the opportunity to narrate events in a new, nonverbal way, which incorporates our conscious and unconscious experiences of the world. Visual images enable us with a new way of writing in which our objectivity (our knowledge of the world that is exterior to us) and subjectivity (our unconsciousness) intersect (25). These notions of visual event and visual culture help us understand, for example, the verbal silence of Guaman Poma as opposed to his iconic loquacity, especially when it comes to understanding the Andean systems of communication. Tom Cummins mentions the silence of the Andean authors about the *toca-pus* (1997, 258–60) and points out that a Western reading of Guaman Poma's chronicle favors this perception of "silence." The indigenous author draws *tocapus*, describes them in their shape, geometric design, and color, and indicates the context in which they appear. But Guaman Poma does not explain what information they convey and how they could be read. The verbal silence about *quipus* and *tocapus* is contrasted with his "visual speech" that is iconic and nonverbal.[13] Andean visual speech and Castilian/Quechua alphabetic speech appear simultaneously in the text. The first explains what the other keeps silent. I will come back later to this distinct speech that is an example of a text in a "contact zone" and, in addition, must be discussed when we talk about graphism and image.

Visual event and visual culture imply the existence of a visual subject. Nicholas Mirzoeff defines visual subject as: "a person who is both constituted as an agent of sight (regardless of his or her biological capacity to see) and as effect of a series of categories of visual subjectivity" (10). The visual subject is the one who sees (agent) and the one who is seen. In this point, the Cartesian rationalism of "cogito ergo sum" meets the main idea of "Optics": "I am seen and I see that I am seen."[14]

Guaman Poma is a visual subject that sees and acknowledges that he is seen. Although he acknowledges being surveilled, as all Andean subjects under the Spanish colonial control, Guaman Poma surveilles as well at the same time that he denounces and asks for punishments and remedies. Mercedes López-Baralt has analyzed the various textual identities that this author utilizes in his chronicle and calls them "masks" (1995). Of these masks, five are visual self-portraits: prince child who is educated as Christian (folio 17), author surrounded by his *informantes* (folio 368), adviser to the king (folio 975), and pilgrim (folio 1105). In the frontispiece, the author represents himself as an Andean prince who, thanks to the authority and power symbolically displayed in his coat of arms, holds the holy kingdoms of Spain and Rome. To understand the importance of this image, I refer to Tom Cummins's analysis (1998) of Guaman Poma's coat of arms in the front page of his chronicle:

> The page is divided by a central vertical axis composed of three coats of arms: the papal arms, the royal house of Spain, and

Guaman Poma's own "fabricated" coat of arms. His coat-of-arms is composed, like that of Leon and Castilla, of the pictorial likenesses of the things to which the words of his name refer: Guaman (falcon) and Poma (puma). The difference is that one sees here an ideographic representation of the Andean parts of his name in distinction to the ideographic representations of territory in the Spanish Royal coat of arms.

Guaman Poma's coat of arms, although it is "fabricated"—false within the European sense of authenticity in that the design of a coat of arms must be given, granted, by the crown in a royal *cédula*—presupposes here that the gift would be granted were the king to know of Guaman Poma's noble heritage and service. Hence Guaman Poma's coat of arms is legitimate in the sense that his status as a noble pre-exists Spanish recognition and is based on Andean precedent. His coat of arms, in a sense, acknowledges the acceptability of the exchange of images between Europeans and Andeans as a sign of a social relationship, and he copies the European-style heraldic figures of a lion and an eagle to indicate his Andean name as a part of this exchange. (94)

The next folios prepare the visual narrative that explains how Guaman Poma's identity changes over time to become a subject of authority, power, and wisdom. Folio 17 shows the author as a child, along with his noble parents, who are being indoctrinated in the Catholic faith and receive the communion from his mestizo half-brother, Martín de Ayala, demonstrating that Guaman Poma is a Christian Indian since a very early age. Folio 368 represents a young adult Guaman Poma who is dressed as an Andean colonial official: he is wearing a Spanish-like shirt and jerkin, cape, shoes, and a hat, but the designs on the fabric reproduce pre-Hispanic *Yarovilca* designs. His hair style may be perceived as Spanish but it coincides with the haircut of pre-Hispanic Andean people. Most importantly, he appears in the center of this folio, surrounded by "old Indians" (*indios viejos*) who are sharing with him their Andean knowledge. He is then an Andean-Spanish subject who is able to collect information from the legitimate Andean sources. The information transmitted by these old Indians is legitimate because their garments and headdresses speak of their noble ancestry. They may be *amautas* (learned men) or even *quipucamayocs* (*quipu* readers). In his verbal text, Guaman Poma refers to all of them as the old Indians who serve him as informants and provide him with the data that will inform his book. This folio closes the first half of his work, named "New Chronicle"

(*Primer Nueva Corónica*). As Mary Louise Pratt explains, the title of this first part is important since "crónica" or "corónica" constituted one of the main official writings for the Spanish representations of the Amerindians: "In writing a 'new chronicle,' Guaman Poma took over the official Spanish genre for his own ends. Those ends were, roughly, to construct a new picture of the world, a picture of a Christian world with Andean rather than European peoples at the center of it—Cuzco, not Jerusalem."[15] Pratt sees this "New Chronicle" as an example of an autoethnographic text, by which people describe themselves while engaging representations that others have made of them. I will come back to the autoethnographic feature of this text later.

Thus, in the first part of his work, Guaman Poma offers his Andean version of human history from ancient times until the last Inca's regime in this "new chronicle." Folio 368 is a conclusive statement on how telling the Andean history has been legitimately possible by an indigenous author. The next twenty folios tell the history of the Spanish wars of Conquest and serve as a transition to the second part of this work: "Good Government" (*Buen gobierno*) in which the early colonial Andean society is depicted in great detail. However, the author will not offer another self-portrait until folio 975, almost at the end of "Good Government."

In folio 975 is an adult Guaman Poma, dressed again as a noble Andean colonial official, who has an audience with the king of Spain. In this drawing, the Indian chronicler responds to the questions of the Spanish king while holding a copy of his book open in front of him. Hand gestures indicate that Guaman Poma is not only presenting his ideas to the king, but he is also giving advice on how to govern the Republic of Indians. He has gone from Andean prince, Christian Indian, and source of information to royal adviser. Guaman Poma represents himself here at the top of his possible competence: he has the knowledge and therefore he has authority to speak. What has happened in the text between folio 368 and folio 975 for this change to take place? In the chapter that follows "New Chronicle," Guaman Poma makes an account of the Spanish conquest by parodying European texts. He presents the Spaniards as beings who ate gold and when they knew about the gold and silver of the Indies and Perú, the wars of conquest started. The conquest brought also civil wars among the greedy *conquistadores* and these wars were brought to an end thanks to the intervention of noble Andeans such as the author's grandfather, Guaman Chaua. The next part, as I mentioned before, is titled "Good Government" and Guaman Poma depicts in great detail the early colonial society of the Spanish Andes, at the same time that he condemns the European exploitation and abuse of the Andean people and the causes for their extermination. After more than 600 folios of critique and denunciations, the Indian chronicler proposes collaboration between the Spanish king and the officers of the Republic of Indians that is summarized in "Chapter of the Question" (*Capítulo de la pregunta*) that starts with folio 975. However, as we know, the advice to the king, as the whole text, never reached its intended main reader.

The last self-portrait offers interesting differences when compared with the former ones. Folio 1105 illustrates an old Guaman Poma who possesses the knowledge of the previous portraits, but is now deprived of power and prestige. He has been expelled from his hometown by Spanish officials and, in the company of his son, a horse and his dog; they travel from Guamanga (Central Andes) to Lima on the Pacific Coast. In the journey, his son abandons him, he loses his horse and dog, and he is obliged to walk to the city alone. In this chapter titled "The Author Walks" (*Camina el autor*), Guaman Poma reveals the sufferings of the Andean people beyond Guamanga, especially the abuses of the extirpators of idolatries in the highlands of Lima, and the corruption of the viceroyalty. Still, he "walks" with his book under his arm with the final goal of turning it in to the appropriate authorities in Lima, so it will be delivered to the Spanish king and eventually printed and published.

In all these folios, the indigenous author poses himself as a visual subject who not only sees to describe, but who also sees panoptically to denunciate and correct. The descriptive gaze seems to dominate most of Guaman Poma's drawings especially in its first part, *New Chronicle*. They can be seen as windows to the Andean pre-Hispanic world and include portraits of Inca rulers, nobles, and scenes of public daily life. The portraits of Incas, *Coyas* (the Inca's wife), captains, noble ladies, and other prominent characters of Inca society, display images of *quipus* and *tocapus* that are described. In contrast, the panoptic gaze has an overwhelming presence in the second part of this text, "Good Government." As I have mentioned earlier, Guaman Poma denunciates, accuses, and claims for remedies by displaying visual examples of what the good government should be, like the drawing of the idealized Andean *escribano de cabildo* or public notary (folio 828).[16]

Autoethnographic Text and Mimicry

I want to go back now to the representation of *quipus* and *tocapus* once they encounter European elements in Guaman Poma's chronicle, which

uses, in my opinion, an ambivalent gaze. By ambivalent gaze I refer to
a gaze that is descriptive and panoptic at the same time. Before I comment on these visual events, I would like to reflect on how I look at
hybrid texts such as Guaman Poma's, especially as an autoethnographic
occurrence of Pratt's "art of the contact zone."

In the context of European imperial expansion and colonization,
Pratt (1999) proposed the concept of "contact zone" to describe the
space for new textualizations as a result of the cultural encounters produced by territorial expansions and colonizations:

> I use this term [*contact zones*] to refer to social spaces where cul-
> tures meet, clash, and grapple with each other, often in contexts
> of highly asymmetrical relations of power, such as colonialism,
> slavery, or their aftermaths as they are lived out in many parts of
> the world today.

In Pratt's view, the contact of two cultures with their respective systems of communications produced a combination of elements in which
textual hybridity took place. This textual hybrid space in early colonial
Spanish America (e.g., the page and the ink) is the "contact zone" of
two or more cultural systems that are confronted by processes of colonization. To understand Pratt's proposal, I summarize here her reasoning to understand why Guaman Poma de Ayala's chronicle is a product
of the contact zone. This account will also bring us to Pratt's proposal
of this Guaman Poma's work as "autoethnographic text."[17]

In the early colonial Andean-Spanish contact zone, hybrid texts are
produced to transmit messages of authority based on knowledge and/
or political power. These texts are usually, but not exclusively, produced by indigenous and mestizo authors, and by the descendants of
the Inca nobility who sought a privileged position in the new colonial
society (e.g., Sayri Tupac, Beatriz Coya, Carlos Topa Inca). Such texts
include visual events among which we may find representations of *quipus*, *tocapus*, iconic images—both Western and Andean—and alphabetic
script. Examples of visual images associated with qualitatively different systems of communication are found in the Andean-Spanish coats
of arms, whose signifying elements are the drawing lines, color, and
culture-specific symbols such as *tocapu* designs and European symbols
such as the eagle, as we can see in the following image. The design of
this coat of arms includes its identification by means of alphabetic script
as belonging to *Doña Beatriz Coya, wife of Martín de Loyola and great-
grandaughter of Huayna Cápac*. In a similar way, the renowned drawing

reproduced by Joan de Santa Cruz Pachacuti Salcamaygua in his 1613 chronicle, claims to depict the main altar of the *Coricancha* temple in Cuzco and utilizes, at least, two visual systems of communication: the iconic image and the written messages of the Indian chronicler, whose intention is to explain the pre-Hispanic Andean cosmogony to his European reader.

There are several theoretical implications from these textual hybridities in this contact zone. In first place, Pratt suggests that Guaman Poma's work, as well as representations made by other Andean subjects, is an autoethnographic text because he describes himself and the Andean people in ways that engage representations of them made by Europeans. In this process, the Andean author responds to the European representations of Indians and takes part in an intertextual dialogue.[18] This process also implies a selective collaboration with elements of different cultures, the old Indians who share their knowledge with him, and the European authors who teach him how to write a chronicle of Indies. Pratt's autoethnographic text connects also with the postcolonial concept of mimicry. In "Of Mimicry and Man: The Ambivalence of Colonial Discourse," Homi Bhabha discusses "mimicry" as an effective strategy of colonial power and knowledge:

> Colonial mimicry is the desire for a reformed, recognizable Other, *as a subject of a difference that is almost the same, but not quite.* Which is to say, that the discourse of mimicry is constructed around an ambivalence; in order to be effective, mimicry must continually produce its slippage, its excess, its difference. The authority of that mode of colonial discourse that I have called mimicry is therefore stricken by an indeterminacy: mimicry emerges as the representation of a difference that is itself a process of disavowal. Mimicry is, thus the sign of a double articulation; a complex strategy of reform, regulation and discipline, which "appropriates" the Other as it visualizes power. Mimicry is also the sign of the inappropriate; however, a difference or recalcitrance which coheres the dominant strategic function of colonial power, intensifies surveillance, and poses an immanent threat to both "normalized" knowledges and disciplinary powers. (87)

As I stated before, Guaman Poma is a visual subject who surveilles the colonial society of the late 1500s and early 1600s. He also knows that he is surveilled, and that Andean people are the object of mimicry by the Spanish authors and notaries. However the object of mimicry unveils a heterogenous subject and this subject performs speech acts, selects information, and puts Andean and Spanish elements together in a collaborative effort that becomes an autoethnographic text. This kind of text is also addressed to different audiences who are in the contact zone and its reception may become unpredictable since the contact zone is a heterogeneous space in which European ideals may not be simply imposed.

Pratt is careful enough to distinguish autoethnographic texts from "autochthonous forms of self-representation," which correspond mainly to pre-Hispanic systems of communication. There are many examples of pre-Hispanic visual texts, such as the iconic narrative of a cosmogony that has been recently uncovered on one of the walls of *Huaca de la Luna* (Temple of the Moon) walls in Tucumé, on the north coast of Perú. Likewise, one can observe the *tocapu* system in pre- and post-Hispanic royal Inca garments (*uncus*) that are preserved in museums. However what is most appealing to the Andean-Spanish visual texts that take place after 1492 are those that are represented in European spaces: the paper and the ink, the coats of arms, and public signs.

Visual Texts and Verbal Texts

The use of genres, artifacts, and spaces that are foreign to the Andean pre-Hispanic modes of representation, brings us to the necessary distinction between "graphic" and "visual texts" that is not new to the field of Andean studies. Scholars such as Tom Cummins, Carmen Arellano-Hoffmann, Joanne Rappaport, and Walter Mignolo, have used "literacy" and "graphism" to refer to non-Western systems of communication.[19] Within this context scholars may examine and interpret the colonial documents and objects beyond their written content, rather as visual images, paying attention to textual occurrences such as, for example, signatures, water seals, the disposition of the lines on the page, and other nonverbal signs. In addition, works of Cummins (2002a) and Arellano-Hoffmann (1999) stress two aspects that may support my reflection on visual texts: in first place, the Western separation between alphabetic script and art is not a consideration in the Amerindian worldview as it is in the European. Amerindian points of view seem to conceive both expressions (script and iconic image) as two sides of one coin.[20] In second place, the Andean communication systems were more abstract and less figurative or representational if we compare them with other Western and Amerindian visual communication systems such as the Mesoamerican pictography. In this way, when confronted with alphabetic script and European iconographies, Andean representation systems experienced more transformations that those from Mesoamerica.

I want to explore now how Andean authors use visual icons to transmit information about their lineage and society, and how they address the European reader to obtain or maintain a secure position in the new colonial order. In the next pages, I review briefly verbal and visual examples of *tocapu* in two Andean chronicles that I analyzed extensively in another work (2005). I then comment the visual transformations in the representation of Andean objects—such as *quipus*—within the pages of these texts and the interaction among elements of Andean communication systems, that I have called "Andean visual literacies" (2006) but decide to call now "visual texts." Within this framework, I intend to explain relations between drawing and writing (in public signs), and Spanish objects—such as shields and coats of arms—that constitute the basis for new Andean coats of arms. Finally, I reflect on the persuasive powers of these communication systems that serve to secure messages of authority and prestige in the pre- and post-Hispanic Andean region.

Quipus and *Tocapus* in Early Colonial Documents

As mentioned before, I have analyzed verbal and visual occurrences of *tocapu* in the works of Guaman Poma de Ayala and compared them with those examples in the *Historia y genealogía de los Reyes Incas* by fray Martín de Murúa. I proposed then that Guaman Poma combined intentionally the substances of two different textualities (alphabetic and visual) and recognized them as *qellqay* or *quilca*, that is, a graphic mark with communicative purposes. If we look at early colonial dictionaries of Quechua such as the ones prepared by Domingo de Santo Tomás (1560) and Diego González Holguín (1608), we have been able to acknowledge a Quechua term for writing, which is precisely *quilca*. The colonial dictionaries indicate that *quilca* had adapted semantically to the Spanish concept of writing, where *quilca* signifies "letter, document" or "letter (of the alphabet)." The verbal form *qellqani* refers to the verb "to write."[21] The entries in these two Quechua dictionaries allow us to perceive other significances. What is inapplicable to some of these significances is the European concept of writing, which we suspect that *quilca* constitutes an Andean creation, or more specifically, an Inca creation. According to these dictionaries, the term *quilca* also signifies "to paint."[22] The word also is used for "embroidery" and "wooden sculpture," referring to specific variations of this form of art, or rather, those which utilize colors.[23] It is interesting to note that in the colonial dictionaries, neither *quipu* nor *tocapu* are related to the word *quilca*. Uniquely, Guaman Poma noted the person who utilizes the *quipu* as a *quipucamayoc* (*quipu* reader) and *quilcacamayoc*, a master of the *quilca* (folios 193, 361). *Quilca* in colonial sources refers to specific forms of certain Inca texts: "But in the *New Chronicle and Good Government*, *quilca* is exemplified as an ambiguous term that enabled Guaman Poma to reunite two non-Andean actions—drawing and writing—with the ancient accounts of knowledge" (Cummins 1998). Despite the relation between *quipu* and *quilca*, Guaman Poma does not manifest any relation between *tocapu* and *quilca*.

Since Guaman Poma and Martín de Murúa used elements of the Andean and European scripts, one can say that both authors proposed a double-coded text addressed to European and Andean readers, who would read either the verbal or the visual texts contained in them. Many scholars agree with this double-coding performed by the indigenous author:

> In a *tour de force*, Guaman Poma expresses his message in two modes simultaneously, his own native mode and the European mode. The modes often become intertwined as they express similar, but not identical, tales. A literal reading of Guaman Poma's Spanish text and a cursory glance at the illustrated figures and what they hold in their hands forefronts the European mode. Operating in the background, at the level of format and configuration, the tale is conveyed in the native mode, without being articulated in words. (Frame 2007, 10)

However in Frame's words, again the alphabetic script seems to be heavily associated with the European reader while the visual text of the drawings seems to address mainly the Andean reader. In a similar way, Martin de Murúa's chronicle has not been seen by most scholars as a double codification, but only as a Spanish chronicle of Indies with illustrations that ornament the verbal text. I think that Murúa's chronicle does offer a double codification, although his main perspective is European, as it happens with Guaman Poma's Andean perspective in his work. I come back to this point later, when I talk about "visual scripts."

I would like to go back now to the visual transformations that *quipus* and *tocapus* experience once they are depicted in the paper. *Quipus* appear in the *New Chronicle and Good Government* alongside Inca authorities who are discussing administrative organization (folio 337), the *quipucamayoc* or main accountant of the empire (folio 362) or local administrators (folio 350).The *quipu* appears also in pages dedicated to the pre- and post-Hispanic *chaskis.*[24] The *chaskis* drawings present an interesting sequence of representations of *quipu*, signs, and the Catholic rosary. While the young pre-Hispanic *chaski*, *Saiapaiac* (folio 204, figure 8) runs with a *quipu* and a sign—that has the word "carta" written on it—in one hand, the colonial *hatun chaski* (folio 825, figure 9) does not carry a *quipu* in his hand but rather a sign/letter, a trumpet to announce his arrival, and a rosary around his neck. The sign/ letter replaces the *quipu*, while the rosary confirms his quality of good Christian. In a similar way, Andean authorities appear with both, *quipu* and book, to denote information and knowledge related to the Inca good government and its extension to colonial times.

In relation to *tocapu*, Guaman Poma draws them and describes them in his *New Chronicle and Good Government* as I mentioned earlier. However, the number of *tocapus* decreases significantly in the chapter of *Conquest* and then in the second part, *Good Government* (2005). I want to stress now the design of *tocapus* to consider iconic spaces within the page that manifest Hispanic and Andean visual systems.

Alphabetic Script, Public Signs, and Coats of Arms

The *tocapus* use to appear, in first place, in royal and war-related garments of Inca nobility and officials. In addition, *tocapus* may be found on shields. At this point, it is important to distinguish between coats of arms, used as a showcase of ethnic and dynastic emblems, from shields that are used as defensive armor during battle. According to Guaman Poma's chronicle, textile activities appear for the first time in the "Third Age of Indians" (*Tercera Edad de Indios*, *Purun Runa*, folio 57). Six folios later, during the "Fourth Age of Indians" (*cuarta Edad de Indios: Auca Runa*, folio 63) Inca warriors who carry shields, wore garments with basic *tocapu* designs. In the next two folios one can observe "the First and the Second Arms of the Inca" (*Primeras*, folio 79, and *Segundas Armas del Inca*, folio 83), which are represented as Inca coats of arms. Within the frame of a Spanish-style coat of arms, the Andean symbols configure the quadripartite organization of *Tawantinsuyu*. The first one

includes elements associated with the first Incas' idolatric practices: the
many-rayed sun in the first-ranked *Chinchaysuyo* quadrant; the moon
in the *Andesuyo* quadrant; the hairy star or *lucero* in the lowest ranked
Condesuyo quadrant; and the three-stepped mountain with the three
caves of *Tambotoco* is shown in the bottom left quadrant that corresponds to *Collasuyo*. Incas believed that their origins were located in the
Collasuyo region, where the *Titikaka* Lake is located. In this illustration,
the quadripartite grid is a schematic diagram of the four *suyus*, pairing
idols with *suyus* in an appropriate rank order.[25]

The second coats of arms presents also a quadripartite distribution,
that corresponds to the "more civilized" era of the late Inkas: a bird that
could be identified with an eagle or hawk (upper left: *Chinchaysuyo*); a
feline (jaguar or otorongo, upper right, *Andesuyo*); two snakes in motion
(*amaro ynga*) that reproduce the aspect of "twoness" that differentiates
Collasuyo from the other suyus (bottom right); and a *mascaypacha* (the
royal Inka tassel, bottom left, *Condesuyo*). The two snakes in motion
usually appear in the coats of arms fabricated by descendants of the
Incas such as *Paullu Inca* and writer Inca Garcilaso de la Vega.[26]

Furthermore, all Inca rulers, except *Manco Cápac* (folio 86) and
Huáscar, who is taken prisoner by Atahualpa's generals (folio 115), display shields with *tocapu* designs and they all appear in battle stance.
Interestingly Frame has pointed out that the Inca rulers wear *uncus* with
diverse *tocapu* designs. Starting with the portrait of Inca Mayta Cápac
(folio 98), *tocapus* coincide with incipient shapes of Arabic numerals in
the following way: $\mathbf{Z}$ = 2 and $+$ = 4. In the following Inca portraits, the
numbers 2, 3, 4, and 8 will be part of most tunics worn by the *Sapa Inca*
(the supreme Inca, i.e., the Inca ruler). This series of portraits includes
a very old *Topa Inga Yupanqui* (folio 110), whose *uncu* is completely cov-
ered by *tocapus* as well.

I have noted earlier visual transformations of *quipu* in Guaman
Poma's drawings. In a similar way, the designs of *tocapus* experience
changes, such as those that I observe in the coats of arms associated
to the twelfth, thirteenth, fourteenth, and fifteenth captains (*doze,
treze, catorze y quinze* capitanes). The twelfth captain (El *doze* capitán,
folio 167) presents Guaman Chaua, grandfather of the author, with
the typical *tocapu* designs of his *Yarovilca-Chinchaysuyo* ethnic group.
Although he is described as a warrior in the verbal text, he does not
carry a shield in the illustration. However, one can observe, at the
bottom left, the coat of arms that the author, Guaman Poma, has
fabricated for himself and his family, and that appears again in the
frontispiece of his chronicle showcasing a hawk and a puma. It is

not casual that the first proposed Hispanic-Andean coat of arms is Guaman Poma's.

The next pages refer to three Andean pre-Hispanic captains that display Spanish-style coats of arms. The thirteenth captain (el *treze* capitán) is the leader of the *Antisuyo, Ninaraua, capac apo*. His coat of arms, located at the bottom right, represent Amazonian animals (jaguar or *otorongo*, and the snake, folio 169). He ostents a crown made of long feathers, most likely papagayo feathers. The fourteenth captain (el *catorze* capitán, *Mallco Castilla Pari*) is the leader of the *Collasuyo* army (folio 171). His coat of arms (bottom left) depicts a bird in an unpartitioned field. His headdress includes a half-moon and a feather. The fifteenth captain (el *quinze* capitán, Mallco Mullo) leads the *Condesuyo*, and displays a coat of arms (bottom left) whose crest is diagonally divided by crossed weapons and has four leg fringes in the quadrants. These symbols are distributed in a similar way to those in Spanish coats of arms (folio 173).

If we compare the drawings of these Inka captains with drawings of Spanish officials, one can observe that Spanish coats of arms are not displayed in the page as it is the case in European portraits, but rather, they are depicted on flags (folios 373, 377, 412). Let us observe the use of these emblems in the representation of a Spanish *conquistador, Martin de Arbieto*, and an Inca warrior, *don Tomás Topa Inca Yupanqui* (folio 462). Both characters wear armor and shields. *Tocapu* designs cover the tunic of the Inca warrior, and his shield as well. Such *tocapu* designs stress him not only as a valiant warrior but also as a noble one, which is confirmed by the use of "don" before his name. These features contrast with the attributes of the Spanish warrior, whose armor is Spanish but does not carry any design that would distinguish him as a Spanish noble.

Public Signs/Letreros

In addition to coats of arms and *tocapu* designs, I want to address a third object that has been already mentioned when I talked earlier about *chaskis* and *quipus*. In Guaman Poma's chronicle, one can observe that the crest of the coats of arms serve also as space for public signs (*letreros*).[27] Small *letreros* named "carta" are placed on the messenger's hands alongside with the *quipu* carried by *Saiapaiac*, the eighteen-year-old pre-Hispanic *chaski* (folio 204). Remember also the *letrero* carried by the *chaski* colonial who does not have a *quipu* in his hands, but a rosary around his neck (folio 825). In both signs the word *carta* (letter) or *despacho* (dispatch) is written and is clearly readable. In my opinion, Guaman Poma wants to assure the right decodification of his message: pre-Hispanic *quipus* do carry information, and they are easily replaced by alphabetic script, which transmits verbal information. From this point, one wonders about the role of alphabetic script within the space of these drawings. López-Baralt states that alphabetic script in these drawings assures the right decodification/reading of the message in the drawing, especially by the European reader.[28] López-Baralt points out that Guaman Poma is familiar with the European methods of the *arte de la memoria* (arts of memory) and states in the first pages of his chronicle that, in order to reach his readers, he will use the rhetorical devices of the arts of preaching, which include visual catequization to expose his program for good government (282). The author then appeals to the means of Western visual communication (paintings) that were used to evangelize those who could not read and write. However, the Andean visual communication systems cannot be reduced to an alternative communication for those who could not read, with the arrival of the Spaniards. Guaman Poma dedicated and addressed his book to the king of Spain and he presented it to him by means of a visual metaphor: "*y ancí por lo escrito y carta nos ueremos*" (And in this way, through the letter and the script, we shall see each other)" (folio 976). Drawing and alphabetic script relate to each other in Guaman Poma's text as the two interwoven elements that make meaning possible. This brings me to my last point in this article: the visual nature of alphabetic script.

Visual Script

In the colonial *letreros* or public signs proposed by Guaman Poma's chronicle, visual images and alphabetic script meet and this does not pose any problem to the European reader, since s/he is used to the combination of both in religious paintings. Guaman Poma insists in the necessity not only of persuasive religious paintings but also of moral public signs. In his chapter dedicated to the "corregimientos," the author draws a "letrero" in which painting and writing work together to communicate effectively its message: "A Jesus and Mary shall be painted (here) and below letters that say: *Beware, Christian, of God and His justice, and do not have pride and do not call justice to punish you.* This should be written in large letters"[29] (folios 517–18, figure 16). The *letrero* then conveys visual-iconic and verbal-written forms of communication. This *letrero* is framed by a Spanish-style coat of arms, which gives authority to its message.

In other *letreros*, Guaman Poma comments on the persuasive powers of alphabetic script and reflects, again, on the necessity of public moral signs (*letreros morales*) in his time:

> And the coats-of-arms and *letreros* shall be exposed in all cities, *villas*, villages, towns, big and small, *so the letter will be in their eyes*. And these letters shall be very large, and then the priests will read them, and the Indian men and women, to give example of justice. (folio 672, figure 17)[30]

This quote corresponds to the written message that shall be included in a blank *letrero* that frame is drawn as a coat of arms. The tassels that accompany this drawing are ambivalent, since they could correspond to both: the Spanish tassels displayed on war shields and the Inca *mascaypacha*. Likewise, the blank field of the coat of arms designs corresponds to the blank *letrero* where moral instruction shall be written. Finally, this *escudo-letrero* (coats of arms/sign) is crowned by a hat that is similar to the one that the author wears as an Indian authority of early colonial Peru. In this way, we can observe once more that for this Andean author, visual images (drawing, *tocapu* designs) and verbal images (alphabetic script) are components of a hybrid way of communication that function is "to have the letter in the eyes" and "to see each other through the letter." Marie Timberlake observes one interesting assumption about woven *tocapus* designs, associated with pre-Hispanic garments, and painted *tocapus* that are associated with colonial versions of these designs (2006). In both cases we are dealing with visual texts, but their perception varies because of their material support. According to Timberlake, there are differences of perception between the woven *tocapu* designs, generally understood by many scholars to have been a primary method to convey Andean history, while painted colonial *tocapus* have often been dismissed as empty signs, decorative elements that function as nostalgic referents to a pre-Hispanic past. In her research for what painted colonial *tocapus* represent, Timberlake's work seeks to demonstrate that painted *tocapus* continued to exhibit the fundamental design components as those manifested in textiles and garments of the pre-Hispanic Andes. Timberlake's proposal brings us to the realization that, despite being drawn, current scholarship neither question nor dismiss Guaman Poma's representations of *tocapu* as empty signs, probably because they appear for the most part as representations of woven *tocapus* and because their author is an iconic native author and artist.[31]

The utilization of *escudos-letreros* (coat of arms/public signs) as textual space for persuasion can be redefined in another possibility that I analyzed in another work and I called "a tocapu made of letters" (2005). I explain here briefly what I find as a pertinent example of "visual script." In his chronicle, Guaman Poma wrote the chapter about the Inca society administration under the visual shape of a *tocapu* design (folios 196–236). The dispositions of the lines in the pages form an upside-down triangle that ends with his signature. One should note the lines that the author wrote on the blank spaces of this triangle (folio 197). In relation to this "writing design" I have proposed more than one possible act of reading. The visual impression of these pages could be that of a *tocapu* design. Other possible visual interpretation is that of a *quipu* in which the vertical lines constitute its strings. The practice of adding phrases—*glosas* in the blank spaces left in the page to explain, expand, or comment certain points is common in the European medieval tradition. However, in the case of Guaman Poma's chronicle, the added lines appear consistently as a complement to what is said in the "main" text (the triangle). In the apparent left blank spaces, the author repeats his obsessions related to colonial corruption and the disappearance of the Indians as a race. Their tone is that one of complaint and accusation: the Indians will disappear as a result of the Spanish bad government. The alphabetic writing has then become, for the Andean reader of this contact zone, a visual text with the shape of a *tocapu*—or even a *quipu*. This is an example of what I call "visual script." Similarly, Martín de Murúa's chronicle offers a verbal representation of a *cumpi* belt, a textile made of woven *tocapu* that was carried by the *Coyas*. Murúa titles the alphabetic transcription as "Memory of a famous Chumbi de lipi or Cumbi, usually worn by the Coyas in the main feasts called çaras; it has one hundred and four and its duplicates. The eight are in the sides, four in each side."[32] In the description that follows, Murúa uses Arabic numbers and letters of the alphabet in organized sequences. At the end of twelve sequences, there is a list of weekdays and activities related to each day. Despite not having decoded the content of this text yet, this example is one of the few found documents in which a Spanish writer decodes or intends to transcribe alphabetically a sixteenth-century Andean text. Likewise, in previous folios, Murúa tells the story of *ñusta Chuquillanto* who speaks with four water springs or *puquios*. Chuquillanto, according to Murúa's tale, is in the middle of the four springs—an allegory of the four *suyus* of the Inca Empire— and a *tocapu*-like drawing follows. This drawing combines geometric designs with words in Spanish and Quechua. Murúa states that the *tocapu*-like drawing intends to represent the story of *Chuquillanto* and her song with the four springs (292). In these examples Guaman Poma's visual texts—that also incorporate alphabetic script—and Murúa's converge. As I mentioned earlier, Murúa's and Guaman Poma's chronicles provide European and Andean examples of how alphabetic script may be understood as a visual text in addition to a verbal text.

Conclusion

Hybridity in the Andean–Spanish contact zone gives place to the simultaneous utilization of different systems of communication that incorporate both, alphabetic script and iconic images.[33] The competence of an Andean author such as Guaman Poma de Ayala who is aware of both (or more) systems of communication, allows him to build texts that are "read" in different ways by diverse readers in the contact zone. Finally, the stress here is the power of visual systems of communication, among which I include the alphabetic script. *Tocapus*, books, rosaries, coats of arms, shields, public signs, *letreros-escudos*, and the alphabetic script in its visual nature, are recognized and read by the early colonial Andean subjects in ways that the Europeans are not used to. In addition, the alphabetic script in contact with non-Western systems of communication that do not reproduce necessarily the phonological structure of a language, was explored by the Andean people in its visual materiality and might have been regarded as a visual text. In this way, alphabetic writing in its visual materiality and Andean visual texts met in the page revealing a hybrid and complex way to transmit information about history, prestige, and authority in the heterogeneous contact zone that characterizes the Andean-Spanish colonial society.

Notes

1. I distinguish between "alphabetic writing" and "alphabetic script." According to the *Oxford English Dictionary Online*,"writing" refers to "the action of one who writes, in various senses; the penning or forming of letters or words; the using of written characters for purposes of record, transmission of ideas, etc." "Script" refers to "Something written; a piece of writing." When I use "alphabetic writing" in this chapter, I emphasize the dynamic process of producing a piece of information. In this process ideological constraints and expectations play a significant role. I use "alphabetic script" to refer to the finished material product: the letters in the paper. Then I use "script" as a material object produced by a technology. When this technology is in process and is imbued by ideology, "writing" is produced.

2. See also *Relation of the Quipucamayos* [1542–1608], cited by Lienhard (1992, 33); and Acosta (1987 [1590] Book 6, Chapter 8).

3. Jared Diamond, author of the best seller *Guns, Germs and Steel*, while exploring the roots of power and inequality, concedes his astonishment that the Incas lacked a writing system (1997, 67).

4. Descartes's study on the reflection of light in his philosophical essay "Optics" established the visual dimension of the Cartesian self "cogito ergo sum" (Mirzoeff 10).

5. Art historians of colonial Spanish America, such as Tom Cummins and Ilona Katzew, and scholars who have analyzed the relations between verbal and iconographic texts in colonial Spanish America, such as Rolena Adorno, Christian Fernández, Mary Frame, and Mercedes López-Baralt, have contributed to set elements of the Spanish American colonial visualities. Their works are cited at the end of this chapter.

6. I summarized works from Nicholas Mirzoeff and Iris Rogoff in N. Mirzoeff, ed. *The Visual Culture Reader*.

7. "Within the systems of auditory signs never space but only time acts as a structural factor, namely, time in its two axes, sequence and simultaneity; the structuration of visual signantia necessarily involves space and can be either abstracted from time, and as immobile painting and sculpture, or superinduce the time factor, as in the motion picture" (Jakobson 701).

8. When the Spaniards arrived to the Andes, they recorded oral Quechua in alphabetic writing. Since then, several written versions of Quechua have developed. In this work, I use the Castilian written form for *quipu* and *tocapu*. Other scholars follow phonological criteria and use instead *kipu, khipu, tokapu, tokhapu*, in which "k" and "kh" intend to reproduce the palatal and glottal features of the sound /k/ in these words.

9. *Quipu* means "knot" in Quechua. There are many works on the *quipu* systems. For rapid information, review Gary Urton's *Khipu Database Project*: http://khipukamayuq.fas.harvard.edu/index.html

10. The most famous Inca garment with tocapus can be found in the pre-Columbian collections of Dumbarton Oaks in Washington DC. This piece, known as "Pachacuti's shirt" was found in Peru's coast and contains a grid of diverse and colorful tocapus that seem to have indicated the ethnic diversity of the Inca Empire.

11. The colonial *caciques* wore tunics probably of *cumpi* (Q'ompi), the quechua name for finely woven cloth, the use of which in pre-Hispanic times was restricted by sumptuary laws. While cumi with tokapu ornamentation had been restricted to Inca royalty, once the Inca state was dismantled, the restrictions on royal regalia were loosened so that in colonial times any noble who could afford it would wore this fine fabric. (Dean, 124).

12. Felipe Guaman Poma de Ayala was native from Guamanga, Central Andes, and he lived approximately between 1550 and 1615. He stated being descent of a noble *Yarovilca* family. Native speaker of Quechua, he learnt to speak, read, and write in Spanish and became an *indio ladino* (*Latin* Indian, i.e., a learned Indian). He worked as interpreter of Cristobal de Albornoz, extirpator of idolatries and probably the person who gave him access to one of the most famous libraries of the early colonial period. Later on, Guaman Poma became notary of Indians. In the late 1590s, he was involved in lawsuits against Spanish officers and Chachapoyas Indians since they were disputing land ownership in Chupas. Unfortunately he lost the lawsuits and was punished and exiled from Guamanga. Scholars think that this loss made him write his major work *First New Chronicle and Good Government* (*Primer nueva corónica y Buen gobierno*), which he turned in to the viceroyalty authorities between 1613 and 1615. The chronicle, thought first as a letter to the Spanish King, became a large manuscript written in Spanish, Quechua, and Aymara, with 1200 folios, including almost 400 ink drawings. Guaman Poma's manuscript never reached his intended reader, the king, and it was lost for centuries until Richard Pietschmann found it in 1908 in the Royal Library of Copenhague. The text remains in this library and a recent digital version is accessible online: http://www.kb.dk/permalink/2006/poma/info/en/frontpage.htm (accessed August 19, 2009). All folios used in this chapter come from this digital edition.

13. Frame 2007, 10.

14. From this point on Mirzoeff will focus on the visual subject that experiences being seen, which uncovers the notion of surveillance and Michel Foucault's idea of *panopticon*: "In 1786 the British philosopher Jeremy Bentham invented a perfect prison that he called the panopticon. The panopticon was an inspection house for the reformation of morals, whether of prisoners, workers or prostitutes by means of constant surveillance that the inmates could not perceive, a system summed up by Michael Foucault in the aphorism 'visibility is a trap.' In Foucault's view, the panopticon was a model for the disciplinary society at large but the practices of visibility were not part of his inquiry. Rather, he simply assumed with Bentham that a straight sight line equated to visibility. For visual culture, visibility is not so simple. Its object of study is precisely the entities that come into being at the points of intersection of visibility with power." (10)

15. Adorno adds another interpretation of "new" in this context: "The notion of historiographic 'newness' as the combination of two, distinctive generic entities had been suggested by the Jesuit José de Acosta with whose works Guaman Poma was familiar. Acosta (1962, 13) had called his own 1588 *Historia natural y moral de las Indias* 'new' because it was in part 'history and in part philosophy.' With or without Acosta as a guide (Guaman Poma referred to Acosta's other works, not the *Historia* that contains the assertion), the notion of 'newness' representing something that was a hybrid or result of a mixture would not have been unfamiliar to Guaman Poma." http://www2.kb.dk/elib/mss/poma/docs/adorno/2002/witness.htm#4.7 (accessed August 19, 2009).

16. In my opinion, the image of this notary constitutes an *alter ego* of Guaman Poma. The Indian chronicler worked as an interpreter and notary of Indians in Guamanga before writing his chronicle. Today, scholars agree that his defeat in the legal arena brought him to write his ultimate text.

17. Autoethnography has been studied extensively in the last decade. Ellis and Bochner understand authoethnography as a form of writing that "make[s] the researcher's own experience a topic of investigation in its own right" (2000, 733). Autoethnography is also "an autobiographical genre of writing that displays multiple layers of consciousness, connecting the personal to the cultural" (739); autoethnographers "ask their readers to feel the truth of their stories and to become coparticipants, engaging the storyline morally, emotionally, aesthetically, and intellectually" (745). These texts are usually written in the first person and feature dialogue, emotion, and self-consciousness as relational and institutional stories affected by history, social structure, and culture. Susan Bennett's Workshop "Autoethnography: Writing about the Self Analytically" list features of an autoethnography as follows: an analytical/objective personal account; about the self/writer as part of a group or culture;often a description of a conflict of cultures; often an analysis of being different or an outsider; usually written to an audience not a part of the group; an attempt to see self as others might; an opportunity to explain differences from the inside; always an attempt to explain one element of self to other; an explanation of how one is "othered." http://www.humboldt.edu/~cpf/autoethnography.html

18. Pratt cites Fernando Ortiz's notion of "transculturation," used by ethnographers to describe the process in which subordinated subjects use materials from dominant groups. In Ortiz's words: "I am of the opinion that the word *transculturation* better expresses the different phases of the process of transition from one culture to another because this does not consist merely in acquiring another culture, which is what the English word *acculturation* really implies, but the process also necessarily involves the loss or uprooting of a previous culture, which could be defined as a deculturation. In addition it carries the idea of the consequent creation of new cultural phenomena, which could be called neoculturation" (102–03).

19. Moreover some scholars have proposed to extend the notion of literacy beyond its alphabetic notion, especially if one seeks to understand the impact of visual events/literacies in the textual production of the New World (Rappaport and Cummins 1998; Mignolo 1995a, 1995b). Ascher and Ascher, for example, refer to them as "visible languages" (1975).

20. In the stories narrated by Chimalpahin, for example, one appreciates the way in which native forms of expression (orality and pictography) are displaced and then replaced by alphabetic script (Mignolo 1992). The *Diferentes historias originales* [1620–1631] of Chimalpahin are the alphabetic transcription in náhuatl of ancient oral stories that are also inscribed in pictography. In this way, paintings and letter join in the space dominated by the alphabetic script (Ruhnau 1999). Mignolo also indicates that in these texts we find the expression "again I have painted" as synonym of "I have written with letters" (1992, 105–107).

21. González Holguín 1989 [1608]: 136, 301, 449; Santo Tomás 1951 [1560]: 182, 357.

22. González Holguín 1989 [1608]: 301; Santo Tomás 1951 [1560]: 188, 357.

23. González Holguín 1989 [1608]: 301, 514, 632; Santo Tomás 1951 [1560]: 61, 131, 357..

24. *Chaskis* were trained runners who carried information in the Andes. Guaman Poma points out that they carried *quipus* the same way in which they started carrying letters in the colonial period.

25. Frame 2007, 35.

26. Fernández traces the Andean tradition behind these signs, as well as the tradition behind the term *amaru*. Fernández analyzes then the motif of the snake from Manco Capac, founder of the Inca dynasty; to Pachacútec, the inac ruler who expanded greatly the imperial territory; Huayna Capac, father of Atahualpa and Tupac Amaru I, the last Inca of Vilcabamba who resisted the Spaniards from his exile in the upper rainforest. Likewise, Garcilaso de la Vega el Inca states having seen the coat-of-arms of Carlos Paullu Topa, descent of Huayna Cápac. This coat-of-arms has two crowned snakes and was approved by royal edict in 1549. The snakes in this Andean context symbolize fertility and reproduction and are seen as mediators between the sky and the earth.

27. It is important to note that the word "letrero" comes from "letra" (letter). According to the Diccionario de la Lnegua Española, "letrero" means "word or set of words that are written to make a public announcement." http://buscon.rae.es/draeI/SrvltConsulta?TIPO_BUS=3&LEMA=letrero

28. López-Baralt, 1988, 409.

29. "One shall paint Jesús, Mary and below letters that tell: Be fearful, Christians, of God and his justice, do not be arrogant and do not call Justice to punish you" (*"A de pintarse un Jesús, María y auajo unas letras que diga: 'Temed, cristianos, a Dios y a la justicia, y no tengáys soberuia y no llaméys a la justicia para que séays castigado'. Se ponga de letras grandes"*). The translation is mine.

30. "Weapons and public signs shall be in the cities, towns, villages and big and small towns of this kingdom as exemplary, and so the letters will be in their eyes. And these letters will be large enough so the priests will read them, the Indian men and women, and so they will see a model of justice" (*"Y las armas y letreros se le ponga en las ciudades, uillas, aldeas y pueblos grandes o chicos deste reyno para exenplo, para que la letra lo tenga en los ojos. Y esta dicha letra sean muy grandes para que los mismos dichos padres lo lean, los yndios y las yndias, que se den exemplo y tema de las manos de la justicia."*) The translation is mine.

31. Even with the importance recognized to Guaman Poma de Ayala as an Indian author and artist, Frame points out reasons for which some scholars have not taken him seriously on the subject of *tocapo*. Sometimes he represents *tocapo* as Hindu-Arabic numerals or possibly alphabetic letters, which they clearly are not. Frame states that Guaman Poma may be signaling to his European audience that these and other *tocapo* are meant to be "read." Frame goes further and suggests that Guaman Poma is signaling that the particular numerical value that he notates in a Hindu-Arabic numeral is meant to be read as a number property that could be embedded in a graphic *tocapu* (2007, 17).

32. The translation is mine. The original text is in Spanish: "Memoria de un famoso Chumbi de lipi o cumbi, que traían las Coyas en las grandes fiestas, çara; lleva ciento cuatro y los duplicados. Los ocho son los extremos, cuatro en un lado y cuatro en otro." (Quispe-Agnoli 2005, 288).

33. To understand this "hybridity," I need to explain my own position in relation to key
terms that I utilize in this chapter, such as "script," "literacy," "graphic," "visual," and
"tangible." Until *La fe andina en la escritura* (Lima: Fondo Editorial de la Universidad
Mayor de San Marcos, 2006), I have used "literacy" to designate both, European and
Andean graphic forms of communication. I have also used "western literacy" to refer to
European systems of communication such as the alphabetic writing and figurative drawings. Likewise I used "Andean literacy" to characterize Andean systems of communications that I consider equivalent to alphabetic writing (*quipus* and *tocapus*). I am aware that
when I say "Andean literacy" I am departing from a term associated with "alternative lit-
erature/literacy" that was proposed by Lienhard's and Mignolo's works in 1991 and 1994
respectively. Arellano-Hoffmann and Schmidt use the German term "Schriftlichkeit"
to denote the tangible and visual nature of the Amerindian communication systems.
Nevertheless terms such as "literacy," "graphic," and "Schriftlichkeit" become uncomfortable in this discussion because both are related to a western referent to "letter." In
addition, Noguez, editor of the Spanish edition of Arellano-Hoffmann and Schmidt's
book, indicates that the closest Spanish translation of "Schriftlichkeit" could be "escrit-
uralidad" (*writing-ability* if I invent the term) (2002, 28). Despite all these efforts to find
an adequate term for communication systems that do not use the phonological principles
of the alphabetic writing; we can only state that this is pending study. This explains my
choice of more globalizing terms such as tangibles/visual texts. I choose "tangibles" and
"visual" because meanings in these texts may be transmitted and decoded by the touch
and the sight.

Bibliography

Acosta, Joseph de. *Historia natural y moral de las indias.* 1987 [1590]. Madrid: Dastin Historia.
Adorno, Rolena. *Writing and Resistance in Colonial Peru.* Austin: University of Texas Press,
    1986.
———. A Witness unto Itself: The Integrity of the Autograph Manuscript of Felipe Guaman
    Poma de Ayala's *El primer nueva corónica y buen gobierno* (1615/1616). 2002. http://www2.
    kb.dk/elib/mss/poma/docs/adorno/2002/index.htm
Arellano-Hoffmann, Carmen. "Quipu y Tocapu. Sistemas de comunicación inca." In *Los Incas,*
    ed. Franklin Pease et al., 261–74. Lima: Banco de Crédito del Perú, 1999.
Arellano-Hoffmann, Carmen, Schmidt, Peer, and Vavier Noguez, coords. *Libros y escritura de
    tradición indígena.* Mexico: Colegio Mexiquense and Universidad Católica de Eichstaett,
    2002.
Ascher, Marcia and Robert Ascher. The Visual Languages of the Inkas. *Visible Language* 9
    (1975): 329–56.
———. *The Code of the Quipu.* Ann Arbor: University of Michigan Press, 1981.
Bennett, Susan. "Autoethnography: Writing about the Self Analytically." http://www.hum-
    boldt.edu/~cpf/autoethnography.html (accessed July 6, 2008).
Bhabha, Homi. *The Location of Culture.* London, New York: Routledge, 1994.
Boone, Elizabeth and Walter Mignolo, eds. *Writing without Words: Alternative Literacies in
    Mesoamerica and the Andes.* Durham: Duke University Press, 1994.
Cummins, Tom. Images on Objects: The Object of Imagery in Colonial Native Peru as Seen
    through Guaman Poma's *Nueva Corónica y Buen Gobierno. Journal of the Steward Anthropological
    Society* 25.1–2 (1997): 237–73.
———. *Let Me See! Reading Is for Them:* Colonial Andean Images and Objects "como es
    Costumbre tener los Caciques Señores." In *Native Traditions in the Postconquest World,* eds.

E. H. Boone and T. Cummins, 91–148. Washington DC: Dumbarton Oaks Library and Collection, 1998.

Cummins, Tom. *Los Quilcacamayoq y los dibujos de Guamán Poma.* In *Libros y escritura de tradición indígena.* Coords. C. Arellano-Hoffmann, P. Schmidt, and X. Noguez, 185–215. Mexico: Colegio Mexiquense and Universidad Católica de Eichstaett, 2002a.

———. *Toasts with the Inca: Andean Abstractions and Colonial Images on Quero Vessels.* Ann Arbor: University of Michigan Press, 2002b.

Dean, Carolyn. *Inka Bodies and the Body of Christ.* Durham: Duke University Press, 1999.

Descartes, René. *The Philosophical Works of Descartes.* London: Cambridge University Press, 1967.

Diamond, Jared. *Guns, Germs and Steel.* New York: Norton and Company, 1997.

Ellis, Carolyn and Arthur P. Bochner. "Autoethnography, Personal Narrative, Reflexivity: Researcher as Subject." In *The Handbook of Qualitative Research*, eds. N. Denzin and Y. Lincoln. 733–68. Thousand Oaks, CA: Sage, 2000.

Fernández, Christian. *Inca Garcilaso: Imaginación, memoria e identidad.* Lima: Fondo Editorial de la Universidad Nacional Mayor de San Marcos, 2004.

Frame, Mary. "Lo que Guaman Poma nos muestra, pero no nos dice sobre *Tokapu.*" *Revista Andina* 44 (2007): 9–48.

Garcilaso de la Vega, el Inca. *Comentarios reales de los Incas.* México: Fondo de Cultura Económica, 1991 [1609].

González Holguín. Domingo. *Vocabulario de la lengua general de todo el Perú llamado lengua Quichua o del Inca.* Lima: Imprenta de Francisco Canto, 1989 [1608].

Guamán Poma de Ayala, F. *El primer nueva corónica y buen gobierno.* [e-facsm] Copenhague: Biblioteca Real, 2001 [1615]. http://www.kb.dk/elib/mss/poma

Jakobson, Roman. "Language in Relation to Other Communication Systems." In *Roman Jakobson, Selected Writings*, 697–708. Paris/The Hague: Mouton, 1971.

Katzew, Ilona. *Casta Painting. Images of Race in Eighteenth-Century Mexico.* New Haven, CT: Yale University Press, 2004.

Lienhard, Martin. *La voz y su huella: escritura y conflicto étnico social en América Latina.* Hanover, NH: Ediciones del Norte, 1991.

López-Baralt, Mercedes. *Icono y conquista.* Madrid: Hiperión, 1988.

———. "*Un ballo in maschera:* hacia un Guamán Poma múltiple." *Revista de crítica literaria latinoamericana* 21.41 (1995): 69–93.

Mignolo, Walter. "La cuestión de la letra en la legitimación de la conquista." In *Conquistadores y conquistados*, ed. K. Kohut, 97–112. Frankfurt a.M.: Vervuert, 1992.

———. "Signs and Their Transmission: The Question of the Book in the New World." In *Writing without Words. Alternative Literacies in Mesoamerica and the Andes*, ed. E. H. Boone and W. Mignolo, 220–70. Durham: Duke University Press, 1994.

———. The *Darker Side of the Renaissance. Literacy, Territoriality and Colonization.* Ann Arbor: University of Michigan Press, 1995a.

———. "Decires fuera de lugar: sujetos dicentes y formas de transmisión." *Revista de crítica literaria latinomericana.* 21.41 (1995b): 9–31.

Mirzoeff, Nicholas, ed. *The Visual Culture Reader.* London: Routledge, 2002.

Murúa, M. de. *Historia del origen y genealogía real de los Reyes Incas del Perú*, ed. Constantino Bayle. Madrid: Consejo Superior de Investigaciones Científicas, 1946 [1590].

Oxford English Dictionary Online. http://dictionary.oed.com.proxy1.cl.msu.edu:2047/entrance.dtl (accessed July 7, 2008).

Pratt, Mary Louise. "Art of the Contact Zone." 1999. http://www.nwe.ufl.edu/~stripp/2504/pratt.html (accessed July 6, 2008).

Quispe-Agnoli, Rocío. *Cuando Occidente y los Andes se encuentran: Qellqay, escritura alfabé-
tica y tokhapu en el siglo XVI. Colonial Latin American Review* 14.2 (2005): 263–98.

———. *La fe andina en la escritura. Resistencia e identidad en la obra de Guamán Poma de Ayala*. Lima:
Fondo Editorial de la Universidad Nacional Mayor de San Marcos, 2006.

Rappaport, Joanne and Tom Cummins. Between Images and Writing: The Ritual of the King's
Quillca. Colonial Latin American Review 7.1 (1998): 271–94.

Rogoff, Iris. "Studying Visual Culture." In *The Visual Culture Reader*, ed. Nicholas Mirzoeff,
14–26. London: Routledge, 2002.

Ruhnau, Elke. Chalco y el resto del mundo. Las *Diferentes Historias Originales* de Chimalpahin
Cuauhtlehuantzin. In *Libros y escritura de tradición indígena*, coords. C. Arellano-Hoffmann,
P. Schmidt and X. Noguez, 435–60. Mexico: Colegio Mexiquense y Universidad Católica
de Eichstaett, 2002.

Santa Cruz Pachacuti Yamqui Salcamaygua, Joan de. *Relación de antigüedades deste reyno del
Perú*. Lima: Instituto Francés de Estudios Andinos y Centro Bartolomé de Las Casas, 1993
[1613].

Santo Tomás, Fray Domingo de. *Lexicón o Vocabulario de la lengua general del Perú*, ed. Fernando
de Córdoba de Valladolid. Lima: Fondo Editorial de la Universidad Nacional Mayor de San
Marcos, 1951 [1560].

Saussure, Ferdinand de. *Cours de Linguistique Générale*. Paris: Payot, 1972 [1907].

Titu Cusi Yupanqui. *Instrucción del Inca Don Diego de Castro Titu Cusi Yupanqui al Licenciado don
Lope García de Castro*. In *Early Americas Digital Archives*, 1570. http://www.mith2.umd.edu/
eada/html/display.php?docs=titucusi_instruccion.xml&action=show

Urton, Gary. *The Khipu Database Project*. Harvard University. http://khipukamayuq.fas.harvard.
edu/index.html (accessed July 6, 2008).

CHAPTER FIVE

Translating Nahua Rhetoric: Sahagún's Nahua Subjects in Colonial Mexico

CRISTIÁN ROA DE LA CARRERA

Franciscan friar Bernardino de Sahagún oversaw the production of the *General History of the Things of New Spain*, an extensive Nahuatl-Spanish encyclopedia of Nahua culture, roughly between 1558 and 1577. His efforts led to the production of an illustrated bilingual manuscript now known as the *Florentine Codex*, the most exhaustive resource ever produced to study a pre-Hispanic culture in the Americas during the sixteenth century. Twelve books arrange the subject into basic categories introducing the readers to various aspects of native life and language in central Mexico. Among these twelve, Book 6 of the *Florentine Codex*, entitled "Rhetoric and Moral Philosophy," records orations employed on various ceremonial occasions. The effort invested in compiling, collating, and translating indigenous speeches was intended to facilitate a larger project of cultural translation to grasp indigenous language, thought, and practices. Nahua oral discourse played a critical role in making a world of metaphors, concepts, and socially meaningful speech available to Christian missionaries who could appropriate some key features of that language to their own ends. As a matter of fact, these speeches came later to inform the development of Classical Nahuatl, that is, Nahuatl standardized by means of alphabetical writing to serve the purposes of evangelization. European categories of rhetoric and moral philosophy were key for the conversion process, as neophytes had to be persuaded by the Christian message and learn to behave according to the new precepts. The political implications that the record of indigenous orations in Book 6 has within Sahagún's larger encyclopedic project bring attention to the development of a colonial knowledge to master indigenous speech and social norms. The appropriation of oral discourse, however, involved a complex mediation process between Nahua and Christian speech traditions that creates new forms of cultural and rhetorical authority. What follows is an attempt to read those voices *in-between* the Nahua speech traditions and missionary ethnography by retracing the process of transforming Nahuatl oral discourse into rhetoric.

The process of cultural translation and more particularly the appropriation of indigenous speech by European missionaries was a means of managing the development of what scholars have termed Nahua Christianity, that is, Christian practice informed by Nahua cultural forms and meanings.[1] Sahagún explains that he started working on his larger project in 1558 by order of his provincial Fr. Francisco Toral, who had asked him to write in Nahuatl what he considered "useful for the indoctrination, the propagation and perpetuation of the Christianization" of the natives and "as a help to...the ministers who indoctrinate them."[2] The statement only partly explains why Sahagún went through the trouble of gathering and editing extensive records on Nahua life, but more importantly it explains the interconnection among three distinct bodies of text: the *General History*—which we best know through the *Florentine Codex*, the *Postilla*, a corpus of doctrinal and devotional writings, and the Canticles, later published as the *Psalmodia Christiana*.[3] The fact that all three texts respond to one and the same command suggests that the *General History* was to provide the linguistic and ethnographic component in a more ambitious writing program. John Schwaller argues that "One must envision the beginning of the total work as the *Historia General-Florentine Codex*, followed by the *Postilla*,...ending with the appendix, which rejects the moral, philosophical basis of the *Florentine Codex* in favor of the Christian system."[4] It follows that Sahagún recorded speeches from indigenous informants to later edit doctrinal and devotional texts. Such an extensive body of scholarship on Nahua culture as the *Florentine Codex* was intended both as an heuristic source for the Christian minister to decode indigenous language and behavior as well as a record to refute the "evil" aspects of native tradition. Sahagún's inquiry on Nahua culture and religion laid the groundwork for the missionaries to expurgate pagan content from native religiosity.

This effort to produce aids for cultural translation involved a substantial and continued investment of resources on the part of the

Franciscan order. The production process of the *Florentine Codex* itself is very complex and has been reconstructed by piecing together fragmented information dispersed throughout Sahagún's work.[5] The earliest material he compiled were the speeches that later became Book 6 on "Rhetoric and Moral Philosophy." The text has been dated to 1547, nearly a decade before Sahagún received the instructions from Toral to produce a source in Nahuatl to serve as an aid for ministry. It remains unclear whether Sahagún actually compiled these speeches himself or he made use of materials previously compiled by Fr. Andrés de Olmos or other Franciscans.[6] In addition to Book 6, Book 12 containing an indigenous narrative of the fall of Tenochtitlan has been dated back to 1555, three years before Toral became provincial. The remaining books were compiled within the various production phases of Sahagún's work: Tepepulco 1558–1560, Tlatelolco 1561–1565, and Mexico City 1565–1570. The Spanish translation seems to have been completed later between 1576 and 1578, and the manuscript known as the *Florentine Codex* was physically produced between 1578 and 1579.[7] The latter is the only complete, clean copy of the twelve books, including Nahuatl text, a Spanish paraphrase, and drawings. It was a slow process of production that yielded various extant manuscripts at different stages, mostly because of the rigorous methodology employed in gathering and revising the materials copied in the manuscripts.

The production of the *Florentine Codex* facilitated the transfer of cultural and linguistic authority from native subjects to European missionaries. Sahagún's work and methodologies were consistent with previous work done by Olmos, who also used pictorial text and statements from indigenous informants in the production of his *Tratado de antigüedades mexicanas.*[8] Around the same time the Book 6 speeches were collected from elders, Olmos completed another collection later published in 1600 by Fr. Juan Bautista as *Huehuetlatolli, o pláticas de los viejos.*[9] The development of common methodologies and the effort to produce similar types of materials among missionaries suggest the compilations were concerted responses to meet the needs of evangelization.[10] That both Olmos and Sahagún, at one point or another, were ordered to compile these sources by their superiors also indicates that their projects were meant to meet the larger demands of evangelization policy. Jorge Klor de Alva argues that the development of Classical Nahuatl as "the literary or 'vehicular' language of instruction, Christianization, and ritualized communication" rested on the cooptation of the native elite.[11] Similarly, Walter Mignolo notes that the alphabetization of indigenous languages relied on models derived from Latin as the language associated with prestigious legacies in science, law, and religion.[12] Control over indigenous speech and literary forms was instrumental not only to meet the goals of proper Christianization, but also to legitimize the friars' authority.

Sahagún took an innovative approach to recording indigenous speech, which certainly made him stand out among his Franciscan predecessors and counterparts. Luis Nicolau D'Olwer believes that Sahagún was reprimanded because he had compiled materials in Nahuatl "outside the limits of catechesis" before receiving the assignment from Toral in 1558.[13] These reprimands most likely stemmed from the collection of speeches for the book on rhetoric, which included prayers to Nahua gods. This approach to indigenous religion is characteristic to the *Florentine Codex* and therefore it seems safe to assume that Sahagún himself had a role in putting together the compilation. Josefina García Quintana shows that Sahagún's collection of speeches is the only one to retain aspects missionaries considered idolatrous.[14] Both Olmos and Juan Bautista, on the other hand, systematically replaced references to indigenous gods with the Christian god, in addition to adapting their texts to educate Nahua audience in the commandments, capital sins, theological virtues, and teachings from the Scriptures. The *Florentine Codex* is unique, for it not only records information about preconquest religious practices or oratorical language, but it records idolatrous speech itself. This was a particular point of concern within some circles of Franciscans and colonial authorities for the fear that the manuscripts could be employed by indigenous people to revive the very practices missionaries had been trying to eradicate.[15] Sahagún, for his part, believed that without detailed knowledge of preconquest beliefs and practices true eradication of idolatries was doomed to failure. His choice, however, was not without risks.

A singularity of Sahagún's approach to Nahua speech is his transcription methodology, which involved adding extra layers of scrutiny to the information he received from his informants. Sahagún explains that he first brought a set of questions to ten or twelve Nahua elders in the town of Tepepulco who spent two years with him discussing various aspects of their culture and gave him pictorial records containing all the information he had requested. Sahagún was accompanied in these exchanges by four Nahua aids, themselves children of Nahua nobles who had been educated as Christians and trained in Latin grammar by the Franciscans at the Colegio de Santa Cruz Tlatelolco. They assisted Sahagún in recording in alphabetical script the information obtained from the elders. After moving to Tlatelolco, he had the text revised, reorganized, and newly transcribed by Nahua assistants whom he considered experts in Nahuatl, Spanish, and Latin. Finally, he repeated a similar process in Mexico City.[16] Not only was he attempting to produce the most complete and accurate possible text by consulting with informants in different locations, but he was also relying on the specialized help of native Nahuatl speakers trained in Latin and Christian doctrine. In addition to their native command of language and culture, Sahagún's students take on a heightened role because of their handling of the transcription and alphabetization process. They are the ones physically putting the manuscripts together and, to a great extent, controlling the presentation of the informants' speech to the reader.

There are some indications in the collection suggesting that Sahagún's Nahua aides played an active editorial role in the production of the *Florentine Codex*'s Book 6. Various headings and introductory paragraphs presenting the speeches provide abundant ethnographic commentary for the benefit of a nonnative reader. These comments describe the social context in which the orations were delivered and provide basic indications regarding their content and style. More significant in terms of cultural translation, perhaps, is that the book's title employs the Spanish words for rhetoric and moral philosophy because of the lack of literal equivalents in Nahuatl,

> Nican vmpeoa: injc chiquancen amuxtli, uncan moteneoa in tlatlatlauhtiliztlatolli: injc qujntlatlauhtiaia inteuan catca: yoan in juh tecpillatouaia, injc qujmatia rethorica, ioan in philosophia moral: in juh neztica in jpan tlatolli.
>
> Here begineth the sixth book, in which are told the various words of prayer with which they prayed to those who were their gods; and how they made formal conversation, through which they displayed rhetoric and moral philosophy, as is evident in the discourses.[17]

The concepts of rhetoric and moral philosophy would have been alien to a Nahua neophyte, but not to a Nahua assistant trained in the liberal arts tradition at the Colegio de Santa Cruz Tlatelolco. As a matter of fact, this voice records and organizes information to facilitate the reading in Nahuatl for an audience developing an understanding of indigenous speech in European terms. Many chapters in Book 6 include extensive ethnographic description of ceremonial behavior and ritual performances. The Nahuatl introduction to a prayer addressed to Tezcatlipoca directs the reader to note that "it is quite apparent how they really believed that all those who died in war went there to the house of the sun, there to rejoice forever."[18] It would make no sense for a Nahua informant to cite a prayer for reassurance regarding a preconquest belief, because the elders themselves were the source of authority. The statement introduces an authorial voice within the Nahuatl text that is situated in-between the informant and a nonnative reader. Miguel León-Portilla attributes these commentaries to Sahagún himself as the director of the compilation, however, many editorial interferences presuppose native command of Nahua language and culture.[19]

The ethnographic text not only provides indications of who the speakers are and the occasions when the orations were pronounced, but it also presents information about beliefs and rituals. The overall tone is that of someone mediating between insiders and outsiders. The clearest examples are found in Chapters 7 and 23 through 40, which have a strong ethnographic tone and deal as much, or more, with ritual practice as with speech. Chapter 7 contains speeches delivered by Nahua priests in confession rituals, and the heading adds the comment that they performed them "when they still practised idolatry."[20] Within a larger sequence of chapters dealing mostly with rituals associated with pregnancy and childbirth, Chapter 29 is devoted to explain that women who died in childbirth became the goddesses called *mocihuaquetzqui*. In the middle of the description, the narrator explains that these goddesses appeared before their former husbands in search of their earthly belongings,

> The demon, the devil, deceived in this manner: many times he manifested himself; he appeared before one like one who had become a *mociuaquetzqui* he addressed, he encountered the one who had been her husband; he sought, he demanded the skirt, the shift, all the equipment of women.[21]

By identifying the apparition of *mocihuaquetzqui* as a manifestation of the devil (*in tzitzimjtl, in coleletli*), the narrator abandons the Nahua belief system for a Christian interpretation. Tzitzimitl was a goddess in the night sky and *tzitzimime*, in the plural, were female demonic beings that ruled in the underworld and who also play a central role in the destruction of the world.[22] The identification of "female demons" with the *mocihuaquetzqui* does not reflect indigenous belief. Moreover, the idea that they could take the image of these women can only be explained as a demonological interpretation of the informants' statement.[23] In fact, the text reproduces the language commonly employed by friars in sermons to allude to the devil.[24] It is important to consider here that this passage introduces a Christian interference into an otherwise noninterpretive, dispassionate description of Nahua ritual and belief. It is unlikely that Shagún could have produced the descriptive Nahuatl text, as it is well-known that he relied on native Nahua speakers to produce, correct, and edit written Nahuatl. The Nahuatl voice dominating the text is consistent with that of a native speaker well trained in the Christian doctrine and vigilant to the cultural and religious differences relevant to the missionary agenda.

The question of how Sahagún and his assistants conceived and went about putting together this book on "Nahua Rhetoric and Moral Philosophy" is, nonetheless, enormously difficult to answer. Among the twelve books of the *Florentine Codex*, Sahagún portrayed Book 6 as the major piece in the collection, both because of its length and content.[25] This suggests that he may have set apart his most valuable materials to be included as chapters within the collection. Alfredo López Austín notes that Sahagún consulted with Nahua specialists to compile the speeches for this book, perhaps using something like an outline.[26] These specialists had relative freedom, as he observes that although Sahagún was soliciting specific information, some material was most likely unexpected. López Austin concludes that Book 6 contains "valuable free exposition which connects some speeches with others and explicates the themes treated."[27] Unfortunately, we lack Sahagún's questionnaires and the book's content make it impossible to reconstruct them even hypothetically as is the case in other books. The fact that Book 6 dates back to 1547, more than ten years before Sahagún systematically interviewed his informants, makes the history of these speeches all the more obscure. It may well be that any part of the prayers, orations, and admonitions were part of the original material and the other pieces were subsequently added because they were good sources for metaphorical language and moral philosophy.

There is also the question of whether the content of Book 6 corresponds to Nahua categories of oral discourse at all. Angel María Garibay makes a strong distinction between *huehuetlahtolli*, "Pláticas de los ancianos," which he considers limited to didactic speech, and other samples of ceremonial speech in the book.[28] Book 6 does not match any indigenous speech typology as evidenced by the retention in the Nahuatl title of the Spanish words "rethorica" and "philosophia moral." López Austin states that the contents of Book 6 "can be classified as prayers to the gods, speeches of the king, paternal exhortations, speeches for ceremonies and solemn occasions... and proverbs, riddles, and metaphors."[29] Evidently, Sahagún's use of the Western categories of rhetoric and moral philosophy serves to organize a heterogeneous array of texts that share similar stylistic features.

The dominant view among scholars, however, asserts the textual unity of Book 6. Miguel León-Portilla considers Book 6 as a collection of *huehuetlahtolli* (the "Ancient Word").[30] However, the acceptance of the expression *huehuetlahtolli* as the Nahuatl word describing the contents of Book 6 does not reflect indigenous usage in the sixteenth or seventeenth centuries. The word is only employed by Juan Bautista Viseo in the title of his 1600 edition of Olmos's compilation of speeches. Fr. Alonso Molina had recorded the word earlier in the sixteenth century, "Veuetlatolli. historia antigua, o dichos de viejos" [Huehuetlahtolli. Ancient history or sayings of the elders.][31] If Molina's definition is correct, then Bautista's use may not refer to a particular genre of Nahuatl speech, but rather the fact that Olmos had collected the speech by using Nahua elders as his informants. In addition, this could be a way of authorizing those speeches, as Olmos had adapted the speeches to convey Christian teachings. Most scholars have opted to retain the word *huehuetlahtolli* as a rough equivalent to Western rhetoric and moral philosophy, but this has meant developing a generic type that differs from Molina's definition and Juan Bautista's usage of the word. Thelma Sullivan defines *huehuetlahtolli* as "'the words of the elders' or 'ancients,' or 'the language of the elders' or 'ancients,'" adding,

> The *huehuetlahtolli* were the rhetorical orations in general—the prayers, discourses, salutations, and congratulatory speeches—in which the traditional religious, moral, and social concepts handed down from generation to generation were expressed in traditional language—that is, rhetorical language.[32]

She observes that Sahagún's compilation of speeches were orations to be delivered on special occasions, and thus concludes that the *huehuetlahtolli* "are both the language of the elders and of the ancients, the rhetorical, ritual, and ceremonial language of...an inordinately ritualistic and ceremonial people."[33] Sullivan's definition of *huehuetlahtolli* as ceremonial language mostly serves to account for the content of Book 6 of the *Florentine Codex* that do not fit the mold of didactic speech and to endow the book as a whole with a conceptual and generic unity. Although this way of looking at the speeches has enormous analytical value, it is ultimately designed to respond to the needs of researchers rather than attempting to reflect the understanding of indigenous speakers.

Josefina García Quintana argues that *huehuetlahtolli* strictly means "ancient word," or "word deposited in the minds of the elders," and notes that the most commonly employed word in the headings of the speeches was *tenonotzaliztli* and *tenonotzaliztlahtolli* (advice, admonition).[34] Her analysis of the category of *huehuetlahtolli* underscores the patrimonial sense of the expression, given that it was the elders who were entrusted with the transmission and preservation of the speeches from generation to generation.[35] Language as possession conveys precisely the conflict of cultural authority implied in the colonial situation where an outsider to an indigenous community records local language and knowledge to make sense of it from the European tradition. The desire to use the speeches to produce insights on local indigenous authoritative traditions explains why the word *huehuetlahtolli* has become conceptually so important in classifications of Nahuatl speeches. It is also quite evident, that this is mainly a category useful for a critical approach to study an alphabetical record of orally transmitted language. It is in this sense, *huehuetlahtolli* may better convey an act of alphabetical appropriation of speech than an actual indigenous category. After all, for Nahua people the role of the elders in the transmission of knowledge was self-evident and did not need to constitute a separate category of knowledge or generic taxonomy.

A brief overview of Book 6 yields five basic thematic units: (1) prayers on behalf of the community's welfare (Chapters 1–8, with a slight variation in 7 where the confession ritual focuses on the individual); (2) orations performed for the installment of a new ruler (Chapters 9–16); (3) admonitions by nobles to their children (Chapters 17–22), descriptions and speeches related to marriage, pregnancy, childbirth, and dedication of children (Chapters 23–40); and (4) Nahuatl idiomatic usage in sayings, riddles, and metaphors (Chapters 41–43). A question about formal speech does not account for the extensive section on pregnancy and childbirth, which includes long descriptive passages dealing with rituals and beliefs. The common thread is the life of the indigenous nobility, but the first two sections focus on collective well-being and rulership, whereas the third and fourth on the fate of individuals. León-Portilla takes the thematic unity of the fourth section to be that of "the principal moments in the life cycle," which would explain its interest from a missionary perspective.[36] The final three chapters are based on specific Nahuatl concepts *tlatlatolli*, "sayings," *çaçanilli*, "riddles," and *machiotlatolli*, which in Book 6 is employed as an equivalent of "metaphor," but this word also has the more general meaning of "simile" and "parable."[37] The contexts of utterance for the various groups of speeches are so different, that only thing they have in common is their tie to the life of the nobility. Another way of looking at Book 6 is mostly as recording instances of the *pillahtolli*, the speech of the nobility. As Klor de Alva argues, this was the language adopted by missionaries to reinforce their hierarchical relationship with native audiences.[38] The overall unity of the book may depend less on how the informants made thematic connections between various speeches than on how Sahagún and his aides organized the materials to model the language of Nahua elites.

An examination of the headings and how they direct the reader to elicit particular content from the text reveals a great deal about the way the text displaces indigenous speech. In addition to providing the context and summarizing the main content of the speeches, there are a number of observations on characteristics of the language. These comments are used to praise the quality of metaphors ("in metaphoras, in machiotlatolli"), speeches ("tlatolli"), thoughts ("sentencias"), and admonitions ("tenonotzaliztlatolli"). The characterizations reiterated again and again are "qualli in tlatolli" (good speeches), "maviçauhquj in tlatolli" (admirable speeches), "maviçauhquj in machiotlatolli in metaphoras" (admirable figures of speech, metaphors), and "quaqualli in metaphoras" (good metaphors). In one case, the comment remarks that a speech pronounced by a dignitary during the ceremony of installment of a new ruler is inferior to the previous ones. Some utterances are identified as *tecpillahtolli*, "courtly language," thus indicating the social connotations of certain language uses. The editorial commentary emphasizes the value of language usage as traits to be isolated and made recognizable for the reader.

The editors certainly were after particular forms of language usage, irrespective of subject matter. Idolatrous content was treated as providing clues about the preconquest belief system or was simply dismissed from the vantage point of Christianity. It is meaningful that the assistants make a strong distinction between language and content. In Chapter 8, for instance, the commentary praises the discourses while simultaneously indicating how they reveal the "follies of ancient times."[39] The ability to distinguish between content and language was critical to the missionary enterprise and may also explain why the samples vary so much in nature. The resulting product for the reader is the language of the nobility in various social contexts: the prayers of the priests, speeches on rulership, advice to children on rules of conduct, formal speech in family occasions (exhortations, prayers, speeches for marriage, pregnancy, birth, and the dedication of children). This suggests that the method to obtain the "good speeches" that the commentary highlights throughout the text may have been rather indirect. The ultimate goal behind the compilation was to employ the language to teach Christian doctrine in the way found in Olmos and Bautista. One of the commentaries assumes a desire on the part of the reader to purge non-Christian content from the text:

> This discourse especially should be memorized, if it is to be used for instruction, for it is a very good discourse; but that which is not necessary to be changed. It is especially useful for the youths, for the maidens.[40]

The stated goal of adapting the speeches for Christian instruction is quite revealing, because it shows the unity of the book lies primarily in the possibility of mining language and concepts rather than on some kind of generic unity.

Translating oral discourse into Nahua rhetoric, therefore, involved a twofold process. First, to authorize the language recorded in the text, procedures were developed to guarantee its integrity. Nahua specialists, who not only had the knowledge but also the social legitimacy to speak authoritatively about what was said on any given occasion, were the source where the text originated. Specially trained assistants later helped Sahagún produce revised transcriptions, polishing errors and making sure oral speech was rendered correctly. Thus the final result retains a certain flavor of authenticity, while providing an ideal rendition of those speeches by the standards of Sahagún's assistants.[41] The second aspect of the translation process takes us away from Nahuatl language and speech to reorganize it within Western understandings of language and social uses of speech. Walter Mignolo points out that generic categories cannot be examined independently of the social practices associated with them, because a culture's organization of knowledge categorizes forms of verbal behavior according to the uses they have for any given society.[42] Defining various forms of speech as "rhetoric and moral philosophy" means that they offer samples of language usage that can carry prestige and influence among indigenous audiences. This process of translation, however, is not simply a mapping of language. As the notion of "moral philosophy" implies, the speeches were also intended to provide knowledge about the relations between language, values, and actions. The idealized version of

Nahuatl speeches in Book 6, thus functioned as vantage point to manage indigenous language, behavior, and thought.

The notion of the Nahuatlization of Christianity primarily conveys this process of rhetorical appropriation where a mastery of language and metaphors was instrumental to making Christianity intelligible for native converts. This process was not without vacillations and rather reveals significant differences from one source to another. Charles Dibble has shown that after the *Coloquios y doctrina cristiana* of 1564, Sahagún's doctrinal writings scarcely employ Nahuatl literary devices, particularly those found in Book 6 of the *Florentine Codex*.[43] Jorge Klor de Alva argues that Sahagún changed his assessment of evangelization after the *Coloquios* and focused his energy on his ethnographic project to identify pagan remnants among Nahua Christians.[44] This may explain why the *Postilla* (1579) lacks literary flourish. If, as Dibble sustains, Sahagún came to associate metaphors with the *cantares*, then he may have avoided them purposefully to fend off pagan content. Seemingly, Arthur Anderson agrees with Dibble's characterization of Sahagún as scrupulous and literarily austere in the *Postilla*, but regards the *Ejercicio cuotidiano*, a short piece containing meditations based on biblical passages for each day of the week, as an exception.[45] It is quite telling that the exception comes from a text that is based on the rewrite of a manuscript Sahagún had originally found circulating among indigenous people.[46] Moreover, the *Postilla* lent itself for adopting the literary style of the *huehuetlahtolli*, but to all appearances it moves away from Book 6. Charles Dibble shows that

> the "Postilla" included the Nahuatl text of Chapters 22 and 40 from Book 6. The page order of the manuscript has been altered in places, some sections are repeated, and the second person singular has been changed to second person plural. Judging from the material here cited, we conclude that Sahagún has included these chapters from Book 6 for the sole purpose of refuting both their content and their metaphorical style.[47]

In other words, Sahagún was deliberately and systematically rejecting the indigenous speech recorded in the *Florentine Codex*.

The conflictive rewriting of Book 6 in the *Postilla* forces us to look at the *Florentine Codex* in a different light. After all, the manuscript of Book 6 was physically produced in 1578–1579 at the same time as the *Postilla*. If Sahagún was eventually to discredit the rhetoric of Book 6, why did he let the Nahuatl text retain the introductory comments praising the quality of the speeches and figures of speech? Moreover, he had already decided that the use of Nahuatl metaphors and concepts had to be limited in Christian sermons and his main interest was to identify the persistence of idolatries. The editorial commentary in Book 6, however, works with the contrary assumption. It is important to recognize in Book 6 the agenda of separating language from religious content. This is an indication of the independent intervention of a Nahua editor invested in legitimizing the language of the speeches as a medium for the propagation of Christianity. It may be surmised that these characteristics were already present in the earlier manuscripts and passed unchecked into the *Florentine Codex*. However, this was not just any copy, but a clean copy to be sent to Spanish authorities. These inconsistencies between ethnographic and doctrinal projects certainly attest to Sahagún's limited editorial intervention in the manuscript's production. Adopting the Nahuatl of Book 6 for the propagation of the Christian message implied granting greater weight and authority to Nahua assistants, and perhaps even some leeway in fashioning and adapting Christian speech and ritual to Nahua practice.

Given these ambivalences, it is not surprising that missionary rhetoric in some ways translates as a cultural loss for Nahua communities. It is not just that the traditional style was abandoned, but rather that Christian preaching was not effectively adapted to Nahua cultural conditions. Louise Burkhart emphasizes the disconnect between Christian rhetoric and indigenous life:

> Indigenous rhetoric emphasized interpersonal persuasion, with a tendency to relate the prescribed or proscribed behaviors to fundamental facts about reality, often expressed in the form of proverbs, and calling upon the wisdom of the ancestors. The friars also engaged in much interpersonal discourse ("you should do this, you should not do that") but tended to validate their statements by referring to third-person events. . . . Assuming that Nahua rhetoricians had developed the style of argument most effective within their cultural context, the friars' divergence from this pattern may have weakened the effectiveness of their teaching.[48]

Part of the problem may lie in the approach followed by missionaries to introduce Christianity to Nahua audiences. Their positions as colonizers and their emphasis on asserting the authority of the Christian message may have hampered their ability to present Christianity as a path to revolutionize Nahua life. Don Paul Abbot observes in Book 6 the type of rhetoric "intended to induce individual conformity to traditional values."[49] The speeches were therefore effective means of transmitting traditional values and maintaining social structures. He also explains how someone like Sahagún may have felt some familiarity with the language, as "the *huehuetlahtlolli* are strikingly similar to epideictic oratory—the classical genus which is probably most typical of Renaissance rhetoric."[50] This similarity between the speeches and epideictic oratory is central for an assessment of their usefulness in evangelization. Epideictic oratory focuses on praise and blame, and its main function is to "defend traditional and accepted values, those which are the object of education, not the new and revolutionary values."[51] Insofar as it is Nahuatl models of epideictic discourse that missionaries are adapting for their sermons, the main move is in the direction of replacing indigenous forms of authority. The problem lies in the truth of that authority before an indigenous audience. In order for missionary speech to work as epideictic discourse it needed that converts recognize it as defending accepted values and protecting community integrity.

Book 6 can be read as an attempt to answer the question of how Christian teaching could effectively engage Nahua life in the context of sixteenth-century evangelization. Sahagún's decision to take a divergent path speaks to his fears regarding Nahua appropriations of Christian practice and belief. This was ultimately an issue of balancing authority in the back and forth between the Nahua and Christian rhetorical traditions. After all, appropriating the authority of Nahua elders could never be effected on a purely formal level and without ceding part of it to Nahua collaborators. Translating Nahua rhetoric could not be simply a matter of cultural functionality either. Walter Mignolo argues we need to pay greater attention to the material aspect of how Nahuas understood that wisdom was preserved and transmitted:

> Sahagún's *Huehuetlatolli*...are paradigmatic examples of the authority of the elders in a society in which oral transmission is more important than written communication, and wisdom is deposited in the living body rather than in the book.[52]

Mignolo's contention is that in "societies in which knowledge is transmitted orally, the elders are the storehouse of wisdom," and thus they are "organizers of knowledge" and "sign carriers."[53] Looking at Book 6 of the *Florentine Codex* from this perspective suggests that a radical transformation is taking place. It is not just that the genre, social practices, and forms of authority associated with them have changed. This, however, does not translate into an assimilation of Nahua rhetoric into the alphabetic tradition and its subjection to European cultural authority. As Carla Mulford argues, "even in written form...the reproduction of the record of the past remains conflicted and conflictual."[54] These were not records likely to reach native audiences as Spanish authorities feared, but they made it possible for forms of cultural authority outside the European Christian scriptural tradition to emerge.

Arthur Anderson has shown how Sahagún's sermons deftly assimilate the model of the *huehuetlahtolli* to introduce the Christian message.[55] He cites sermons transcribed and translated by Barry Sell that ask parents, "Why do you not urge them to know the *Persignum Crucis*, the *Pater Noster*, the *Ave María*, the *Credo*, the *Salve Regina*, the [fourteen] articles of the faith and the commandments of God?...You will go to hell if you do not meet your obligations."[56] Each sermon, he adds, "is introduced by what amounts to an invitation to parents to add to their store of domestic *huehuetlatolli* a Christian one based on the sermon's theme."[57] If the intended goal of the sermons was ever accomplished, Sahagún and his assistants may have developed a technology to inscribe Christianity into the indigenous body. Rather than simply dispensing with the elders, the sermons are introducing new traditions and forms of authority into the community's oral performances. This practice, moreover relied on Nahuas themselves for incorporating the new speeches and transforming their traditions from within, as Anderson puts it

> Sahagún must have thought them important, too, as a means of fixing Christian worship, ideals, and principles in the minds of his converts. For the intelligent Nahua was noted for his retentive memory, being able on one hearing to repeat complex texts word for word. With repetition they remained fixed in his mind. That was one reason the *huehuetlatolli* were so effective.[58]

The possibility of repetition eliminates the main limitation of alphabetical writing of displacing authority from the body. The procedure, however, demands a continuous back and forth between missionary authority and community as seen in the case of the *Ejercicio cuotidiano* edited by Sahagún's assistants. The result is a hybrid form of cultural authority where speech is appropriated and rewritten under missionary direction, but keeps reverting back to the mnemonic appropriation of indigenous agents.

As a translation of oral discourse into Nahua rhetoric, Book 6 trans-
forms the conditions of enunciation of Nahua speech. In doing so, it
displaces the enunciation of indigenous speech by intersecting its traditional forms of cultural authority with scriptural practices that weaken
their functionality in relation to local community life. This displacement, however, introduces enormous fluidity into speech. Sahagún's
case reveals that not only the alphabetical record of Nahuatl speech
could be made malleable for missionary use, but also made room for
intermediary roles. If the alphabetical record eliminates the need for
the body of the elders and bypasses traditional forms of legitimating
knowledge in indigenous communities, it also draws new trajectories
for the "Ancient Word." By retaining the body of elders as a point of
origin, it inscribes a space where speech can follow a trajectory back
into the bodies of Nahua audiences. In this trajectory, native Nahuatl
speakers with Christian training inscribed their intervention to negotiate the difference. In this process of cultural appropriation, one certainly
cannot fail to perceive Sahagún's ambitious and visionary approach to
Nahuatl speech, but one must also envision how his Nahua assistants
carve a place for themselves as translators of Nahua rhetoric.

Notes

I am indebted to Scott Sessions for his suggestions and commentaries.

1. Dibble "The Nahuatlization of Christianity," 225–33, explains how missionaries needed to
   rely on Nahua language and metaphors to make Christianity intelligible to Nahua audiences.
   Burkhart takes the idea a step further to argue that "Christian rhetoric was made indigenous
   by its adoption of Nahua form" (14).
2. Sahagún, *Florentine Codex*, 1: 53.
3. On Sahagún's doctrinal encyclopedia, see Luis Nicolau D'Olwer, *Fray Bernardino de Sahagún
   (1499–1590)*, translated by Mauricio J. Mixco (Salt Lake City: University of Utah Press,
   1987), 35–41; Anderson, "Sahagún's 'Doctrinal Encyclopaedia,'" 109–22; and Schwaller.
4. Schwaller, 13.
5. Dibble, "Sahagún's *Historia*," 9–23. For a study of the various manuscripts produced
   under Sahagún's supervision and their composition process, see García, *Fray Bernardino de
   Sahagún*.
6. On the composition of Book 6, Garibay (425–27, 438–439) advances the theory that
   Fr. Andrés de Olmos compiled two groups of documents, one gathered from commoners
   and another from nobles, the latter of which Sahagún appropriated the second group of texts
   for Book 6 of the *Florentine Codex*. Hanson adduces further circumstantial evidence in support of this thesis (29–35). However, based on stylistic and linguistic differences between the
   two groups, Sullivan maintains that Olmos's and Sahagún's compilations come from different localities and must be regarded as independent from each other (79–109).
7. Dibble, "Sahagún's *Historia*."
8. Wilkerson, 27–77, and Hanson, 30.
9. Sullivan, 79–80.

10. Hanson, 29–30, envisions the development of evangelical and ethnographic methods within a larger group of Franciscans and comments on the difficulty of documenting Sahagun's context when there are few extant materials from other friars such as Martín de Valencia, Jacobo Testera, and Andrés de Olmos.
11. Alva, "Language," 146.
12. Mignolo, 44–53.
13. Sahagún, *Fray Bernardino*, 30–31.
14. Quintana, "Exhortación," 137–82.
15. A royal cédula signed in Madrid April 22, 1577, ordered all of Sahagún's manuscripts to be collected and prohibited their publication. It also ordered, "no consentir que por ninguna manera persona Alguna escriua cosas que toquen A superstiçiones y manera de biuir que estos Indios tenian en ninguna lengua" [to not permit anyone whomsoever to write on the superstitions and ways of life that these Indians had in any language], Recogida de ejemplares, June 22, 1577, Patronato 275, R.79, Archivo de Indias.
16. Sahagún explains his methodology in his prologue to Book 2 on "The Ceremonies," *Florentine Codex* 1: 53–54.
17. Sahagún, *Florentine Codex*, 7:1.
18. Ibid., 11.
19. León-Portilla, *Bernardino de Sahagún*, 118.
20. Sahagún, *Florentine Codex*, 7:29.
21. Ibid., 163.
22. Brundage, 62.
23. Brundage, 174, explains that the expression *mocihuaquetzqui*, "one who has stood up like a woman," equated these women to warriors. This specifically refers to mortal women who die in childbirth.
24. Burkhart, 42.
25. León-Portilla, "Bernardino de Sahagún (1500–1590), 10.
26. Austín, 134.
27. Ibid.
28. Garibay, 1:402.
29. Austín, 133–34.
30. León-Portilla, *Bernardino*, 115.
31. *Vocabulario en lengua castellana y mexicana y mexicana y castellana* (Mexico: Porrúa, 1977), 157.
32. Sullivan, 82.
33. Ibid., 109.
34. Quintana, "Exhortación," 139–40.
35. Quintana, "El Huehuetlatolli," 62–64.
36. León-Portilla, *Bernardino*, 117.
37. Molina, 50v.
38. Alva, "Language," 146–49.
39. Sahagún, *Florentine Codex*, 7:35.
40. Ibid., 99.
41. Quintana, "Exhortación," 144, refers to Sahagún's compilation of speeches in Book 6 as "los más auténticamente nahuas" [the most authentically Nahua ones].
42. Mignolo, 186–216.
43. Dibble, "Nahuatlization of Christianity."
44. Alva, "Sahagún's Misguided Introduction," 83–92.
45. Anderson, "Sahagún's 'Doctrinal Encyclopaedia,'" 114.
46. The note reads: "Este exercicio halle entre los yndios, no se quien le hizo ni quien se le dio tenia muchas faltas e incongruidades mas con verdad se puede dezir que se hizo de nueuo que no que se emendo. Este año de 1574 fray Bernardino de Sahagun" [I found this *Ejercicio*

among the Indians. I know not who made it, nor who gave it to them. It had many errors and inconsistencies and it can be truly said that it was made all over again rather than simply corrected. This year of 1574. Fray Bernardino de Sahagún.] Fray Bernardino de Sahagún, Comiença un exercicio en lengua mexicana sacado del sancto Euangelio y distribuido por todos los dias de la semana contiene meditaciones deuotas muy prouechosas para qualquier cristiano que se quiere llegar a dios, Vault Ayer MS 1484, The Newberry Library.

47. Dibble, "Nahuatlization," 230.
48. Burkhart, 191.
49. Abbot, 257.
50. Ibid., 260.
51. Ibid., 261.
52. Mignolo, 112.
53. Ibid., 116.
54. Carla Mulford, "*Huehuetlatolli*, Early American Studies, and the Problem of History," *Early American Literature* 30.2 (September 1995): 147.
55. Anderson, "Old Word-New Word," 85–91.
56. Ibid., 88.
57. Ibid.
58. Ibid., 90.

Bibliography

'Abbot, Don Paul. "The Ancient Word: Rhetoric in Aztec Culture." *Rhetorica* 5.3 (1987): 251–64.

Anderson, Arthur J. O. "Old Word-New Word: *Huehuetlatolli* in Sahagún's Sermons." In *Current Topics in Aztec Studies: Essays in Honor of Dr. H. B. Nicholson*, edited by Alana Cordy-Collins and Douglas Sharon. San Diego: San Diego Museum of Man, 1993, 85–91.

———. "Sahagún's 'Doctrinal Encyclopaedia.'" *Estudios de Cultura Náhuatl* 16 (1983): 109–122.

Brundage, Burr Cartwright. *The Fifth Sun: Aztec Gods, Aztec World*. Austin: University of Texas Press, 1979.

Burkhart, Louise. *The Slippery Earth. Nahua-Christian Moral Dialogue in Sixteenth-Century Mexico*. Tucson: University of Arizona Press, 1989.

Bustamante García, Jesús. *Fray Bernardino de Sahagún: una revisión crítica de los manuscritos y de su proceso de composición*. México: Universidad Autónoma Nacional de México, 1990.

Dibble, Charles E. "The Nahuatlization of Christianity." In *Sixteenth-Century Mexico: The Work of Sahagún*, edited by Munro S. Edmonson. Albuquerque: University of New Mexico Press, 1974, 225–233.

———. "Sahagún's *Historia*." In Fray Bernardino de Sahagún. *Florentine codex. General History of the Things of New Spain*. Translated by J. O. Anderson and Charles Dibble. Monographs for the School of American Research, Number 14. 13 vols. Santa Fe, NM: School of American Research, 1950–1982, 1: 9–23.

García Quintana, Josefina. "El Huehuetlatolli—antigua palabra—como fuente para la historia sociocultural de los nahuas." *Estudios de Cultural Náhuatl* 12 (1976): 61–71.

———. "Exhortación de un padre a su hijo. Texto recogido por Andrés de Olmos." *Estudios de Cultural Náhuatl* 11 (1974): 137–82.

Garibay, Angel María. *Historia de la literatura nahuatl*. 2 vols. México: Editorial Porrúa, 1987.

Hanson, Craig A. "Olmos and Sahagún." *Chipping Away on Earth: Studies in the Prehispanic and Colonial Mexico in Honor of Arthur J. O. Anderson and Charles E. Dibble*, edited by Eloise Quiñones Keber. Lancaster, CA: Labyrinthos, 1994, 29–35.

Klor de Alva, Jorge. "Language, Politics, and Translation: Colonial Discourse and Classic Nahuatl in New Spain." In *The Art of Translation*, edited by Rosanna Warren. Boston: Northeastern University Press, 1989, 143–62.

———. "Sahagún's Misguided Introduction to Ethnography and the Failure of the *Colloquios* Project." In *The Work of Bernardino de Sahagún. Pioneer Ethnographer of Sixteenth-Century Aztec Mexico*, edited by Jorge Klor de Alva, H. B. Nicholson, and Eloise Quiñones Keber. Albany, NY: Institute for Mesoamerican Studies, 1988, 83–92.

León-Portilla, Miguel. *Bernardino de Sahagún: First Anthropologist*. Translated by Mauricio J. Mixco. Norman: University of Oklahoma Press, 2002.

———. "Bernardino de Sahagún (1500–1590): un juicio lapidario sobre su historia." *Caravelle* 55 (1990): 5–11.

López Austín, Alfredo. "The Research Method of Fray Bernardino de Sahagún: The Questionnaires." In *Sixteenth-Century Mexico: The Work of Sahagún*, edited by Munro S. Edmonson. Albuquerque: University of New Mexico Press, 1974. 111–49.

Mignolo, Walter. *The Darker Side of the Renaissance: Literacy, Territoriality, and Colonization*. Ann Arbor: University of Michigan Press, 1995.

Molina, Fray Alonso. *Vocabulario en lengua castellana y mexicana y mexicana y castellana*. México: Editorial Porrúa, 1977.

Mulford, Carla. "*Huehuetlatolli*, Early American Studies, and the Problem of History." *Early American Literature* 30.2 (September 1995): 146–51.

Recogida de ejemplares. June 22, 1577. Patronato 275, R.79. Archivo de Indias.

Sahagún, fray Bernardino de. Comiença un exercicio en lengua mexicana sacado del sancto Euangelio y distribuido por todos los dias de la semana contiene meditaciones deuotas muy prouechosas para qualquier cristiano que se quiere llegar a dios. Vault Ayer MS 1484. The Newberry Library.

———. *Florentine Codex. General History of the Things of New Spain*. Translated by J. O. Anderson and Charles Dibble. Monographs for the School of American Research, Number 14. 13 vols. Santa Fe, NM: School of American Research, 1950–1982.

Schwaller, John Fredrick. *Guías de Manuscritos en Náhuatl*. México: Universidad Nacional Autónoma de México, Fundación de Investigaciones Históricas, 1987.

Sullivan, Thelma D. "The Rhetorical Orations, or *Huehuetlatolli*, Collected by Sahagún." In *Sixteenth-Century Mexico. The Work of Sahagún*, edited by Munro S. Edmonson. Albuquerque: University of New Mexico Press, 1974, 79–109.

Wilkerson, S. Jeffrey K. "The Ethnographic Works of Andrés De Olmos, Precursor and Contemporary of Sahagún." In *Sixteenth-Century Mexico: The Work of Sahagún*, edited by Munro S. Edmonson. Albuquerque: University of New Mexico Press, 1974, 27–77.

CHAPTER SIX

Practicing Methods in Ancient Cultural Rhetorics: Uncovering Rhetorical Action in Moche Burial Rituals

LAURIE GRIES

The word research is probably one of the dirtiest words in the indigenous world's vocabulary. When mentioned in many indigenous contexts, it stirs up silence, it conjures up bad memories, it raises a smile that is knowing and distrustful. . . . It galls us that Western researchers and intellectuals can assume to know all that it is possible to know of us, on the basis of their brief encounters with some of us. It appalls us that the West can desire, extract and claim ownership of our ways of knowing, our imagery, the things we create and produce.
—Linda Tuhiwai Smith, *Decolonizing Methodologies: Research and Indigenous Peoples*

As the study of cultural-rhetorical practices in the field of rhetoric and composition grows in a post-*Comparative Rhetoric* era, scholars are beginning to uncover the distinct rhetorical traditions of various communities without resorting to the deficiency model often produced in comparative work. Scholars such as Malea Powell, Damián Baca, LuMing Mao, and Kermit Campbell, in particular, model various ways in which to recover ancient rhetorical-cultural practices that are not rooted in Greco-Latin traditions. In "Studying the Chinese Rhetorical Tradition in the present" (2007), for instance, Mao demonstrates how we can "re-present" ancient rhetorical traditions by "both anchoring it in its own context and its *own terms* [my emphasis]."[1] Studying cultural practices of Pre-Columbian societies *on their own terms* is a tempting methodology for uncovering the unique rhetorical traditions of Latin American ancient societies—rhetorical traditions which need and deserve to be theorized from a rhetorical perspective, yet up until now have largely gone unacknowledged in our field. However, many of these ancient rhetorical practices are nonverbal and have literally been buried in the sand since the beginning of the Common Era. In addition, as of date no verbal accounts recorded by many Pre-Columbian ancient societies have ever been recovered; thus we are often forced to rely on cultural symbols transcribed onto material artifacts to uncover their rhetorical traditions. Under such circumstances, the methodological application of studying Pre-Columbian rhetorical traditions *on their own terms* becomes especially challenging.

In his own work, Mao acknowledges the complexities of studying any ancient culture *on its own terms*. As Mao explains, while we can certainly try to situate ourselves in the context of the "other" and study their rhetorical practices on their own terms all the time, we cannot literally do so because our present location always impacts how knowledge is both produced and consumed.[2] Moreover, we are far removed from some rhetorical practices in terms of time that we cannot possibly 100 percent accurately represent the Other's point of view. This latter point is especially important to acknowledge; when any researcher begins to study the rhetorical practices of an ancient and/or Other culture, the researcher enters a complex, hierarchical relationship between him or herself and the researched. This relationship is particularly complex when archaeology and history are involved; as Gerald Vizenor, Edward Said, and others remind us, archaeology and history, as part of Western social science, have been part of the longstanding occidental project responsible for erasing and distorting the traditions and lives of other cultures. Therefore, even as we attempt to recover an ancient society's rhetorical traditions *on their own terms*, we must be cautious about representing ancient rhetorical traditions that we "dig up" from the past. As part of the European and U.S. academic project, we cannot escape this risk of perpetuating an Orientalist logic that has historically and continually plagues contemporary scholarship.

In their studies of Chinese rhetorics, both Mao and Xing Lu demonstrate how Chinese terms embedded in ancient Chinese discourse can be useful in describing ancient Chinese rhetorical traditions while avoiding an Orientalist logic. Mao advocates for continuing to explore how embedded terms within ancient discourse "influenced and affected the rhetorical behaviors of their users and how they interacted with each other at different historical moments."[3] Yet again, such exploration is made easier when we have access to an ancient culture's verbal records that include their own terms to describe their communicative practices as they occurred in particular moments of time. Confucius' *Analects*, for instance, has proved to be a productive site for recovering ancient Chinese rhetorical traditions recorded during the spring and autumn period through the Warring States Period (ca. 479 BCE–221 BCE). As this project on ancient Peruvian mortuary practices will illustrate, however, sometimes rather than having access to an ancient cultures' verbal records, all we can recover and rely on are nonverbal cultural material artifacts that have buried in the earth for thousands of years. How then do we accurately recover nonverbal ancient rhetorical practices *on their own terms* if we do not have a society's own "terms" to begin with?

In this chapter, I propose that when studying nonverbal cultural artifacts from beyond the Greco-Roman rhetorical tradition, we listen to the embodied discourse in the ancient practices themselves to uncover the rhetorical actions of those very practices. As W. J. T. Mitchell so persuasively argues in *Picture Theory* (1994), every picture has a metalanguage of its own; as such, they are "capable of providing a second-order discourse that tells us—at least shows us—something about pictures."[4] I argue that nonverbal cultural artifacts have this same potential; if we listen close enough, these cultural artifacts speak to us and render the terms with which we can begin to uncover their rhetorical actions.

Cultural artifacts have the potential to reveal their own rhetorical desires. They invite us to ask what they want, not only in their initial moment of creation but throughout time, as their desires shift with each new encounter. They, not us, have the agency to shed light on their own rhetorical traditions.[5] Even if we cannot know their intent and/or their effect, cultural objects speak through an embodied discourse and uncover their rhetorical actions to us. To illustrate ways in which we can begin to uncover the embodied discourse and rhetorical actions of nonverbal cultural artifacts from Pre-Columbian societies, I turn to the ancient royal tombs of Moche[6] elite rulers, which I first encountered on a seven-week trip to Peru in the summer of 2006. I describe the ritual symbolic construction of the burial chambers evident in the intentional placement of certain artifacts such as human bodies, earthenware, and gold and silver ornaments. In *Sex, Death, and Sacrifice in Moche Religion and Visual Culture* (2006), art historian Steve Bourget offers one of the most thorough and recent interpretations of the purpose behind these distinct Moche mortuary rituals; such as many cross-cultural redressive rituals, he posits Moche burial rituals were most likely employed to transmit ideological values of the ruling class and maintain the prevailing sociopolitical paradigm. From this perspective, the royal tombs of Moche elite rulers could be read as a rhetorical genre intended to maintain sociopolitical order in ancient Moche polities.

However, even as I argue for the need to acknowledge the royal tombs as a rhetorical genre, I refrain from speaking *for* the mortuary rituals *about* their original intentions. As W. J. T. Mitchell advises in *What Do Pictures Want* (2004), I also refrain from interpreting the funerary ritual practices as a "vehicle of [rhetorical] meaning or instruments of power."[7] To do so would *assign* agency to the ancient Moche funerary rituals from a Eurocentric perspective and thus perpetuate the Orientalist logic that we must work so hard to avoid. We must, as Bruno Latour insists in *Reassembling the Social* (2005), resist imposing our own metalanguage *onto* actors, whether human or nonhuman, and recognize that we "possess only some *infra*-language whose role is simply to help [us] become attentive to the actor's own fully developed metalanguage."[8] Therefore, in studying the ritual mortuary practices of ancient Moches, I listen to the Moche burials to illustrate how the royal tombs embody the nonverbal discourse of *duality, concealment*, and *inversion* which, in turn, uncovers the rhetorical actions of the mortuary rituals. I then present Bourget's interpretation of what rhetorical function these mortuary rituals might have had in the kairotic moments in which they were encountered. Rather than adopting Bourget's interpretation, however, I draw on it to demonstrate what cautions we must take as we begin to excavate rhetorical traditions of Pre-Columbian societies. I ultimately argue that as we strive to identify the rhetorical purpose of ancient cultural practices through rhetorical analysis, we must be leery of employing the same methods of *duality, concealment*, and *inversion* that the ancient Moche used to construct their royals' tombs. We must practice self-restraint in assigning rhetorical meaning to those rhetorical acts, which have yet revealed to us their original intentions and effects. As rhetorical scholars drawing on archaeology and history to help uncover Pre-Columbian rhetorical traditions,[9] we need in the simplest of terms, to acknowledge what we can safely claim and what we cannot. In the case of Moche mortuary rituals, even though the rhetorical meaning of these actions is not revealed to us under any certainty, a rich description of the tombs still sheds light on the rhetorical genres of a people with a deep and rich pre-Incan past. We need to embrace the genre of this rich rhetorical tradition; however, rather than jump quickly into assigning it rhetorical meaning, we need to move slowly and carefully and let it reveal its meaning to us. In letting go of our need to appropriate the purpose and meaning of ancient rhetorical traditions, we confront our own desires to master the "other" through interpretation. Through refrain, we honor; through listening to rather than speaking for, we let go of that part of ourselves that must explain. Through restraint, we embrace only those actions of which we can be certain.

Digging up Ancient Moche Mortuary Practices

The Moche culture, considered by some scholars as one of the first state-level societies in the Andes, flourished on the north Pacific coast of Peru for nearly 700 years between 100 and 800 CE (see figure 6.1). According to "traditional" European notions of writing,[10] the Moche had no writing system; however, as evident in the recovery of Moche material artifacts uncovered through long-term archaeological investigation, the Moche inscribed in pottery, metalworks, and textiles, all of which are semiotic in nature and capable of transmitting ideas, beliefs, and values. Fortunately, Moche studies has grown extensively since Moche field archaeology gained momentum in the 1970s; today a rich abundance of these artifacts have been excavated from various archeological sites. Much of the artistic style of these artifacts is actually narrative and thus provides glimpses into the daily, administrative, and religious lives of the Moche people. The narratives are so sophisticated, in fact, that today the Moche art is considered one of the highest ranking symbolic arts in the world. As distinguished professor of anthropology Izumi Shimada claims, in ancient Andean civilizations, for certain, no other culture has matched the sophistication of symbolic art created by the Moches.[11]

Moche studies scholars read this symbolic art like a text and consider the art in and of itself as a language capable of shedding light on this ancient Pre-Columbian society. One of the leading experts in Moche iconography, Christopher Donnan, for instance, claims that Moche art follows such consistent rules of expression that we can think of Moche art as a system of language in its own right, which uses "artistic nouns" and "artistic adjectives" to represent the cultural values, beliefs, and traditions of the Moches.[12] Garth Bawden (*The Moche*, 1996) claims that actually the artistic style, iconography, and architecture does not represent the social lives of the broader public (8–9); rather "Moche art functioned to communicate the text and the context of elite power to the public" (118). Like Donnan, Bawden categorizes Moche visual symbols as a language constructed of basic components that can help us

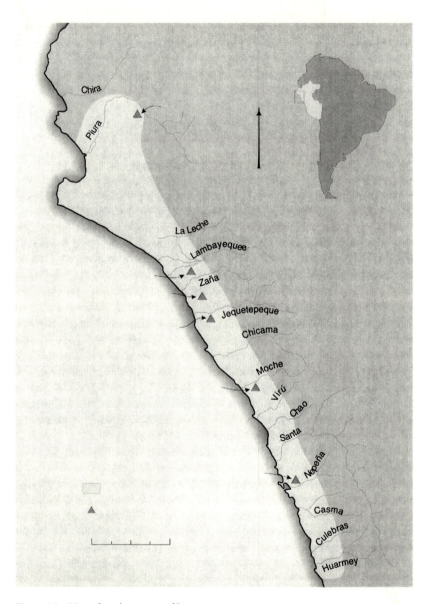

Figure 6.1   Map of northern coast of Peru.

Source: Map by Donald Mclelland, Courtesy of Christopher Donnan. *Royal Tombs of Sipan*, p. 12 (1994).

determine the social structure and religious beliefs of elite Moche society. W. J. T. Mitchell would say that these artifacts do not necessarily want to be a language; they simply want "equal rights" with language and to be seen, not interpreted, as "complex individuals occupying multiple subject positions and identities."[13] Regardless, in recognition of their semiotic potentials, archeologists have interpreted these naturalistic and highly representational artifacts in an effort to reconstruct ancient Moche society.

Over the years Moche studies scholars have reached consensus about some interpretations of Moche society while others are still up for debate. For instance, in studying these artifacts, Moche studies scholars agree that the Moche was an agrarian society whose longstanding survival success can largely be attributed to their extensive networks of irrigation canals, which permitted agriculture to flourish in the coastal desert in northern Peru. Scholars also agree that Moche were also industrious miners and engineers who could access precious natural resources such as gold, silver, and copper for trade and quickly rebuild their infrastructure in times of environmental crises. Consensus has not been reached, however, about the Moche political organization.[14] While some Moche studies scholars believe in a single conquest state model, others believe in a dual kingdom model, or a federation model. The material artifacts left by the Moche have also led many scholars to propose that the Moche society consisted of at least two independent polities, which may have separated the Moche culture into northern and southern regions and consisted of organizational differences. Even though consensus has not been reached about how the Moche organized themselves politically, however, analysis of Moche material culture indicates that the Moche peoples across time and place did have a shared artistic style, which leads scholars to conclude that the Moche had a shared system of power based in shared political and religious ideology.[15]

As of date, at least 350 Moche burials have been excavated, which have been particularly important to archeological and anthropological investigation of what role material culture might have played in the social and political organization of Moche society. When investigating these burial chambers, archeologists have discovered that Moche graves were not simply used to dispose of decaying corpses. Extensive examination of Moche burials indicates that delayed burials were common and that burial chambers were periodically revisited and reopened by certain members of Moche society.[16] Whether revisiting and reopening the burial chambers was to preserve bodies and artifacts from environmental destruction or to make secondary offerings, the exact purpose is unclear; nevertheless, archaeological evidence indicates that Moche burial chambers were often reopened so that the deceased bodies could be viewed and manipulated again.[17] Archaeological investigation also reveals that Moche funerary practices were highly consistent across the Moche Empire and involved intricate rituals in which funerary attendants deliberately placed bodies and artifacts in specific positions for specific purposes.

The royal burial tombs at Sipan—one of the administrative and religious centers in the latter stages of Moche culture located in the Lambayeque Valley near the city of Chiclayo—have proved to be particularly important to Moche scholars in revealing Moche cultural beliefs and values as well as political and social structure. In 1987, after seizing artifacts from a looting at the site of Sipan and spending nearly twelve years excavating the site, prominent Moche archaeologist Walter Alva and his crew unearthed the tombs of at least ten high-ranking individuals, revealing a complex set of ritual burial practices that date back between 200 and 300 CE. For the first time, when investigating these extensive burial chambers, archaeologists believe they have conclusive evidence that the Moche buried their deceased according to the individual's status and role during life. As Izumi Shimada explains, the tombs at Sipan reveal the Moche had the following three distinct social classes: (1) a line of hereditary lords with exclusive access to gold and other valuable artifacts; (2) a "priest" or noble buried flanked to the lords in their royal tombs; and (3) the lord's personal attendants that include warriors, female attendants, and perhaps artisans.[18] The distinct artifacts placed in the burial tombs and the presence or lack of accompanying human subordinates indicates an individual's status or role. As such, each burial chamber is uniquely constructed according to class and thus, as Jean-Francois Millaire argues, Moche burials can be understood as "precise composition[s], tailored for each and every deceased person, according to that individual's position in a collectivity at a precise moment in time" (374). This burial ritual has been confirmed in subsequent excavations of elite burial chambers as well, namely the tombs uncovered at the site of San Jose de Moro in Jequetepeque, Peru, which, along with the tombs of the Lord of Sipan, create the most extensive evidence of elite Moche burial practices yet uncovered.

The royal tombs at Sipan and San Jose de Moro are also especially important because for the first time, archaeologists believe they have found evidence in the tombs that the Sacrifice Ceremony was an actual event in which priests, who conducted this ceremony, dressed in the same attire and used the same objects as depicted in Moche art.[19] According to leading Moche studies scholars, the Sacrifice Ceremony[20] was part of the state religion and was the most important of a complex system of ceremonies performed by elite Moche nobles to increase social solidarity among Moche society members. During these ceremonies, Moche studies scholars have deduced that Moche high priests recreated myths and traditions in performances that legitimated their elite status in Moche society and thus solidified Moche societal and political structure. When one of these high priests died, officiates took elaborate and deliberate measures to bury the priest-nobles with the same attire they wore to perform rituals as well as with other ornamental objects used when performing ceremonies. According to Donnan and other Moche studies scholars, while the tombs at Sipan housed the remains of male high priests, known as the Warrior Priest and the Bird Priest, the tombs at San Jose de Moro, constructed nearly 300 years later, housed the remains of two high priestesses—all of which have been identified by scholars in Moche iconographic themes as playing leading roles in the Sacrifice Ceremony. Although these tombs are constructed differently, since they were constructed in different polities and at different points in time, all tombs included ritual accoutrements, the extensive layering upon layering of which creates a complicated composition that is oriented toward rhetorical action.

The figures 6.2 and 6.3 give you some sense of just how complicated and deliberate these mortuary practices are. As these pictorial reconstructions of tomb 1 at Sipan make clear, human bodies, ceramic pots, and metalworks were intentionally situated in certain places and specific positions around the noble's bodies in elaborate compositions unique to each particular principle ruler. When seen from our vantage point, these deliberately constructed tombs become artifacts, which, as Clay Spinuzzi (2003) helps us understand, "emerge from cultural-historical activity . . . [and] bear the material traces of an ongoing activity, represent problem solving in that activity, and thus tend to stabilize the activity in which they are used" (39). Situated in their own context, these burial tombs act as a *medium* not only through which symbolic messages are communicated and rituals are performed but also in which images and forms appear.[21] By *medium* here I draw on W. J. T. Mitchell (2004) to define the royal tombs as a medium that is more complicated than a simple set of materials, codes, or conventions that transmit messages between individuals. As a medium, the tombs are "a complex social institution that contains individuals within it, and is constituted by a history of practices, rituals, and habits, skills and techniques, as well as a set of material objects and spaces."[22] Thinking of the royal tombs as a medium in this light necessitates a methodology

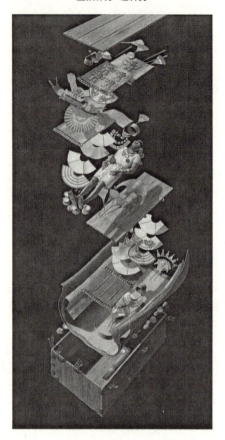

Figure 6.2   Tomb 1 at Sipan as it might have initially been constructed.

Source: Painting by Percy Fiestas, Photograph by Guillermo Hare, Courtesy of Christopher Donnan, *Royal Tombs of Sipan*, p. 124 (1994).

in which the tombs in and of themselves can be studied as a culturally specific genre with an "embodied discourse" that uncovers the rhetorical actions taken to construct these complex burial chambers. In this chapter, I *begin* to develop such a methodology; the methodology I model at this point is more of what might be called a methodology of restraint that attempts to work within the confines of a genre that has not yet revealed to us its precise rhetorical purpose but clearly has rhetorical actions. It is a methodology that reigns in our expert knowledge to create space for the genres themselves to identify their own rhetorical traditions.

Figure 6.3   Exploded view of contents of tomb 1 at Sipan.

Source: Painting by Ned Seidler, Courtesy of Christopher Donnan, *Royal Tombs of Sipan*, p. 63 (1994).

Much of the colonialist existence of the past few hundred years has silenced Native voices. The stories which we have like to tell were largely appropriated and retold by non-Aboriginal "experts" in such fields as anthropology, art and history and especially in the political realm. Not surprisingly, the appropriated stories distort the realities of our histories, cultures and traditions. Underlying this paternalistic and damaging practice is the supposition that these "experts" have the right to retell these stories because of their superior status within the cultural and political constructs of our society.

−Gerald McAlister and Lee Ann Martin,
The Indigena Project

Before locating the theoretical terms, which uncover the rhetorical actions embedded in the unique genre of the royal tombs of Sipan and San Jose de Moro, we need to unpack the concept of genre itself. From a rhetorical perspective, as Carolyn Miller has suggested, genres are best "centered not on the substance or the form of discourse but on the action it is used to accomplish."[23] In addition, as Spinuzzi (2003) draws on Mikhail Bahktin to make clear, genres are culturally and historically situated ways of "seeing and conceptualizing reality" that convey a worldview, shape ideology, and are developed so that people can accomplish certain activities. In this sense, genres are simultaneously "oriented toward" *addressivity* and *history*. In regard to addressivity, genres are addressed to certain audiences and, because they are delivered at kairotic moments for particular reasons, are mutable, dynamic, and reshapable.[24]

> In regard to history, genre represents ways that participants in a given social sphere have developed to deal with particular activities within that sphere.... Such genre habits are extremely powerful because they provide us with *ready-made strategies for interpreting not just discourse in a genre, but the world as seen through the "eyes" of that genre* [my italics]. (Spinuzzi 43)

Archaeological investigation indicates that the Moche funerary rituals used to construct the royal tombs of high priests in both Sipan and San Jose de Moro were so intricately orchestrated, demanding much time, energy, and cultural knowledge, that these Moche burial rituals were more than likely practiced by officiates with some form of authority in Moche society.[25] When nobles who conducted the Sacrifice Ceremony died, archaeologists have surmised that these funerary officiates conducted complex, deliberate rituals to construct the elite noble's burial chambers. These mortuary practices vary to some degree across time and place; like any genre, Moche mortuary rituals respond to transitory technological, economic, religious, and political influences and change shape in both form and effect. However, many of the funerary practices are so consistent that, even as we must refrain from concretizing interpretations of their rhetorical meaning, it is safe to say that in their orientation to both *addressivity* and *history*, the Moche mortuary practices constitute a rich rhetorical genre that uncovers its own embedded rhetorical actions.

Before describing the mortuary rituals used to construct the royal tombs of Sipan, it should be noted here that the scientific process used to excavate these chambers is so complex and fascinating that an entire museum has been constructed to retrace the steps and display the findings from this archeological project. When visiting the Museum of the Royal Tombs of Sipan, which is located in Lambayeque, Peru, you encounter the cultural objects excavated from the royal tombs in the same sequence the archeologists encountered them during the actual excavation. The museum display includes the actual skeletal remains of the nobles in tombs 1 and 2 as well as a reconstruction of the royal chambers exactly as it was found when it was uncovered. This reconstruction of the chambers makes it glaringly clear that the original burial chambers were constructed with deliberate intentions to achieve specific social actions.

Alva and Donnan have argued that the deliberate placement practices used to construct the royal chambers are so pervasive and consistent that symbolic meaning must be ascribed to these mortuary practices. As Mao reminds us, when studying any ancient rhetorical practice, we always ascribe its relevancy to who we are and what we are. In their interpretations of this rhetorical genre, Moche studies scholars claim the mortuary rituals reflect Moche cultural beliefs in transcendence and the afterworld, which in turn were perpetuated to achieve sociopolitical action. As a rhetorician who tends to think of rhetoric as symbolic action yet acknowledges that intention, meaning, and purpose cannot always be ascribed to rhetorical practices, I would argue that that from our vantage point, the symbolic meaning attached to the deliberate mortuary rituals of the royal tombs described in the following text can never been fixed with any certainty. Although the royal tombs at Sipan and San Jose de Moro did in fact leave "ready-made strategies" that *could* very well and even *may* likely have been employed to achieve this sociopolitical action, and even as we acknowledge that rhetorical action is embedded in this rich rhetorical tradition, we must be careful of how we interpret these strategies to avoid creating a culture of *manifest manners*. As Gerald Vizenor (1994) writes, *manifest manners* are the "absence of the real in the ruins of tribal representations. The simulations of manifest manners are treacherous and elusive histories....Tribal realities are superseded by simulations of the unreal, and tribal wisdom is weakened by those imitations, however sincere."[26] No matter our intention, ascribing rhetorical meaning through interpretation of these practices is thus a risky project that should be taken slowly until the Moche burial rituals reveal to us *what they want us to know*. For now, although exact rhetorical purpose is indeterminate, what can be heard as we listen to the echoes of these tombs is an embodied discourse that reveals their rhetorical actions to us. I turn now to excavating that discourse so we can begin to listen to the ancient voices of the royal tombs. Cultural artifacts are actors that, through their own devices, render the world in new ways. They ask for nothing more than for us to see the world through their eyes and acknowledge the voices of their actions.

Excavating the Theoretical Discourse of Moche Mortuary Practices

One of the most repeated symbolic funerary rituals revealed in the royal burial chambers at Sipan that uncovers the rhetorical actions of Moche mortuary rituals is the deliberate placement of ornaments,[27] ceramic vessels, and human bodies in symbolic *duality*. If a necklace was hung around a warrior priest, for instance, the right side of the necklace was strung with gold beads while the left side was strung with silver beads. Also, silver and gold objects placed in the tomb on opposite sides of the body were of similar size and shape, if not the exact same object. More over, many objects such as nose and ear ornaments were made of complementary gold and silver halves. The *duality* described here does not just apply to metal works; *duality* is also evident in pairings of vases and human bodies. For instance, if one vessel found in the burial chamber was fired, an exact replica of the same vessel was found in the tomb that was not fired. Also, decorations would be positioned on the same place on two vases, yet appear in opposing forms. Similarly, in what has been labeled tomb 1, two younger males flanked the warrior priest (see figure 6.2). The young male on the right side of the warrior priest rested on his back in the same position and orientation as the warrior priest. However, the other male, who was laid in the same position on the other side of the warrior priest, was placed in the opposite direction. Similarly, in tomb 2, two women flanked the elite ruler but while one rested on her back, the other rested on her belly.

According to Moche studies scholars (Bourget 2006; Moseley 1992; Russel and Jackson 2001; Shimada 1994), the *duality* in Moche mortuary practices is consistent with the dualist organization found throughout much religious apparatus in the Moche Empire. The principle of duality found in the funerary rituals was expressed not only in the Moche temple architecture, but also in sacrificial rituals, and in Moche iconography found in murals and on ceramic vessels and metal jewelry. Archaeologists such as Garth Bawden (1996) have situated the overarching principle of duality found in Moche cultural artifacts in the broader context of Pre-Columbian Andean conceptions of the universe.

According to interpretations of Andean world-views, cosmic order was suffused with opposing forces that create a "harmonious balance" of life on earth. In this context, the duality found in the mortuary rituals "reflects a universal social quality whereby dichotomous cultural perceptions are mediated in differential ritual space."[28] As will become clear with Bourget's interpretation of Moche burial rituals in the next section of this chapter, Moche studies scholars surmise that the dual placement of cultural objects does not only reflect cultural beliefs about cosmology. These ritual practices infuse the secular with the nonsecular, or more specifically, the political with the supernatural.

Agency

This infusion of the secular and nonsecular is also evident, according to Moche studies scholars, in the mortuary ritual of *concealment* embodied in the tombs at San Jose de Moro and Sipan. In the tombs of the high priestesses at San Jose, ritual officiates enacted the ritual of concealment by placing large hammered metal sheets over the priestesses' bodies, which included silver-copper alloy facial masks. Unlike this simple measure taken to conceal the identity of the priestesses in the royal tombs at San Jose de Moro, funerary officiates took extensive measures to conceal the elite priests' identities in the tombs at Sipan. In tomb 1, for instance, funerary officiates orchestrated an elaborate layering of large facial and body ornaments on the ruler's body. During the excavation of this tomb, Donnan and Alva first encountered nose ornaments large enough to conceal all the distinctive facial features of the ruler, including the mouth, nose, and chin. Yet the ritual officiates apparently did not rely solely on these particular ornaments to conceal the identifiable features of the deceased ruler. Underneath these large nose ornaments, a large gold sheet hammered in the shape of cheeks, chin, mouth, and upper neck was placed over the lower face of the deceased. As Alva and Donnan note (1994), this hammered gold form was not meant to be worn in life because perforations allowing the ruler to breathe were absent.[29] Beneath this gold layer, yet another set of ornaments was found that included an individual gold nose covering, band of teeth, and two eye coverings, which were placed directly over the corresponding facial parts of the deceased ruler (see figure 6.4). In conjunction with the two previously mentioned attempts to deliberately mask the recognizable facial features of the elite ruler, this final layering of gold facial ornaments ensured that the ruler's personal identity would be concealed as he lay deceased in his burial chamber.

Artifact

This elaborate orchestration of symbolic *duality* and *concealment* in the tombs at Sipan and San Jose de Moro has perplexed archaeologists and Moche studies scholars and driven them to find answers as to why the

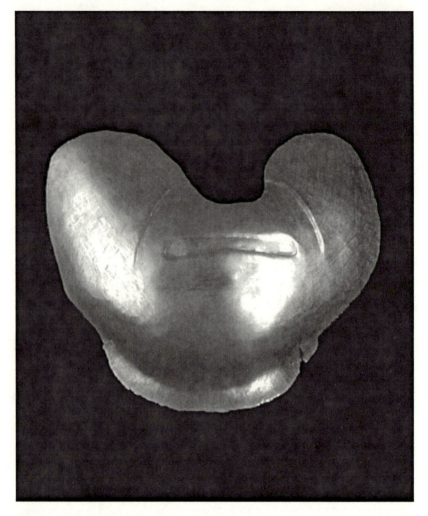

Figure 6.4   Gold facial ornaments.

Source: Photograph by Christopher Donnan, Courtesy of Christopher Donnan, *Royal Tombs of Sipan*, p. 90 (1994).

Moches would go through such elaborate measures of symbolic *duality* and *concealment* when burying the elite nobles of their society. Since no verbal texts were recorded by the Moches to explain these delib- erate actions, some archaeologists and scholars have turned to a small inventory of basic themes depicted on various ceramics and murals for hints, which Donnan claims we might correlate to themes such as the Nativity Theme in Christian art.[30] As already noted, by comparing the cultural objects found in the tombs at Sipan with depictions of the Sacrifice Ceremony theme, scholars have hypothesized that the Sacrifice Ceremony was an actual event, which helps to identify what role the nobles buried in the royal tombs might have played in Moche society. However, although it is evident from the construction of the tombs that *duality* and *concealment* were deliberate and thus had a rhetorical function, the Sacrifice theme does not help in explaining why *duality* and *concealment* were employed in the Moche burial practices of elite rulers. Scholars have thus turned to the Burial Theme, which was depicted on at least sixteen ceramic pots from the last phase of the Moche culture, to see why the Moche might have employed these specific mortuary practices. The Burial Theme[31] is a narrative of a burial for an elite Moche noble, which consistently depicts four separate activities that Bourget claims provides insight into Moche beliefs in the afterworld and more specifically their beliefs about the metaphysical transformation of their elite nobles.

One vessel on which the Burial Theme is presented is a stirrup bottle located in the elaborate tomb of the second priestess at San Jose de Moro. The Moche ritual of *inversion* is evident in the deliberate placement of this vessel. Apparently, the bottle with the Burial Theme was placed in special niche in an inverted position between two other pairs of vessels, which are similar in decoration but opposite in orientation. This practice of inversing certain offerings was a common funerary ritual in many constructing Moche burials, which, Bourget claims, indicates that the funerary ritual officiates were fully aware of the concept of ritual inversion and "decided to physically reassert the concept by carefully arranging the bottle in this precarious position."[32] Study of the iconography of the Burial Theme leads archeologists to suggest that the ritual *inversion* practiced in constructing the tombs of Moche elite represents the Moche metaphysical belief in the transformation from death to the afterlife. As Bourget surmises, "it provides the internal logic of the ritual system reuniting in a cycle: Life—Dying—Death—[Inversion]—Afterlife" (224). Thus, from his perspective as an art historian, ritual *inversion* is one of the "main conceptual tools" along with *duality* and *concealment* that Moche funerary officiates employed to explain and represent cultural beliefs about transcendence (210). Although Bourget does not frame his interpretation in rhetorical terms, he argues that these conceptual tools also had a rhetorical function, which connects the secular with the nonsecular; working in conjunction with one another, these conceptual tools preserved the existing ruling kinship in Moche society. I summarize his interpretation in the following text to demonstrate what rhetorical actions we could assign the mortuary ritual practices should we embrace Bourget's explanation. I then turn, however, to problematizing my own rhetorical analysis to demonstrate how our habits to interpret, to explain, to find meaning sometimes oversteps our boundaries into a culture of *manifest manners.*

Uncovering Rhetorical Actions in Moche
Mortuary Rituals

According to Bourget, whom I rely on extensively throughout this section, perpetuating beliefs about transcendence in the mortuary burial rituals as described earlier had a direct role in maintaining the prevailing sociopolitical structure of Moche society. To understand this role, it is important to realize that archaeologists such as Bawden believe the Moche power structure was situated in enduring principles of communal ancestry and kinship in Andean society.[33]

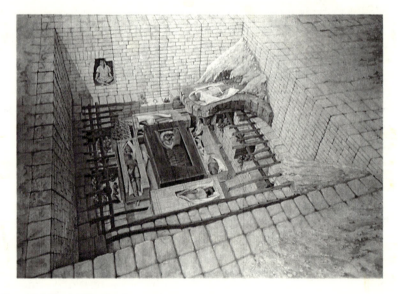

Figure 6.5 "Burial Chamber."

Source: Painting by Percy Fiestas. Photograph by Guillermo Hare.

In this structure, Moche leadership would be "derived from group-shared supernatural authority, inhibited the formation of a strong ruling elite, qualitatively separated from the populace at large by divisions of class and genealogy."[34] As Bourget explains, in order to avoid potentially dangerous instability to political order, which often occurs when an elite ruler in kinship political structures dies, the Moche society might have created an illusion of the ruler's two bodies—a physical body, known as the body natural, and the political body or rulership, known as the body politic (235). In the Moche case, "the solution [to possible political disorder] may have consisted of the creation of a sort of generic persona adopted by successive rulers and high ranking individuals who exercised office over the centuries in sociopolitical centers such as Sipan" (236). To preserve the identity of the immortal ruler, the high warrior priests, who masqueraded as the immortal ruler when performing ceremonies and rituals, would always have been masked, which would explain why the rulers identity were concealed by large facial and body ornaments in the burial chambers and why rulers in Moche iconography were always depicted as anthropomorphic creatures such as the commonly depicted Iguana and Wrinkle Face[35] (236). By concealing recognizable features and masking the personality of the standing/living ruler, the Moche high officials created an everlasting impression of the rulership in the eyes of society members who either witnessed the original burial chamber or reopened the burial chamber some time thereafter (237).

In Bourget's interpretation, the act of ritual *duality* and *inversion* in conjunction with *concealing* the ruler's identity would have played a major role in perpetuating cultural beliefs in the immortality of the Moche ruler and thus perpetuated beliefs in an everlasting ruler. In this interpretation, the *duality* found in the funerary practices could have symbolized the "duality transcending life and death with the dual reinstatement of two similar rulers—one in the world of the living and the second one in the afterworld—like two slightly different but related terms at the end of an unbroken continuum" (236). The inversion of a vessel depicting the Burial Theme found in tomb 2, as already noted, is also of particular importance in Moche studies scholars' minds to the transmittal of cultural beliefs about the transformation from death to afterlife. Bourget claims the inverted vessels serve as "tangible evidence that ritual inversion is not speculation by the analyst but rather that it clearly inhabited the mindscape of the Moche people" (213). In *The Realm of Rhetoric*, Chaim Perelman explains

al intention instead
f imposes supposition

"choosing to single out certain things for presentation in a speech draws the attention of the audience to them and thereby gives them a *presence* that prevents them from being neglected" (35). Similarly, the inverted vessels in the niche might have been deliberately given a special presence in the burial chamber to articulate the significant value of the transcendence from life to death. This belief in turn would have been necessary to perpetuate in order to maintain the impression of an everlasting rulership.

The Moche's deliberate act of making it seem as if an immortal ruler exists in their culture could, according to Bourget, have been a direct result of some high-ranking officiates claiming "a form of filiation or direct descent from certain beings with supernatural attributes or sacred persons" (235). Creating and maintaining the impression of an everlasting rulership would not have been possible without deliberate concealment of the deceased ruler's identity. As already noted, wide nose and ear ornaments found at Sipan and other sites were used to conceal all distinctive facial features such as the mouth, nose, and chin of rulers. The funerary officiates had to conceal the ruler's identity to perpetuate belief in the Moche ruler's immortality and thus maintain his or her status as ruler over more subordinate members of Moche society. Bourget acknowledges that "the apparently seamless transition from one given ruler to the next could have been enacted and maintained through the proclamation of ritual utterances to the effect that the ruler had not in fact died but rather had journeyed into the 'afterworld,' where he was reinstated" (236). However, actual speech would not have been necessary to achieve this purpose. As discussed earlier, cultural artifacts speak through visual display and act rhetorically as "they emphasize some meanings even as they diminish or conceal others."[36] Certainly, the act of concealing the identity of the recently deceased ruler deflected attention away from the reality of the ruler's mortal death. This concealment would have been necessary for the impression of an immortal ruler to be revealed to not only members of society who may have witnessed the original funerary ritual but also members of society who revisited and reopened the burial chambers some time after the original burial.

To sum up, if we accept Bourget's interpretation, when a high priest/noble died, Moche funerary rituals employed to construct the royal tombs were practiced for reasons far beyond paying respect for the deceased (184). The complex Moche rituals were "meant to establish and maintain an elaborate belief system concerning life, fertility, death, and another form of life after death" (224). Perpetuating this belief system through Moche funerary rituals, in turn, would have been a deliberate action aiming "to protect and maintain political authority by diminishing the threat posed by the untimely death of an individual ruler" and to preserve both the heritage and future of Moche society. (238). After all, if revisiting and reopening burial chambers was a common practice enacted either to preserve the contents of the graves or for secondary ritual practices, then the funerary rituals were created not only for the immediate audience but also for a future audience. Thus, in Bourget's interpretation, the actions of *duality, concealment,* and *inversion* would have been the conceptual tools purposefully used to perpetuate prevailing ideologies that maintain the Moche social structure and political order from generation to generation.

From a rhetorical perspective, if we accept ritual as rhetoric, these "main conceptual tools" could certainly be interpreted as rhetorical actions embodied in the discourse and embedded in the genres of the royal tombs. In the academic world, ritual has been commonly understood to be:

1. repeated (e.g., every Sabbath)
2. sacred (related to the Holy, of utmost significance)
3. formalized (consisting of prescribed, unchanging movements such as bowing or kneeling)
4. traditional (not being done for the first time, claiming an ancient history or authorized by myth)
5. intentional (nonrandom actions, done with awareness of some reason or meaning). (Grimes 56)

Yet rituals are also rhetorical. Suzanne Langer (*Philosophy in a New Key* 1942), for instance, defines ritual as "non-discursive symbolism" that operates much like language[37] in that "ritual is the most primitive reflection [and expression] of serious thought, a slow deposit, as it were, of people's imaginative insight into life" (157). Rituals should not be interpreted simply as acts of self-expression.[38] When a ritual is performed, it is not a compulsive act. Rather it is expressive in the logical sense and articulates a complex, permanent *attitude,* which is always linked with "exigencies of current life, colored by immediate cares and desires, by specific memories and hopes."[39] These exigencies are often a crisis of some sorts, which occurs on either an individual or community-wide level. In response to community-wide crises, some sort of redressive action is taken, either formally or informally,

verbally or nonverbally, by representative members of the troubled
social system.[40]

Transculturally and transhistorically, redressive acts include ritual practices that are often interpreted as nonrational from a Greco-
Roman rhetorical perspective, but these redressive ritual practices,
which are part of social dramas enacted in many ancient cultures, are
not irrational.[41] These redressive ritual practices reflect and articulate
permanent attitudes of a particular culture. Consequently, as David
Kertzer points out in *Ritual, Politics, and Power* (1988), ritual as "the
propagation of a message through a complex symbolic performance"
can be interpreted as a form of rhetoric (181). Yet, again, the purpose
of rituals is not simply expressive. As Donovan Ochs explains, "All
cultures, much like humans, seek to preserve themselves and, in ritual,
the culture engages in symbolic activity to this end.... Viewing ritual
from a rhetorical perspective permits one to learn how communication through symbols is used to both adapt to and resist changes that
threaten the continuity of the audience—the collective itself."[42] Besides
articulating cultural beliefs, rituals also have both epistemic and sociological purposes in that they create knowledge and serve social and
political functions.[43] As such, redressive ritual practices can reveal the
rhetorical actions that certain members of a culture employ in attempt
to restore and maintain social and political order.

In the Moche case, archeologists have argued that redressive rituals
performed by Moche elite would have been important as in other cultures to maintain sociopolitical order during times of crisis. Although
exact crisis experienced by the Moche have yet to be pinpointed,
Moche studies scholars and archaeologists assume that the crises for
the Moche might have come from both within and beyond the Moche
polities. In some contexts, cultural crisis might have been caused by
disastrous weather conditions. The Moches lived along the Pacific
shore of Northern Peru at the foothills of the Andean mountains in
a location where the El Nino current creates periodic disastrous rains
and floods. Several administrative and/or ceremonial complexes were
abandoned and/or reconstructed multiple times perhaps because of
structural damage caused by natural disasters. During such crises, natural disasters might have threatened the ruling elite's authority and even
induced revolt or other social instabilities.[44] Some scholars have surmised that the imperial desires of the neighboring Wari Empire would
have also necessitated the need for redressive rituals to maintain sociopolitical stability. As already noted, redressive rituals might also have
been internally caused by inequalities between ruling elite and lower

classes, which might have created a high degree of social tension. The thick adobe walls surrounding many of the administrative sites suggest the presence of both internal and external strife, from which the walls could have been shielding the royal elite.[45]

Assuming that one or more of the above situations are likely to have occurred, as it is natural to assume that the Moche periodically experienced moments of sociopolitical instability, we could deduce that the rhetorical actions of *duality, concealment,* and *inversion* in the genres of the royal tombs were enacted as redressive rituals intended to maintain sociopolitical order at the time of crises. Whether the crisis resulted from environmental damage to political and administrative structure or internal or external threats against the dominant order of society, creating the impression of an everlasting ruler through the actions of *duality, concealment,* and *inversion* would help maintain the prevailing power and social structures by preserving dominant ideologies, both religious and political in nature. These rhetorical actions then could be seen as playing an important role in the rhetorical traditions of Moche elite.

However, in the Moche case we need to practice restraint and problematize our own interpretations of the Moche funerary rituals' rhetorical meaning. We need to ask ourselves if we can base our rhetorical analysis on the suppositions of other's interpretations. As Jeffrey Quilter writes in his survey of the present state of Moche studies (*Moche Politics,* 2002), Moche studies as a field of study is relatively young and must

> be careful in not too quickly attempting to fit the evidence we have into interpretive straightjackets. It is not a question of waiting for more evidence, for more evidence will always be arriving in our journals and on our desks. We should just be very careful not to allow the tentative conclusions, the conjectures, suggestions, and hypotheses to become reified into "facts" that are then used to develop more "facts" that are equally shaky because of the poorly developed foundations on which they rest. (188)

In this same vein, as we begin to excavate the rhetorical functions of ancient cultural rituals in Pre-Columbian societies, we must be leery of the interpretive frameworks in which we situate rhetorical traditions. Drawing on methods of archeologists and anthropologists can help us uncover the rhetorical actions of ancient cultures and we should be grateful to the long, hard hours they put into their own scholarship. However, as we begin to perform our own excavations into the rhetorical traditions of ancient Pre-Columbian societies, we need to be constantly aware of our own desires and acknowledge our own limitations. In many cases, such as with the Moche culture, the best we may be able to do is look to the metalanguage embodied in the rhetorical traditions themselves to uncover their rhetorical actions. Refraining from taking the next step into interpretation of these actions should be done only with caution (if not avoided altogether) to avoid distorting and/or erasing those peoples whose rhetorical traditions we aim to recover. Although Vizenor might argue that we can never completely avoid *recovering* these ancient indigenous cultures as we attempt to listen to their rhetorical traditions, through a methodology of restraint, we can practice resistance even as we proceed forward in our pursuit of Pre-Columbian rhetorical traditions. Interpretation is often colonization in disguise. It posits reality in the hands of the interpreter. Interpretation fills our Eurocentric desire to explain and to give meaning. It speaks over that which speaks on its own terms and in the process, distorts and conceals.

Conclusion

In this chapter, I have attempted to listen to the royal tombs of Moche elite rulers for what they have to reveal to us about their rhetorical actions. I have argued that these tombs constitute a rhetorical genre that needs to be acknowledged as we seek to recover the rhetorical practices of Pre-Columbian societies. Even as I work to identify this genre by excavating the theoretical terms of *duality, concealment,* and *inversion,* I advocate for a methodology of restraint in which we curtail our own desire to interpret the rhetorical meaning of a genre that has not yet revealed to us its precise rhetorical purpose. I believe that situating rhetoric in redressive rituals can be useful for identifying the rhetorical traditions of ancient cultures that relied on nonverbal ritual practices to commit rhetorical action. I even demonstrate how a rhetorician studying the nonverbal ritual practices of ancient societies might employ rhetorical or genre analysis to uncover rhetorical actions taken by elite members of the Moche society to maintain sociopolitical order during a time of crisis. However, I ultimately argue that we must be cautious of taking interpretive leaps in our attempts to locate the rhetorical traditions of ancient Pre-Columbian societies. For if we do so, we run the risk of employing the same rhetorical strategies the Moche used to construct the royal tombs of Moche elite. We run the risk, in other words, of *concealing* the actual effects that Moche mortuary rituals served throughout time as various audiences encountered the royal tombs. We run the risk of *inverting* the realities of Moche society in our hopes to identify meaning and purpose of rhetorical traditions, that have only just begin to reveal themselves to us. We run the risk of *creating dualities* between verbal and nonverbal, European and non-European, orality and writing even as we attempt to subvert them. I have attempted to argue here that in effort to minimize these risks, we should instead practice restraint and be satisfied with what we can accurately and responsibly accomplish. As we attempt to uncover rhetorical traditions of ancient Pre-Columbian societies, we must move slowly and carefully; we must listen to what these traditions have to reveal to us.

Self reflective

can we have an EMBODIED experience with the artifact?

Notes

1. Mao, 226.
2. Ibid., 222.
3. Wang, 176.
4. Mitchell, *Picture Theory*, 38.
5. For more on the agency of objects, see Latour, *Reassembling the Social*.
6. The actual name of the indigenous peoples referred to today as the "Moche" is unknown. The name Moche refers to the peoples who inhabited the Northern coast of Peru between 100 and 750 CE and the "culture reflected by its distinctive artistic and architectural remains." Bawden, 6. Also commonly referred to as Mochica, the Moche evolved out of earlier indigenous cultures known as Cupisnique and Salinar, coexisted with the Gallinazo and Cajamarca and Recuay cultures, and was superseded by the Chimu culture. Shimada,1. Although the exact language that the Moche used is uncertain, some Moche scholars claim the Moche might have spoken Yunga or Muchika, which the name Mochica is thought to derive. Quilter, 155.
7. Mitchell, *What Do Pictures Want?*, 36.
8. Latour, 49.
9. Richard Enos and Robert Gaines argue that immersing one's research in archaeology and history is needed to locate and acknowledge a broader spectrum of rhetorical traditions unique to distinct cultures beyond those that have been included in the Greco-Roman tradition. See Enos, 7–20; Gaines, 61–73.
10. For an important discussion on how "the materiality and the ideology of Amerindian semiotic interactions were intermingled with or replaced by the materiality and ideology of Western reading and writing cultures," see the chapter titled "The Materiality of Reading and Writing Cultures" in Mignolo, 76.
11. Shimada, 7.
12. Donnan, 8.
13. Mitchell, *What Do Pictures Want*, 47.
14. See Quilter's "Moche Politics, Religion, and Warfare" for an excellent survey of the different theories of Moche political organization offered by Moche studies scholars.
15. Bawden, 8.
16. Millaire, 371.
17. Ibid., 377.

18. Shimada, 105.
19. Alva and Donnan, 223–24.
20. For a complete description of the Sacrifice Ceremony, see Chapter V titled "Moche Warfare and the Sacrifice of Prisoners" in Alva and Donnan's Royal Tombs of Sipan, 127–42.
21. Mitchell, 208.
22. Ibid., 203 and 213.
23. Miller, 151.
24. Spinuzzi, 41–43.
25. Alva and Donnan (1994), Millaire (2004).
26. Vizenor, 8.
27. For a clear depiction of duality at work in Moche ornaments, see Alva and Donnan's *Royal Tombs of Sipan*. Some Moche ornaments can also be observed in The Michael C. Rockefeller Memorial Collection, Bequest of Nelson A. Rockefeller (1979) located on the Metropolitan Museum of Art Web site as of February 2009: <http://www.metmuseum.org/toah/ho/05/sac/ho_1979.206.1225.htm>
28. Bawden, 143.
29. Alva and Donnan, 87.
30. Donnan, 158.
31. For a complete description of the Burial Theme, see Chistopher Donnan and Donna McClellan's *The Burial Theme in Moche Iconograpy* (Dombarton Oaks, 1979) as well as Chapter 4 in Steve Bourget's *Sex, Death, and Sacrifice in Moche Religion and Visual Culture*, 186–224.
32. Bourget, 214.
33. Bawden, 175.
34. Ibid., 175–76.
35. Iguana and Wrinkle Face represent specific individuals who played major roles in three often-depicted scenes: burial, mythic combat, and the "Scene of the Decoders." Donnan, 320.
36. Prelli, 12.
37. Langer defines language as "essentially an organic, functioning *system,* of which the primary elements as well as the constructed products are symbols." Langer, 135. She distinguishes between discursive symbolism or "language" proper and nondiscursive forms of language, that is, presentational symbolism (97). Langer writes that "the transformation of experience into concepts, not the elaboration of signals and symptoms, is the motive of language (126).
38. Langer (1942), Turner (1975), Ochs (1993).
39. Langer, 153.
40. Turner, 39.
41. Ibid., 47.
42. Ochs, 120.
43. Turner, 47.
44. Haas, "Class Conflict and the State in the New World."
45. Quilter, 160.

Bibliography

Alva, Walter and Christopher Donnan. *Royal Tombs of Sipan*. 2nd edition. Los Angeles: Fowler Museum of Cultural History, 1994.

Bawden, Garth. *The Moche*. Peoples of America Series. Malden, MA: Blackwell, 1996.

Bourget, Steve. *Sex, Death, and Sacrifice in Moche Religion and Visual Culture*. Austin: University of Texas Press, 2006.

Butters, Luis James Castillo. "Five Sacred Priestesses from San Jose de Moro: Elite Women Funerary Rituals on Peru's Northern Coast." *Revista Electronica de Arqueologia PUCP* 1, no. 3 (2006).

Donnan, Christopher B. *Moche Art of Peru: Pre-Columbian Symbolic Communication.* UCLA Latin American Center: California, 1978.

Enos, Richard. "Recovering the Lost Art of Researching the History of Rhetoric." *Rhetoric Society Quarterly* 29 (1999): 7–20.

Gaines, Robert N. "De-Canonizing Ancient Rhetoric." In *The Viability of the Rhetorical Tradition,* edited by Richard Graff, Arthur E. Walzer, and Janet M. Atwill, 61–73. New York: State University of New York Press, 2005.

Haas, J. "Class Conflict and the State in the New World." In *Transition to Statehood in the New World: Toward a Synthesis,* edited by Grant D. Jones and Robert Kautz. Cambridge, England: Cambridge University Press, 1981.

Kertzer, David I. *Ritual, Politics, and Power.* New Haven, CT: Yale University Press, 1988.

Langer, Suzanne K. *Philosophy in a New Key.* Cambridge, MA: Harvard University Press, 1942.

Latour, Bruno. *Reassembling the Social: An Introduction to Actor-Network-Theory.* Oxford: Oxford University Press, 2005.

Lipson, Carol and Roberta A. Binkley, eds. *Rhetoric Before and Beyond the Greeks.* Albany: State University of New York Press, 2004.

Mao, LuMing. "Studying the Chinese Rhetorical Tradition in the Present: Re-presenting the Native's Point of View." *College English* 69, no. 3 (January 2007): 216–37.

Mignolo, Walter D. *The Darker Side of the Renaissance.* Ann Arbor: University of Michigan Press, 1995.

Millaire, Jean-Francois. "The Manipulation of Human Remains in Moche Society: Delayed Burials, Grave Reopening and Secondary Offerings of Human Bones on the Peruvian North Coast." *Latin American Antiquity* 15, no. 4 (2004): 371–88.

Miller, Carolyn R. "Genre as Social Action." *Quarterly Journal of Speech* 70 (May 1984): 151–67.

Mitchell, W. J. T. *Picture Theory: Essays on Verbal and Visual Representation.* Chicago: University of Chicago Press, 1994.

———. *What Do Pictures Want?: The Lives and Loves of Images.* Chicago: University of Chicago Press, 2004.

Moseley, Michael E. *The Incas and Their Ancestors: The Archaeology of Peru.* London: Thames and Hudson, 1992.

Ochs, Donovan J. *Consolatory Rhetoric: Grief, Symbol, and Ritual in the Greco-Roman Era.* Columbia: University of South Carolina Press, 1993.

Perelman, Chaim. *The Realm of Rhetoric.* Notre Dame, IN: University of Notre Dame Press, 1969.

Prelli, Lawrence. Introduction to *Rhetorics of Display,* ed. Lawrence Prelli. Columbia: University of South Carolina Press, 2006.

Quilter, Jeffrey. "Moche Politics, Religion, and Warfare." *Journal of World Prehistory* 16, no. 2 (2002): 145–95.

Russell, Glenn S., and Margaret A. Jackson. "Political Economy and Patronage at Cerro Mayal, Peru." In *Moche Art and Archaeology in Ancient Peru,* edited by Joanne Pillsbury, 159–75. New Haven, CT: Yale University Press, 2001.

Shimada, Izumi. *Pampa Grande and the Mochica Culture.* Austin: University of Texas Press, 1994.

Smith, Linda Tuhiwai, ed. *Decolonizing Methodologies: Research and Indigenous Peoples.* London: Zed Books, 1999.

Spinuzzi, Clay. *Tracing Genres through Organizations: A Sociocultural Approach to Information Design.* Acting with Technology Series. Cambridge, MA: MIT Press, 2003.

Turner, Victor. *Dramas, Fields and Metaphors: Symbolic Action in Human Society.* Ithaca, NY: Cornell University Press, 1975.

Vizenor, Gerald. *Manifest Manners: Postindian Warriors of Survivance.* Hanover, NH: Wesleyan University Press, 1994.

Wang, Bo. "A Survey of Research in Asian Rhetoric." *Rhetoric Review* 23, no. 2 (2004): 171–81.

CHAPTER SEVEN

Rhetoric and Resistance in Hawai'i: How Silenced Voices Speak Out in Colonial Contexts

GEORGANNE NORDSTROM

The reality of the United States' enterprise of colonization in places such as Hawai'i is only now beginning to become a part of the national conversation. Since history is most often written by the victor, the experiences of indigenous peoples and other marginalized ethnic groups in colonized locations are frequently portrayed in such a way so as to cast the colonizer in a specific favorable light and downplay oppressive practices. Such rhetorical manipulation of the historical record in mainstream Western discourse has resulted in the production of a specific picture of Native Hawaiians and the immigrant laborers brought in to work the plantations as passive, content, and welcoming of the civilizing agenda of the benevolent colonizers. Perhaps more problematic is that such narrated reality has often conflated all non-Caucasians in Hawai'i—Native Hawaiians an immigrant settler—into a simplistic monolithic exotic other. Because of this, the different ways Native Hawaiians and settlers in Hawai'i resisted the colonial agenda rhetorically has often been overlooked. But life in the islands was never simple and idyllic, and the rhetorical responses to colonization reflect the complexity of life in the archipelago. However, to understand the rhetoric employed in Hawai'i to resist colonization and subsequent marginalization, it has to be read within the unique sociopolitical and historical context in which it is enacted and the cultural traditions it draws from.

The indigenous people have been most obviously oppressed and disenfranchised in Hawai'i, and examining texts produced by Native Hawaiians can provide insight into their experiences of and efforts to resist colonization. Similarly, literature written by Asian immigrants in this specific context sheds light on the identity politics involved with being a non-white settler working in the impoverished conditions of the plantation. In this chapter, I will look at the rhetoric of three works that exemplify such struggles. First, I will discuss songs from *The Queen's Songbook* to show how Queen Lili'uokalani, the last reigning monarch of Hawai'i, used the traditional Hawaiian rhetorical strategy of *kaona*[1] in songs written during the last four decades of the nineteenth century to send messages of resistance to her people before and after the overthrow of the monarchy. Next, I will detail how Milton Murayama, through the publication of his book *All I Asking for Is My Body* in 1959, established a particular ethos by using Pidgin (Hawai'i Creole English) to affirm the experiences and identity of plantation-era immigrant workers in Hawai'i. Lastly, I will look at contemporary Hawaiian scholar Noenoe Silva's 2004 *Aloha Betrayed: Native Hawaiian Resistance to American Colonialism*, to demonstrate how her book works rhetorically in its documentation of events that counter the dominant historical narrative to reaffirm Native Hawaiian identity. The examination of these three authors' works will offer insight into some of the ways context-specific rhetorical strategies have been used to resist the silencing that has accompanied colonization in Hawai'i.

I have arranged my discussion of these three texts chronologically, beginning with Queen Lili'uokalani, followed by Murayama, and closing with Silva. However, while arranging them thus facilitates understanding of the way social and political events evolved in Hawai'i, it is also important that the accounts of resistance examined here begin and end with Hawaiian voices. Discussions of the plantation era capture how colonization exploited people and land for the sake of power and money—a recurring theme in America's move west. However, examining how the rhetoric Native Hawaiians have and continue to employ to respond to colonization provides a counternarrative to that which has been reproduced in media and in the history books—that Hawaiians welcomed American dominance in their islands. I have framed my discussion of the rhetoric in each of these texts within concepts from traditional Western rhetorical theory. I do so not to privilege Western theory, but because in many ways the theoretical concepts that deal with the purpose of rhetoric, meaning-making, and the role of audience can be generally applied in any context; however, although these theoretical frames provide departure points, as I will demonstrate throughout, understanding how these rhetorical concepts are deployed is contingent upon viewing them within a specific sociopolitical and cultural context. So that the rhetoric employed by each of these writers can be more fully understood, I will begin by providing a brief historical contextualization of the events that occurred since Hawai'i's first contact with Captain James Cook in 1778.

Hawai'i: A Brief Contextualization

Before 1778, Native Hawaiians, their language, and their culture thrived in the archipelago of Hawai'i. However, Captain James Cook's arrival in the Hawaiian Islands that year triggered a string of events that would eventually lead to the devastating decimation of the Hawaiian population. In his book, *Before the Horror: The Population of Hawai'i on the Eve of Western Contact* (1989), David Stannard argues that the Native Hawaiian population ranged from 800,000 to well more than 1,000,000 when Captain Cook arrived. Contact with the west—particularly through diseases such as smallpox—took its toll on the Hawaiian people; by 1900, the population of Hawaiians had declined to 37,656.[2] In the century between contact and the overthrow of the Hawaiian monarchy in 1893, Native Hawaiians went from being a strong and thriving people to fighting to keep their culture, language, and people alive.

The establishment of plantations played a key role in efforts to colonize Hawai'i and the marginalization of Native Hawaiians. In the 1830s, a Honolulu mercantile firm founded by New England businessmen sent William Hooper of Boston, Massachusetts to establish a sugar plantation in the islands.[3] In 1835, the first plantation was founded at Koloa, Kaua'i, marking the beginning of Hawai'i's plantation era.[4] Caucasian businessmen like Hooper saw the Native Hawaiians and their system of government as standing in the way of their efforts to civilize the islands. Hooper wrote the following about his enterprise:

> I have succeeded in bringing about a place, which if followed up by other foreign residents, will eventually emancipate the natives from the miserable system of "chief labour" which has existed at these Islands, and which if not broken up, will be the effectual preventative to the progress of civilization, industry and national prosperity...The tract of land in Koloa was [developed] after much pain...for the purpose of breaking up the system aforesaid

or in other words to serve as an entering wedge...[to] upset the whole system.[5]

That many Native Hawaiians quickly refused to work as laborers on the plantations further cemented the perceptions that Native Hawaiians were impeding progress.

Although at first, Hawaiians were recruited to work on the plantations, the Natives of Hawai'i, whose tradition is to act as stewards of the land which in turn takes care of its people, found that plantation work went against their relationship of reciprocity with the land. Moreover, Hawaiians, whose population had decreased dramatically since first contact, were able to sustain their livelihoods from the land through fishing and farming, making them more resistant to plantation life. Although the gradual obtainment of exclusive water rights for sugar plantations beginning in 1853 further devastated the Native Hawaiian lifestyle that had relied on a complex agricultural system, few Hawaiians resorted to working on the plantations.[6]

The plantation owners interpreted this lack of interest by Native Hawaiians as laziness and did not hesitate to man their labor force from outside the islands when the Hawaiians proved unwilling. Takaki writes, "Hooper soon became frustrated by the inefficiency and recalcitrance of the Hawaiian laborers and began to employ a few Chinese...[noting in a correspondence that] 'A colony of Chinese would, probably, put the plantation in order.'"[7] The president of the Royal Hawaiian Agricultural Society echoed Hooper's sentiments about Hawaiian laborers, stating, "We shall find Coolie labor to be more certain, systematic and economic than that of the native. They are prompt at the call of the bell, steady in their work, quick to learn, and will accomplish more [than Hawaiian laborers]."[8] Hooper's model was quickly followed by other plantation owners, and these mostly American businessmen and sons of American missionaries thus initiated a mass immigration of laborers to the islands.

The first immigrant laborers came from China in 1852, and by 1872 there were 2,038 Chinese in Hawai'i.[9] They were soon followed by Portuguese (1878), Japanese (1885), Koreans (1904), and other small groups from Europe.[10] The Japanese became the largest immigrant group brought in to work on the plantations; by 1924 their population totaled 120,074.[11] It is important to note that although the members of these ethnic groups were all brought to Hawai'i to work on the plantations, they were kept stratified in distinct, separated living areas.[12] Marginalization of non–Caucasians in Hawai'i increased as the economic and political power of American businessmen in the islands grew. Queen Lili'uokalani, the last reigning Hawaiian monarch and a prolific writer in both her native language and English (as will be discussed later), provides a Native Hawaiian perspective of the American capitalistic enterprise in her autobiography, which she wrote in English, *Hawai'i's Story by Hawai'i's Queen* (1964). I quote at length what the Queen writes of the American businessmen's usurpation of power in Hawai'i, as it is most eloquently stated in her own words as someone who witnessed these events:

> For many years our sovereigns had welcomed the advice of, and given full representations in their government and councils to, American residents who had cast in their lot with our people, and established industries on the Islands. As they became wealthy, and acquired titles to lands through the simplicity of our people and their ignorance of values and of the new land laws, their greed and their love of power proportionately increased; and schemes for aggrandizing themselves still further, or for avoiding the obligations which they had incurred to us, began to occupy their minds. So the mercantile element, as embodied in the Chamber of Commerce, the sugar planters, and the proprietors of the "missionary" stores, formed a distinct political party, called the "down-town" party, whose purpose was to minimize or entirely subvert other interests, and especially the prerogatives of the crown, which, based upon ancient custom and the authority of the island chiefs, were the sole guaranty of our nationality. Although settled among us, and drawing their wealth from our resources, they were alien to us in their customs and ideas respecting government, and desired above all things the extension of their power, and to carry out their own special plans of advancement, and to secure their own personal benefit. (177–78)

Many of these settlers felt that acquiring this personal benefit which Queen Lili'uokalani alludes to could be expedited by Hawai'i becoming an American territory.

Not only did these Americans have an economic advantage, they also had the United States military behind them. In 1893, with the help of the U.S. marines, in an event President Cleveland later called an "act of war" and a "substantial wrong,"[13] the Hawaiian monarchy was overthrown by the same Americans whom the Hawaiians had welcomed into their lands. In 1895, Queen Lili'uokalani was imprisoned

in her palace for eight months after an aborted attempt by her support-
ers to restore her to the thrown. Following the overthrow, the push for
Americanization became even more overt. In 1894, English replaced
Hawaiian as the official language of instruction in all Hawai'i schools,[14]
and the Hawaiian language was officially banned in 1896. This act
not only represented the political dominance of the American businessmen, but also the disdain for all things considered un-American,
including language.

The effects of privileging Standard English on Native Hawaiians
were devastating, and there are many *mo'olelo* (stories) among Hawaiians
that tell of the abuses their ancestors suffered when caught speaking
Hawaiian. With the marginalization of their language coincided an
increasing displacement of Hawaiians in their own land. In the events
that propelled the territory toward statehood, all ethnic groups residing in the islands were frequently portrayed as "Hawaiians," or *locals*.[15]
Arguably, acknowledging Native Hawaiians as a distinct ethnic group
would encourage recognition of Hawaiian land claims and the legitimacy of their active protests to the overthrow and later to statehood,
whereas conflating Native Hawaiians into the term local perpetuated
the marginalization of their culture.

Amidst this political backdrop, Hawai'i Creole English, or "Pidgin"
as it is commonly called in the islands, emerged as the language identified with being local. Until the 1970s, a period of time credited with
the beginning of the Hawaiian renaissance, communication in Hawai'i
has been acknowledged[16] as occurring in two ways: through Standard
English, and its deficient counterpart, Pidgin. Yet, although the speaking of Pidgin has often been correlated with inferiority in the dominant discourse, many of its speakers perceive it as an act of resistance.[17]

Speaking Pidgin is most commonly associated with Hawaiians and
immigrant laborers in Hawai'i. The presence of large Hawaiian communities whose members mostly speak Pidgin is representative of
(1) that Pidgin was originally based on Hawaiian not English, thus
the speaking of it has been noted as an act of resistance to colonization
particularly since their native language was banned; and (2) as immigrant laborers first learned this Hawaiian-based Pidgin, Hawaiians,
particularly those in close proximity to plantations, seemed to have
socialized with the immigrant laborers and their descendants more
regularly than with the Caucasians. However, at some point, the local
Asian community, most notably those of Japanese descent, surpassed
the Hawaiians on the social ladder; sociolinguistic scholar Charlene
Sato writes, "Today [1991], Hawai'i's middle class is primarily

Caucasian and Asian, while the working class is largely composed of native Hawaiians, Filipinos, and recent Asian and Pacific island immigrants."[18] Hawai'i's story, until recently, has been most often told by members of the two dominant ethnic groups, from their perspective, and to their advantage.

After the turn of the century, the Caucasian population in Hawai'i increased as a result of the general "move west" enabled by the new railroads connecting the east and west coasts on the continent. Many of these new families could not afford the elite private schools that had been established in the early 1800s "for missionary and other privileged *haole* children."[19] The Caucasian community whose children were attending public schools began expressing concern that "Caucasian children should not be interacting with Pidgin English-speaking '*local*' children."[20] This eventually led to the establishment of the English Standard Schools in 1924, where children had to pass English proficiency tests in order to be admitted to designated public schools around the islands. The schools, which remained in place until 1948, were attended "almost exclusively by Caucasian children," which "further stratified Hawaiian society."[21] Language use was also correlated with patriotism—Sato notes, not only was Pidgin "declared *not* a language," but also "branded un-American."[22] Thus, local Asians were aware that speaking Pidgin made them seem like outsiders. To be American meant to speak Standard English.

After World War II, there was another dramatic push for Americanization, this time by the local Asian community. Many local Asians had fought as Americans in the war or volunteered in the American war effort. At the same time, they lived under the threat of being "relocated" to concentration camps, with curfews exclusively for Asians, and other forms of discrimination. The local *haoles* who maintained political and economic power in the islands generally opposed statehood because if Hawai'i were a territory, the positions that afforded them such legal and economical power would be jeopardized. However, the local Asians saw statehood as a path toward liberation from the slave-like conditions of plantation labor. A. A. Smyser, the *Honolulu Star-Bulletin*'s political editor at the time, states, "The goal [of statehood] was democracy for all in Hawai'i, to give our Asian population a political voice equal to their numbers."[23] To counter anti-Japanese sentiments, Governor Burns made the case for the local Japanese by "praising their war record, their political skill and their patriotism."[24] In this political climate, speaking Standard English, so as to sound more American, took on even more significance.

It is important to note that contrary to the media coverage at the time, there are many stories of protests against statehood by Native Hawaiians, but as noted by Hawaiian activist George Kanahele, "The Hawaiians as a community were only on the periphery of the power struggle" during the post–World War II period.[25] Ultimately, the drive to become American by many in the local Asian community culminated in statehood in 1959. But the post–World War II era also heralded in other perspectives about what it meant to have rights—changes that would challenge colonialism not just in Hawai'i but around the world.

During the 1950s through the 1970s, civil rights movements took shape around the world. Unprecedented challenges to imperial colonialism and oppressive states were happening globally with dramatic effects. In South Africa, the anti-Apartheid movement was underway; The Maori in New Zealand were fighting to reclaim their land rights and sovereignty; On the continental United States, the black civil rights movement as well as protest to the Vietnam War were shaking the country. Against this global backdrop, particularly in the 1970s, Hawaiians were experiencing what some have termed a renaissance.[26] As Kanahele articulates in his 1979 article "The Hawaiian Renaissance," Hawaiian *mele* (song) was regaining its popularity, the practice of *hula kahiko* (ancient hula) and male *hula* as well as other Hawaiian traditions, such as feather work and *kapa*[27] making, were being revived. And then in 1975, the building and sailing of the Hokule'a, a traditional Hawaiian voyaging canoe, was to come to symbolize Hawaiians' reclamation of their traditions and culture.

But everyone did not embrace the Hawaiian political and cultural renaissance. While all efforts at cultural revitalization have not had an end goal of political sovereignty, ethnic groups who have settled in Hawai'i have frequently seen them as such and thus as a challenge as threat to claims that settler identity is tied to the islands. Resistance to the Hawaiian sovereignty movement manifested both in silent opposition and legal battles. In 1996, Harold Rice challenged the Hawaiian-only vote for trustees of the Office of Hawaiian Affairs (OHA) to the U.S. Supreme Court. Rice claimed that allowing only those of Hawaiian descent to vote for OHA trustees (state offices), amounted to racism and was, as such, in violation of the fourteenth and fifteenth amendments to the Constitution. Rice won his case in 2000. Other attacks against institutions whose purposes are directed toward the betterment of Hawaiians followed, including suits against the Department of Hawaiian Homelands, also a state agency. Most notably, there have been several lawsuits against Kamehameha Schools, a private school established by one of the last reigning monarchs of Hawai'i whose mission is to educate children of Hawaiian ancestry, charging that the school's policy of giving preference to children of Hawaiian descent is racist.

It is within this politically charged context that the texts examined here are written—each representing a different period, each employing rhetorical strategies to counter the dominant narrative in ways that convey the unique experiences of that time.

Queen Lili'uokalani's *Mele*

Aristotle articulates rhetoric as "an ability in each case, to see the available means of persuasion."[28] Although the ways in which language can be and is used to persuade in a particular rhetorical situation has remained the focus of rhetoric, the scope of rhetoric altered in the twenty-first century. For Aristotle and other classical rhetoricians, such as Cicero and Quintilian, rhetoric encompassed specific forms of public discourse, specifically the political, forensic, and ceremonial.[29] The most significant divergence from the classical Western perspective in many current understandings of rhetoric lies in the expansion of rhetoric to include literature and all language acts. For Aristotle, rhetoric was confined to public speech; literature was not included in its scope. Kenneth Burke best explains the reasoning behind including literary works in the scope of rhetoric; he asserts in the *Philosophy of Literary Form* (1973) that all literary acts "embody attitudes, of resignation, solace, vengeance, expectancy..." (3), and thus works of poetry (which Burke argues include both critical and imaginative works), are to be considered "symbolic action" (8). However, arguably, the distinction between the literary and public discourse that Burke works to discount is a Western construct. Hawaiians, for example, view most if not all literary acts as inherently political, and they thus fall into Aristotle's purview of what constitutes rhetoric. Haunani Kay Trask in "Writing in Captivity: Poetry in a Time of Decolonization," writes,

> Like most Native people, I do not perceive the world of creative writing as divided into categories of prose and poetry or fiction and nonfiction...Life is a confluence of creativities: art is a fluid political medium, as politics is metaphorical and artistic...Our Hawaiian chiefs, for example, announced war through the use

of ominous metaphor; and woe to those who misunderstood the chiefly references.[30]

The Hawaiian perspective that *mele*, *oli* (chants), and *mo'olelo* are political in nature firmly establishes these Hawaiian traditions in what Aristotle would consider rhetoric. Moreover, as I will show in the following discussion of the *mele* written by Queen Lili'uokalani, it is the Native Hawaiian peoples understanding of the rhetorical strategies associated with these Hawaiian traditions that prompts them to look for and decode political messages that often go unrecognized by outsiders.

During the events leading up to the overthrow and following her imprisonment, Lili'uokalani sent messages of resistance to her people through her *mele*. While the specific content of the *mele* are rhetorical as will be discussed later in this section, the Queen also relied on what Burke has termed identification to establish her ethos so as to ensure her subjects would look for the Hawaiian rhetorical strategy of *kaona* in the *mele*. Aristotle writes that "character is almost, so to speak, the most authoritative form of persuasion," and that successful persuasion also relies on putting the audience in a particular emotional state.[31] In the case of Lili'uokalani, Burke's identification theory demonstrates how the Queen's position as an *ali'i nui* (high chief) facilitates establishing her moral character and simultaneously puts her audience in a certain frame of mind. For Burke, identification results in "ambiguities in substance," for to identify with someone also articulates your difference. Burke writes, "In being identified with B, A is 'substantially one' with a person other than himself. Yet at the same time he remains unique, an individual locus of motives."[32] This complexity of identification, its work to articulate "consubstantiality" and at the same time uniqueness, aptly relates to the Queen's relationship with her people and provides a means to understanding other rhetorical strategies she employed.

By identifying with her subjects as a Hawaiian monarch, Lili'uokalani could rely on her people to assume several things. First that she was *pono*,[33] for as Lilikalā Kame'eleihiwa notes in her book *Native Lands and Foreign Desires* (1992), *ali'i nui* were expected to maintain the highest moral character, and there were repercussions if they did not. If an *ali'i nui* was considered not *pono*, through the practice of *imihaku*,[34] the *ali'i* could be deposed or even killed (48).[35] Thus, by her very position, her moral character was established with her people. Moreover, as an *ali'i*, as with any monarch who is respected, she was expected to direct her people to a *pono* course of action. Kame'eleihiwa explains that *maka'āinana* (commoners) understood that if they "follow the 'powers that be,' then the politicians and the state would intervene on their behalf."[36] Thus, as subjects, the Hawaiian people expected that the Queen would direct them in a way that was *pono*, and that she had their best interest in mind. That was her duty. Thus by identifying herself with her subjects as a monarch, she could rely on their shared knowledge of the traditions of Hawaiian society. At the same time, she could also establish her uniqueness as a monarch and thus trust in her people's understanding that she would try to provide direction and model appropriate behavior.

This understanding of shared traditions would allow the Queen to employ the Hawaiian rhetorical strategy of *kaona* to convey messages to her people. Kame'eleihiwa in *A Legendary Tradition of Kamapua'a: The Hawaiian Pig God* (1996) explains how *kaona* works, saying, "there are always several layers of *kaona* in any good example of Hawaiian prose" (ix); there is the meaning at face value, the reference to ancient times, and through allusions and metaphor, to ancient events. Then, Kame'eleihiwa acknowledges another possible level that is "known only to the raconteur and 1 or 2 special members of the audience...while everyone else remains oblivious to the message."[37] She goes on to articulate the importance of *kaona* in Hawaiian tradition, saying, "Hawaiian poetry and narrative were critically judged by their audience as sophisticated or simple, depending on the levels of *kaona* or hidden meanings, presented."[38] Thus, it would be expected for *kaona* to be embodied in any *mo'olelo* or *mele*—the Queen was expected to employ *kaona* and her people were expected to look for it to decipher the meaning of her texts. These understood roles are best explained by Wayne Booth's theory of collaborative meaning-making wherein "authors imagined ideal audiences for their works and readers generally were willing to take on the role assigned to them... [resulting in] a collaborative effort at communication."[39] The tradition of *kaona* in Hawaiian *mele* and *mo'olelo* indicates that Lili'uokalani would be able to employ this strategy and that her audience would assume their role as decipherers of the *kaona*.

Hawaiian scholar Noenoe Silva discusses how *mele* provided a perfect vehicle for the Queen to send messages to her people. She writes,

Since the advent of the print media starting in 1834, mele also became a genre of resistance to cultural imperialism.... Mele was a primary genre through which women were able to express their political views... [moreover], the understanding that mele should contain these several layers of meaning made the genre particularly well suited to communicating thoughts and feelings undetected but yet in plain sight of hostile forces.[40]

Silva goes on to discuss several of the Queen's *mele* and their overt political message—that is overt for those who understood the *kaona* and its respective references. For example, in her examination of the *mele* "He 'Ai na ka Lani," Silva discusses one level of *kaona*. According to Silva, the first two lines of the *mele* can be translated as "The royal one is dining now/You should all be silent." However, the word for dine (*'ai*) is also the word for rule; thus the first two lines can also be translated as "The royal one is ruling now/You should all be silent."[41] By substituting an alternative meaning for the word *'ai*, a different meaning of the phrase, or its *kaona*, is conveyed. For a foreigner, with limited knowledge of Hawaiian, to be quiet while one is eating may not be something to take note of, particularly if that person holds a high-ranking position. However, to say "The royal one is ruling now/You should all be silent" has a completely different meaning—suggesting no one should question the rule, which takes on even greater significance considering that American settlers were challenging the Hawaiian monarchy. This alternate meaning, revealed only if looked for by an audience expecting *kaona*, could be relied on to go undetected by most if not all non-Hawaiians.

Silva goes on to discuss several songs that the Queen smuggled out of her rooms while she was held captive and how through these songs she opened a dialogue with some of her imprisoned subjects.[42] These *mele* were printed in the newspaper *Ka Makaainana*, and sent messages of allegiance and hope to her people. For example, Silva translates one poem as saying, "Sacred is the aloha that comes/For my people in the spray of bullets"[43]; and another, "Say that there is life through her majesty/Who sacrifices her life for the lāhui/So that you patriot(s) may live."[44] These *mele* were responded to by the imprisoned subjects, and as Silva notes, "the mele acted like a conversation between people who were physically unable to talk to each other because they were imprisoned."[45] Despite being censored, the Queen was thus able to use *mele* and *kaona* as a rhetorical strategy to send messages of unification and resistance to her people.

The Queen's inherent understanding of the *kaona* in any text likely allowed her to exploit plays on meaning in order to mislead a foreign audience. Her rhetorical adeptness is perhaps most apparent when translations of her works are paired next to each other. In *The Queen's Songbook,* which is a collection of Lili'uokalani's *mele*, all the songs are translated by Hui Hānai, the book's editors and several of the songs have translations which the Queen wrote herself. The editors write of the Queen's translations: "Her translations are free-form, for her primary purpose was to make the songs 'singable' in English and thus acceptable to non-Hawaiian audiences."[46] In light of Silva's work, however, I contend that the Queen used the translation to mask the true meaning of her *mele*. I am not fluent in Hawaiian, so I will rely solely on the translations provided by the Queen and Hui Hānai, and I will only examine one verse in one song to provide example. In the *mele* "Ka Wai 'Apoi Lani," the Queen translates the last stanza as, "Cold words and looks reprove/Oh, turn not thus away/Give kind greetings, words of love/And a heart that beats within."[47] However, Hui Hānai translates the same stanza as, "Words come like a pressing needle/Don't shy away from your subjects/While you have this responsibility/While you feel so strongly about this."[48] The meaning and attitude in the two translations differ significantly. In the Queen's translation the attitude determining the way in which the meaning is conveyed implies someone who has been wronged, but comes above it to forgive. The second translation indicates an attitude of resolution to stand firm despite being attacked. The different readings convey altered pictures of the Queen. No doubt it was in her best interest to seem the resigned and forgiving victim to her foreign captors. However, translating the lines with their alternate meaning, their *kaona*, the Queen demonstrates her loyalty to her subjects and dedication to the sovereign nation.

I have only discussed a small sample of the *kaona* in the Queen's *mele* here and the way she used these *mele* to speak to her people to convey messages of hope, loyalty to the Hawaiian nation, and resistance; however, there are numerous examples in the Queen's songbook, some of which Noenoe Silva discusses at greater length in her book *Aloha Betrayed*. What is important to note is that understanding the Queen's rhetorical strategies provides an alternative history of the colonization of Hawai'i—it demonstrates that Hawaiians did not welcome Western rule as has often been suggested in American accounts of this period. Hawaiians respected their monarch and looked to her to tell them how to act during this painful and tumultuous time. And her *mele* suggest she dictated patience, telling her people to wait for the right time to make their move to reclaim governance of their country—not resignation and acceptance of foreign rule. Unfortunately, despite the Queen using *mele* as a rhetorical platform to send messages of hope and resistance to her people, her attempts to secure support for the reinstatement of the Hawaiian nation were largely ignored by the U.S. government.[49] As history has shown, the Queen never regained her throne. During this same period, many of the American businessmen who had taken part in the overthrow of the Hawaiian government were reaping the rewards of the flourishing plantation economy. Similar to the plantations that were the backbone of the economy in the southeast United States, the romantic and idyllic lifestyle associated with Hawai'i's plantation life masked abuse and oppression. I turn next to Milton Murayama's *All I Asking for Is My Body* to offer insight into how literature written in Pidgin plays a significant role in the struggle by immigrant laborers to assert their identity.

Milton Murayama's *All I Asking for Is My Body*

The first section of *All I Asking for Is My Body* was serialized in the *Arizona Quarterly* in the summer of 1959.[50] The specific sociopolitical climate of the time is significant: 1959 is post–World War II and Korean War, and Hawai'i is about to become a state. During this period, Hawai'i was mostly viewed by outsiders (i.e., those residing on the continent) through the cultural lens constructed and reproduced in postwar Hollywood films such as *From Here to Eternity* (1953), *South Pacific* (1958), and later in *Blue Hawai'i* (1961). Films such as these worked to paint a specific picture of islands in the Pacific in general and Hawai'i in particular: life was simple and fun, the natives were an homogenous ethnic group, and Euro-Americans were not only well-received but waited for and welcomed—indeed the exploits and love affairs of the foreign *haole* took center stage in these films. Murayama's novel offers a very different view of life in Hawai'i—one that locals to Hawai'i can more readily identify with than the images previously reproduced in film. In this section, I will discuss how writing in Pidgin becomes a rhetorical vehicle for Murayama to both reaffirm local identity and identify with a local audience.[51]

When *All I Asking for Is My Body* was being considered for publication as a book in the early 1970s, the editors asked Murayama to correct the "grammatical error" in the title. However, as Stephen Sumida writes, "[Murayama] refused to falsify the work and its subject."[52] To publish the book, Murayama and his wife formed their own publishing house, Supa Press, and *All I Asking for Is My Body* became their first release. The rhetorical act of refusing to change his language to conform to the accepted standards, despite risking the loss of cultural capital associated with publishing, provides the framework for the reading of his work as disruptive. To understand the conflict about language use, Murayama negotiated and what his decisions about publication meant to his Pidgin speaking audience necessitates understanding the ambiguous attitudes toward Pidgin held by the local community.

The attitudes toward Pidgin in the local community in Hawai'i have always been conflicted, with speakers secretly acknowledging their use of the language in "at home" contexts but frequently denying its use in academic settings. These ambiguities are reflected in responses to a survey conducted by Sato of 986 graduating students gauging sentiments about Pidgin. Sato notes the range of the responses to the survey: "Pidgin English fosters illiteracy. Pidgin is a lazy way to talk: it promotes backwards thinking" and "banning Pidgin would violate our freedom of speech...its our way of making Hawaii different from anywhere in the United States."[53] The responses of these students indicate that while Pidgin does inform identity ("its our way of making Hawaii different"), this position is held in check by the sentiment that speaking Pidgin indicates an inferior way of thinking. This lack of legitimization of their language has led Pidgin speakers to be hesitant to assert their identities and experiences as valid representations of human experience. A scenario in which a group of people is denied the value of their own experiences can result in cultural assimilation—loss of language and loss of identity. Likewise, speakers of marginalized languages often interpolate the ideology of the dominant culture to varying extents in an attempt to reconcile their position in the dominant society.

In a context such as this, legitimizing a language in print, considering the value placed on publication in Western society, represents a sort of "contact zone" where competing ideologies collide. Contact Zones, as defined by Mary Louise Pratt in *Arts of the Contact Zone* (1999) are "social spaces where cultures meet, clash, and grapple with each other, often in contexts of highly asymmetrical relations of power, such as colonialism, slavery, or their aftermaths as they are lived out in many parts of the world today." Thus, validating a marginalized language through publication can provide an avenue of resistance—a social space where the epistemologies of different language-speakers come face to face. Print and publication have long been privileged in Western society; having a particular language and its corresponding discourse legitimized in book form can work to change the perspectives of a group speaking a language formally perceived to be inferior. Anne Wysocki and Johndan Johnson-Eilola discuss the significance of the book in their article "Blinded by the Letter" in *Passions and Pedagogies* (1999). In speaking of the colonization of Mexico, they write, the Spaniards "were so steeped in book culture that they believed the Mexica had no sense of history—because the Mexica had recorded their pasts in paintings rather than in books—and hence that the Mexica lacked intelligence and humanity" (357). Despite that the above occurred several hundred years ago, the value placed on publication has changed little and recording a language in a formal publication can work to counter preconceived notions of inferiority.

Ironically, despite the overt rhetorical act to validate Pidgin and its speakers by writing in Pidgin, Murayama seems caught up in the ambiguous feelings about Pidgin. Publication for him is a contact zone in which he attempts to reconcile the dominant discourse about Pidgin and his own feelings about language and identity. Odo discusses Murayama's use of Pidgin, saying, "Murayama intended to reach the broadest possible audience with this book and thus limited his use of pidgin, confining it to conversation and...tempering the language to make it accessible to standard English speakers."[54] Indeed Murayama explains the forces influencing his representation of Pidgin in the book; he says, "I wanted my pidgin to be understood by the editors and readers of those [*Harper, New Yorker*] magazines."[55] Thus while one intention of Murayama's was to give us a story that would allow history to be "remembered...with love, with all the warts showing,"[56] he is obviously caught between using Pidgin to give us this realistic portrayal and accommodating the dominant culture's aesthetic values. Murayama seems to negotiate the ambiguities associated with Pidgin, to resist and at the same time yield to the demands of a continental readership. Murayama does not completely accommodate his English-speaking audience, yet neither does he represent his language authentically—he is residing in a borderland. The rhetoric of providing a version of history in all its complexities is actually accomplished, but perhaps not the way he intended. His use of Pidgin combined with his tempering of it reflects the mixed attitudes toward Pidgin as a characteristic of local culture and identity *as well as* an inferiority marker. Arguably, his negotiation of the two positions does not completely annihilate the effect of using Pidgin. Within the publishing arena in which any use of Pidgin was perceived as being counterproductive from the perspective of editors, his decision to use any Pidgin at all can and should be recognized as a rhetorical statement of affirmation for Pidgin speakers. Indeed, in claiming the right to publish the tempered Pidgin as he did, he may have risked not being published at all. Publishing thus becomes a contact zone wherein power is negotiated; one could easily argue that Murayama gained ground.

Even though Murayama's Pidgin is arguably "watered-down," his use of Pidgin as a representation of the vernacular used in everyday life in the novel acts rhetorically to reaffirm identity of Asian plantation workers. Ancient rhetoricians acknowledged the importance of speaking in the vernacular of the everyday life to create a bond with one's audience. Cicero asserts, "the very cardinal sin [of a rhetorician] is to depart from the language of everyday life and the usage approved by the sense of the community."[57] Moreover, he advocates speaking in language and with style that "townspeople and rustics alike"[58] can relate to, so that "the audience, even if they are no speakers are sure they can speak in that fashion."[59] Thus, the use of vernacular allows the audience to identify with the speaker and thus his purpose—to become "consubstantial" to use Burke's term. Use of language that differs from that of an audience—a language perceived privileged by the dominant culture, and not one's vernacular—can work to alienate an audience. Burke explains that identifying oneself with a specialized activity "makes one a participant in some social economic class."[60] Therefore, if Murayama had exclusively used Standard English, no matter how authentic his portrayals of plantation and *nissei*[61] life, there is a strong likelihood that local readers would not have identified as easily with the story. His use of Pidgin thus works as a platform for Murayama to establish identification with his audience.

The writing of Pidgin allows the reader to identify with the work and thus the agency attained from the platform through which the work is disseminated, a published book, takes on a deeper meaning. The legitimization by Western society of the word in print is arguably interpolated in a colonized location such as Hawai'i. Thus, seeing their language in print reverses for Pidgin speakers what Johnson-Eilola and Wysocki noted as the response to the absence of books: instead of having no sense of history, of lacking intelligence and humanity, a history has been reclaimed and intelligence and humanity asserted. Language in publication can have a powerful effect; and the influence of this is the correlating legitimization of the story being told. The hardships and relationships that may have previously been guarded secrets can now be compared to the trials Western authors such as Dickens and Twain depict in their novels. The story of *nissei* Japanese, not having enough food to eat, struggling under an oppressive plantation where no one can get ahead, feeling conflicted between cultures, assumes a significant place in the chronicles of historical experiences as told through literature. History gets reclaimed, identity begins to be reestablished as unique, not inferior. Providing an account in print often correlates to a sense of permanence and authenticity of that account. Thus, writing in Pidgin can have the rhetorical effect on the audience of reaffirming cultural identity, validating a history not previously acknowledged. It can privilege a cultural lens previously designated as inferior, or worse, nonexistent, by the dominant discourse. These are utopian outcomes, but even a fraction of these effects can have a positive influence on a culture whose language had been "forbidden in the classroom, declared not a language, [and] branded un-American."[62] As Murayama desired to provide an account of history so that it would not be lost,[63] this may have been his intent for this audience. Whatever Murayama's intent, this authoring of an identification through the use of Pidgin to tell this story arguably created the expectation in the Pidgin speaking readership that stories written in Pidgin would reveal some part of life they could recognize.

Noenoe Silva's *Aloha Betrayed: Native Hawaiian Resistance to American Colonialism*

Fast forward almost half a century to 2004: most Native Hawaiians have been raised speaking Standard English as their first language and have had to learn Hawaiian in an academic setting. The nuances and *kaona* Queen Lili'uokalani knew her people would be able to understand and interpret has, for many Hawaiians, been resurrected mainly through committed research. Efforts to recapture their language, traditions, and historical record have simultaneously brought to the forefront the injustices suffered by Native Hawaiians over the last 150 years of colonization. Equally important in the body of scholarship that recasts the actions of American businessmen and the U.S. government as deceitful, self-serving, and illegal is its role in painting a different picture of Native Hawaiians as proud, intellectual, brave defenders of their kingdom. Noenoe Silva's *Aloha Betrayed: Native Hawaiian Resistance to American Colonialism* is such a work—it is rhetorical not only because it falsifies the common narrative reproduced about the events preceding, during, and following the overthrow, but also because it gives Hawaiians a very different legacy as compared to the one described by the colonial enterprise from which to move forward from. In addition, Silva's book demonstrates that while language and rhetorical strategies are sometimes easily identifiable to a Western audience, understanding the overall rhetoric of text necessitates reading it within a specific sociopolitical, historical, and cultural context.

Silva's book provides a countertext to history books written by the dominant Western culture. Written in English, it is accessible to all English-speaking readers and thus may work to make known this alternate history. However, arguably, the book is even more significant for Hawaiians. Silva clearly states the rhetorical aim her book in the introduction; she writes, "This book refutes the myth of passivity through documentation and study of the many forms of resistance by the Kanaka Maoli [Native Hawaiians] to political, economic, linguistic, and cultural oppression."[64] Silva begins her book with an account of the first newspaper controlled in every aspect by Native Hawaiians and written in Hawaiian—which allowed it to be largely unreadable to many in the missionary establishment. The articles and stories demonstrate that Hawaiians actively celebrated their cultural traditions despite condemnation of these traditions by the missionaries. The newspaper also provides accounts of struggles and confrontations with the encroaching establishment. Her analysis begins a history of Native Hawaiians that directly contradicts accounts of Hawaiians as compliant and docile in the face of impending colonization. She continues by recasting King Kãlakaua's cultural revival efforts—representative in his commissioning of the writing and printing of the Hawaiian genealogy chant the *Kumulipo* and providing public performance avenues for *hula* and *mo'olelo*—as acts of resistance to the American oligarchy and the imposition of their Western religion. In the book, she also succeeds in providing a portrait of Queen Lili'uokalani as a powerful rhetorician, who used numerous "genres of resistance [in attempts to] rescue her nation from the United States."[65] Silva best explains what articulating these acts by Native Hawaiians mean to today's Native Hawaiians:

> What does it matter that this history of resistance is documented and analyzed? What does it matter that we read what Kanaka Maoli wrote in their own language a hundred or more years ago? We might just as well ask: How do a people come know who they are? How do a colonized people recover from the violence done to their past by the linguicide that accompanies their colonialism.[66]

The purpose of *Aloha Betrayed* is to reaffirm Native Hawaiian epistemology, history, and identity. As such, out of the three texts examined here, it is most easily identifiable as an example of rhetoric in the classical Western sense. The book can be viewed as fitting in all three of the classical Western categories: political, forensic, and ceremonial. Of the three categories Aristotle writes, "Deliberative advice [political] is either... 'exhortation' or... 'dissuasion'... In the law courts [foren-sic] there is either accusation or defense... In epideictic [ceremonial], there is either praise or blame."[67] Silva's book defends her Hawaiian *kupuna* (ancestors), refuting the "myth of passivity" (forensic), thus praising their acts as heroic (ceremonial). The book is also aligned with Aristotle's political genre in that it advocates a course of action toward a specific end: Silva writes, "Now we must decide how to govern our-selves and how we want to live together as a lāhui."[68] To redefine the actions of her *kupuna* as resisting colonizing efforts, Silva revisits the past so as to provide a departure point for future efforts for reclaiming the Hawaiian nation.

Just as her book is more readily identifiable as being rhetorical in the classical sense, Silva's work also facilitates knowledge that has mostly remained unavailable—a basic goal of all good rhetoric as articulated by Aristotle. For Aristotle, rhetoric is most aptly applied to facilitate deci-sion on matters about which true knowledge is unavailable. As most of what has been widely accepted as truths about Hawai'i, her people, and her monarchs, until recently was authored by members of the col-onizing culture, Silva's research reconstructs a truth that had previously been largely silenced. Her means for accomplishing this entails "docu-mentation and study" of historical records that included "microfilmed copies of seventy-five newspapers in the Hawaiian language."[69] Such resources act as a type of example in the classical Western rhetorical sense. However, despite Silva's strategies fitting neatly into our under-standing of classical Western rhetoric, meaning-making is still only fully realized by examining the material through a cultural and his-torical context. In the case of accounts in the newspapers, for example, Silva looks at actual archives and interprets them using the tradition of *kaona* to explain the resistance of Hawaiians during the 1800s. It is by reading these texts through what she calls a "Kanaka-centered lens" that enables her to reconstruct acts of resistance by Hawaiians. Silva is thus able to explain documents from a Kanaka Maoli perspective and offer an alternative historical account of a people that works to reaffirm their culture and identity.

Conclusion

Rhetoric is a powerful tool in any colonial enterprise: it influences what a people know of themselves and points to a course of action. When a people are robbed of their language, their rhetoric is also lost. Indeed, this is why a common practice in all colonial agendas is to replace the indigenous and ethnic languages with that of the colonizer's. However, as successful as this practice has been in colonized locations such as Hawai'i in securing the dominance of the colonizer, it has not always gone unchallenged. And, if the moments of resistance are understood and made public, it acts as a reaffirmation of identity for those oppressed within a colonizing regime. To fully understand how silencing has been countered, it is necessary to view rhetoric in the context of the sociopolitical, historical, and cultural context in which it occurs. To understand the full impact of writing in Pidgin, for example, one must have a sense of the ambiguities surrounding Pidgin, its role in the local community in Hawai'i as both an identity and inferiority marker. Analyzed against this contentious backdrop, Milton Murayama's negotiation of Pidgin in *All I Asking for Is my Body* can be seen not only as more than an act of resistance but also a representation of the dichotomous attitudes toward the language and its speakers. Such a work thus acknowledges the conflict Pidgin speakers face and validates their experiences.

Until recently, Hawai'i's story has mostly been told by the colonizer—American missionaries and businessmen have commonly been portrayed as benevolent benefactors, even saviors, and Native Hawaiians as willing and docile. But, examining the rhetoric produced during the period of the overthrow through a *Kanaka Maoli* lens provides a different picture of Native Hawaiians—it shows they were linguistically savvy and exploited linguistic tools in the fight to save their land and way of life. When faced with physical repercussions for voicing opposition, Queen Lili'uokalani drew from the rhetorical traditions of her culture to send messages of resistance and hope to her people in the medium of *mele*, which she could rely on to go undetected by most Hawaiian-speaking foreigners. Understanding this rhetorical work recasts perceptions about Native Hawaiians and counters what Noenoe Silva has termed the "myth of passivity." Indeed, Silva's work expands on the examples of Queen Lili'uokalani's *mele* discussed here to provide a fuller historical account of the actions of Native Hawaiians, and her work thus reaffirms the identity of Native Hawaiians by providing a legacy that directs a course of action for Native Hawaiians struggling for sovereignty today.

As I suggested in the opening of this chapter, many Western rhetorical concepts can be applied in cross-cultural contexts—ideas such as Booth's collaborative meaning-making, Burke's consubstantiality and identification, and of course the ancient rhetoricians' treatise on style and audience, to name a few. However, applying Western rhetorical theory does not account for divergence in culture, experience, and unique rhetorical strategies such as *kaona* that give life to rhetoric. As the experiences of Native Hawaiians and immigrant Asian laborers demonstrate, silencing rhetoric jeopardizes a people's epistemology; however, as I hope to have shown here, reclaiming that rhetoric can have the equally powerful effect of reaffirming knowledge, identity, and culture—and of rewriting history.

Notes

1. *Kaona* will be explained in the section on the Queen's *mele*.
2. Kawamoto, 193.
3. Takaki, 21.
4. Reinecke, 39.
5. Qtd. in Takaki, 22.
6. McDougall 2008.
7. Takaki, 22.
8. Ibid.
9. Reinecke, 40.
10. Ibid., 55–59.
11. Ibid., 57–58.
12. At the historical Hawai'i Plantation Village located in Waipahu on O'ahu, that this stratification between ethnic groups was preserved through living conditions is evidenced in the way immigrant life is represented. An advertisement for this historical site reads: "The Plantation features 30 original and replica homes and buildings representing each ethnic group's lifestyle from 1900–1930." (http://www.hawaiiweb.com/oahu/sites_to_see/hawaii_plantation_village.htm)
13. Kawamoto, 199.
14. Ibid., 197.
15. Local is a contested term in Hawai'i and is often used to refer inclusively to Native Hawaiians, *local* Asians, and (sometimes) Caucasians (see Sato 1985; Kawamoto 1993; Watson-Gegeo 1994 for examples of this). This approach suggests that the experiences of any one of these ethnic populations adequately describes that of another; however, this idea of what it means to be local can be problematic, particularly in the case of Native Hawaiians. In the introduction to *Asian Settler Colonialism: From Colonial Governance to the Habits of Everyday Life in Hawai'i*, Fujikane explains how identifying as local has been used to mask complicity in the marginalization of Native Hawaiians.
16. I say acknowledged here because there is clear indication that many Hawaiians were working to preserve their language.
17. Kimura 1983.
18. Sato "Language Change in a Creole Continuum, " 1991, 125.
19. Haole is used to refer to "White person, American, Englishman, Caucasian…formerly any foreigner" (Pukui and Elbert; Sato "Linguistic Inequality in Hawaii." 1985, 262.
20. Kawamoto, 201.
21. Ibid., 202.
22. "Linguistics…" 1985, 267.
23. Borreca 1999.

24. Qtd. in ibid.
25. Kanahele, 2.
26. Renaissance is a contested term for this period—some object to it because its literal definition, "rebirth," implies that Hawaiian culture and traditions were dead; however, others align it with the European Renaissance experienced following the Dark Ages that realized a resurgence of cultural and political thought (see George Kanahele, "The Hawaiian Renaissance"). I use this term to represent the latter.
27. *Kapa*: cloth "made from *wauke* or *mamaki* bark; formerly clothes of any kind or bedclothes" (Pukui and Elbert).
28. Aristotle, 37.
29. Ibid., 47–48.
30. Trask, 18.
31. Aristotle, 38–39.
32. Burke, *Rhetoric of Motives*, 1969, 21.
33. In Pukui and Elbert's Hawaiian Dictionary, the definition of *pono* is almost a page long, which implies the complexity of this term. Some of the concepts associated with *pono* include the following: "goodness, uprightness, morality, moral qualities, correct or proper procedure, excellence, well-being, benefit, behalf, equity." However, *pono* can also mean hope.
34. *'imi haku* is the accepted practice of seeking a new chief (Pukui and Elbert), particularly when one's current chief is not upholding his obligations to his/her people.
35 .It is worth noting that the deposing would have to be at the hands of her own people, not outsiders.
36. Kame'eleihiwa 1992, 48.
37. Kame'eleihiwa 1996, ix.
38. Ibid., viii–ix.
39. Bizzell and Herzberg, 1491.
40. Silva, 184–185.
41. Ibid., 185.
42. Ibid., 187–90.
43. Ibid., 187.
44. *Lāhui* in this context is used to mean, "Nation, race, tribe, people, nationality; great company of people." (Pukui and Elbert); Silva, 189.
45 .Silva, 190.
46 .Lili'uokalani, xxiii.
47 .Ibid., 185.
48 .Ibid., 184.
49. In addition to her *mele*, during this time the Queen actively tried to counter the United States's control in Hawai'i in numerous ways including through the publication of her autobiography, *Hawaii's Story by Hawaii's Queen,* in which she provides an account written in English of the events leading up to the overthrow and her imprisonment that differs significantly from the common perceptions perpetuated on the U.S. continent at this time, and in 1896, she traveled to Washington to plead the case of her people to President Cleveland.
50. Sumida 1991.
51. Literary analysis of *All I Asking for Is My Body* has been taken up by many scholars, thus I will not directly look at the actual storyline here. Rather I will solely focus on the rhetorical act of Murayama's writing in Pidgin.
52. Sumida, 112.
53. Sato, "Sociolinguistic Variation," 1991, 654.
54. Murayama, 105.
55. Ibid.
56. Quoted in Sumida, 117.
57. Cicero, 291.

58. Ibid., 340.
59. Ibid., 339.
60. Burke, *Rhetoric of Motives,* 1969, 28.
61. Second generation Japanese.
62. Sato, "Linguistic Inequality in Hawaii," 1985, 267.
63. Sumida, 117.
64. Silva, 1.
65. Ibid., 11.
66. Ibid., 3.
67. Aristotle, 48.
68. Silva, 203.
69. Ibid., 2.

Bibliography

Aristotle. *On Rhetoric: A Theory of Civic Discourse.* Translated by George A. Kennedy. 2nd ed. New York: Oxford University Press, 2007.

Bizzell, Patricia, and Bruce Herzberg. "Modern and Postmodern Rhetoric." In *The Rhetorical Tradition: Readings from Classical Times to the Present,* edited by Patricia Bizzell and Bruce Herzberg, 1181–1205. Boston: Bedford/St.Martins, 2001.

Borreca, Richard. "For Hawaii, At Long Last…" *Honolulu Star-Bulletin,* October 18, 1999. http://starbulletin.com/1999/10/18/special/story4.html. (accessed May 2003).

Burke, Kenneth. *A Rhetoric of Motives.* Berkeley: University of California Press, 1969.

———. *The Philosophy of Literary Form: Studies in Symbolic Action.* 3rd ed. Berkeley: University of California Press, 1973.

Cicero. From *De Oratore.* In *The Rhetorical Tradition: Readings from Classical Times to the Present,* edited by Patricia Bizzell and Bruce Herzberg, 289–343. Boston: Bedford/St. Martin's, 2001.

Fujikane, Candace. Introduction to *Asian Settler Colonialism: From Colonial Governance to the Habits of Everyday Life in Hawai'i,* edited by Candace Fujikane and Jonathan Okamura, 1–43. Honolulu: University of Hawai'i Press, 2008.

Kame'eleihiwa, Lilikala K. *A Legendary Tradition of Kamapua'a: The Hawaiian Pig God.* Honolulu: Bishop Museum Press, 1996.

———. *Native Lands and Foreign Desires: Pehea Lā E Pono Ai? How Shall We Live in Harmony?* Honolulu: Bishop Museum Press, 1992.

Kanahele, George. "The Hawaiian Renaissance." May 1979. Kamehemeha Schools Archive. http://72.14.253.104/search?q=cache:JZhBMu0B6JcJ:www.lava.net/cslater/kanahele.pdf+Hawaiian+renaissance&hl=en&ct=clnk&cd=2&gl=us&client=firefox-a. (accessed June 2008).

Kawamoto, Kevin. "Hegemony and Language Politics in Hawaii." *World Englishes* 12, no. 2 (1993): 193–207.

Kimura, Larry, and William Wilson. *Native Hawaiians Study Commission Minority Report.* U.S. Dept. of Interior, 1983.

Lili'uokalani. *Hawaii's Story by Hawaii's Queen.* Tokyo: Charles E. Tuttle Company, 1964.

McDougall, Brandy Nalani. e-mail correspondence, May 27, 2008.

———. *The Queen's Songbook.* Edited by Hui Hanai. Honolulu: Hui Hanai, 1999.

Murayama, Milton. *All I Asking for Is My Body.* Honolulu: University of Hawai'i Press, 1959.

Odo, Franklin S. Afterword to *All I Asking for Is My Body,* by Milton Murayama. Honolulu: University of Hawai'i Press, 1959.

Office of Hawaiian Affairs. "OHA Vision and Mission." April 9, 2008. http://www.oha.org/index.php?option=com_content&task=blogcategory&id=23&Itemid=127. (accessed June 2008).

Pratt, Mary Louise. "Arts of the Contact Zone." In *Ways of Reading*, edited by David Bartholomae and Anthony Petroksky. New York: Bedford/St. Martin's, 1999.

Reinecke, John. *Language and Dialect in Hawaii*. Honolulu: University of Hawai'i Press, 1964.

Sato, Charlene. "Language Change in a Creole Continuum: Decreolization?" *University of Hawai'i Working Papers in ESL* 10, no. 1 (1991): 127–47.

———. "Linguistic Inequality in Hawaii: The Post-Creole Dilemma." In *Language of Inequality*, edited by N. Woltson and J. Manes, 255–72. Berlin: Mouton, 1985.

———. "Sociolinguistic Variation and Language Attitudes in Hawaii." In *English around the World: Sociolinguistic Perspectives*, edited by Jenny Cheshire, 647–63. Cambridge: Columbia University Press, 1991.

Silva, Noenoe. *Aloha Betrayed: Native Hawaiian Resistance to American Colonialism*. Durham, NC: Duke University Press, 2004.

Stannard, David E. *Before the Horror: The Population of Hawaii on the Eve of Western Contact*. Honolulu: Social Science Research Institute, University of Hawai'i, 1989.

Sumida, Stephen. *And the View from the Shore: Literary Traditions of Hawaii*. Seattle: University of Washington Press, 1991.

Takaki, Ronald. *Strangers from a Different Shore*. Boston: Little, Brown and Company, 1989.

Trask, Haunani K. "Writing in Captivity: Poetry in a Time of Decolonization." In *InsideOut: Literature, Cultural Politics, and Identity in the New Pacific*, edited by Vilsoni Hereniko and Rob Wilson. Lanham: Rowman and Littlefield, 1999.

Watson-Gegeo, Karen Ann. "Language and Education in Hawai'i: Sociopolitical and Economic Implications of Hawai'i Creole English." In *Language and the Social Construction of Identity in Creole Language Situations*, edited by Marcyllena Morgan and Mervyn C. Alleynean, 101–20. Los Angeles: UCLA Center for African American Studies, 1994.

Wysocki, Anne, and Johndan Johnson-Eilola. "Blinded by the Letter: Why Are We Using Literacy as a Metaphor for Everything Else?" In *Passions and Pedagogies and 21st Century Technologies*, edited by Gail Hawisher and Cynthia Selfe, 349–68. Logan: Utah State University Press, 1999.

CHAPTER EIGHT

Rhetoric, Interrupted: La Malinche and Nepantlisma

DAMIÁN BACA

We have come here to Tenochtitlan
to give you strength,
Tlaxcaltecas, Huexotzincas.
How will the Lord Xicotencatl hear Nelpiloni?
ea, have courage, ah.
Our chief, Quauhtencoztli,
comes roaring.
Xacaltencoz tells the Captain (Cortés),
and our mother, Malintzin,
that we have arrived at Acachinanco,
ea, have courage!
. . .
Go to the aid of our Lords.
Those who have arms of metal
destroy the city,
they destroy all that is Mexican,
ea, have courage!

—*Cuicapeuhcáyotl/Cantares*
Mexicanos

In 1550, the *Cuicapeuhcáyotl* was translated into Roman letters and renamed *Cantares Mexicanos*, some thirty years after the brutal destruction of *Tenochtitlan*, the Aztec spiritual and administrative center.

Nahuatl alphabetic texts naturally postdate this destruction after which Franciscans taught Aztecs to inscribe their own language using the Western alphabet. Before genocide and conquest, Mesoamerican discursive traditions were strongly reinforced by *amoxtli*, the pictographic manuscripts which served in the transmission and performance of *Huehuetlatolli*, a Nahuatl expression for ancient word and wisdom of the elders.[1] The postconquest era saw a rapid and violent transition period from a predominantly pictographic culture to an alphabetic one within a single generation. Pictographic rhetorical practices did not become extinct, of course, as *amoxtli* revisions continue to be produced today.[2]

The *Cantares Mexicanos* document emerges during an era of the colonization of both time and space, between pictographic and alphabetic rhetorics and the memories embedded in those rhetorics. Referenced in the *Cuicapeuhcáyotl/Cantares Mexicanos* is "our mother, Malintzin," the adolescent sexual slave and translator for Hernán Cortés who has since become a central figure in the Conquest, denigrated as La Malinche, the first symbolic traitor and progenitor of Mexican-origin peoples. Malinche/Malintzin, like the *Cantares Mexicanos*, is intertwined in the colonization of history and geography, an extension of cultural, spiritual, gendered, and linguistic plurality. In this chapter, I consider whether it is indeed possible to rethink Malinche's historical agency as a manifestation of *Nepantlisma*, a rhetorical strategy rooted in the spaces between multiple means of identification, between the languages and memories of Mesoamerican and Western worlds. I attempt to answer this question by proposing how, and in what sense, Malinche could be seen as a decolonial figure, as a subversive rhetorician in the rewriting of historical memory and the European invention of the Americas. This work is motivated, in part, by a question that has the histories told by Rhetoric and Composition studies in focus[3]: in what ways can one read an historiographical agenda as not simply yet another version of rethinking Greco-Latin history but as possessing a necessarily decolonial interruption of enduring Western macro-narratives? I take time to mention Rhetoric and Composition's overarching historical imaginary due to the glaring omission of Mesoamerican and Mexican peoples in the framework of rhetoric history and rhetorical theory, both ancient and new. Repeated omissions can be found in the majority of the field's publications which fail to devote a single line to five hundred years of intellectual contributions from Central and South America as well as the development of highly complex rhetorical traditions long before the Conquest. How might Rhetoric and Composition scholars read Malinche as a theoretical, rhetorical, and historiographical paradigm, as a "new" vantage point that contributes to allegedly expanding notions of rhetoric across nations and cultures?

I am not interested in nostalgic attempts to generalize or encapsulate what the historical Malintzin might have thought or experienced. Moreover, emerging studies of rhetorical theory need to consider more than individual agency in order to include a much broader array of structural conditions that impact communicative events. My interest here is in the collective imagination inherent in the practices of Chicana and Chicano subjects whose communal identities are informed by the legacies of Malinche. Notably, I make a distinction between *Nepantlisma* and the field's currently fashionable expressions "alternative rhetorics" and "rhetorics of difference." Whereas the first is grounded in the material complexity of intercultural relations and the overlapping of different and conflicting cultural exchanges between Mesoamerica and the West, the latter expressions remain embedded within Anglo- and Eurocentric frameworks. *Nepantlisma* is a decolonial articulation "in between," in between time, cultures, and creative invention. This is a rhetoric of adaptation for the symbolic descendents of Malinche, those who have the ability to interrupt colonizing macro-narratives as they cannot interrupt themselves.

Malinche and Nepantlisma

> The high priest of the pyramids feared La Malinche's
> power of language—how she could form strange syllables
> in her mouth and Speak to the gods without offering
> the red fruit of her heart. He had visions of a white
> man who could change her ways with an obsidian knife.
> —Alicia Gaspar de Alba

At the dawn of the sixteenth century, only eight years after Christopher Columbus stumbled upon the Caribbean, the woman who would eventually become known as Malinche was born in Teticpac. Betrayed by her own mother, Malinche was sold into slavery and lived among the Chontal Maya as a slave. Careful negotiations with cultural assimilation are encoded through the very etymology of her legendary name. Malinche is the Aztec name for Malinalli, her birth name. Malinalli was presented as a servant to conquistador Hernán Cortés in 1519 when his armed forces landed in Veracruz. While Gerónimo de Aguilar, one of Cortés's soldiers, had learned the Chontal Maya language variety common to Mexico's eastern coast, Cortés was lacking in Nahuatl literacy and experienced difficulty communicating with Mexican valley populations such as those in *Tenochtitlan*, the Aztec imperial center. Malinche's extensive knowledge of Chontal Maya and Nahuatl dialects and customs, her ability to interpret Aztec pictography, and her eventual mastery of Castilian caught the attention of Cortés. Soon, Malinche became Cortés' foremost interpreter, advisor, mistress, and mother of his child. Nahuatl, as an adjective, can be translated as "well-sounding" or pleasing to the ear. From this, the term Nahua is used collectively for all peoples who spoke the Nahuatl tongue. However, the term can also signifies cleverness and skill, and the derivation is probably from the root *na*, to know.

In *Mestiz@ Scripts, Digital Migrations, and the Territories of Writing*, I analyzed Malinche as an archetypal border crosser, as a subversive product of conflicting and intertwining worlds. My rhetorical framework was and remains informed by the late Gloria Anzaldúa and her decolonial invention of "new mestiza consciousness." In her landmark *Borderlands/La Frontera: The New Mestiza*, Anzaldúa writes,

> In a constant state of mental nepantlism, an Aztec word meaning torn between ways, la mestiza is a product of the transfer of the cultural and spiritual values of one group to another. Being tricultural, monolingual, bilingual or multilingual, speaking a patois, and in a state of perpetual transition, the mestiza faces the dilemma of the mixed breed: which collectivity does the daughter of a dark-skinned mother listen to? (25)

Nepantlisma, then, is a state of dwelling in a border-space, a symbolic space where several languages and cultural values overlap. A borderlands subjectivity is furthermore a movement between cultural spaces, a perpetual transition between worldviews. Inventing from *Nepantlisma*, from a position of suspension between two contradictory frames of reference, does not attempt to produce or perform a harmonious union between Mesoamerica and Spain. It instead implies being "torn between ways" (78) and forms new possibilities that do not rely upon linear or hierarchical dichotomies.

Under the dominant trope of conquest and conversion, Malinche symbolically evokes the historical conditions of subjugation that surround Mexico's imposition. Malintzin's role as translator for Cortés would thus constitute a dramatic means by which she is instilled with the commemoration of her own colonial defeat. I suggest instead that

Malintzin's *Nepantlisma* enacts resistance to European conquest and serves as a model of adaptation without assimilation. This counternarrative is encoded and expressed primarily in the multifaceted figure of Malinalli/Malintzin Tenepal/Malinche: Malinalli the betrayed daughter, Malintzin Tenepal as "the one who speaks" through multiple languages, and Malinche, symbolic betrayer and re-envisioned figure of resistance and empowerment.

Expanding Malinche's historical act of translation from its linguistic conception to its present-day symbolic and rhetorical potential adds significantly to her role as translator and cultural mediator. If understood as Mexico's first subversive rhetorician in the face of European invasion and conquest, Malinche performs history's primary role of resistance. The sexual struggle and predicament of Malinche forms an opposing paradigm against the virginal purity of Christendom's Mary, the Holy Mother. Malinche embodies multiple contradictions and sets them into motion through translation. Her variable combinations of rhetorical interweaving effectively resist the linear and hierarchical configuration of conversion. Thus it is not Malinche that is converted but the European model of Christian conversion itself that is undermined and revised through her dynamic mediation. Anzaldúa's *Nepantlisma* contributes significantly to Malinche's role as subversive rhetorician. Malinche is the key mediator between indigenous Mexicans—though not necessarily Aztec, as Malintzin was not Aztec—and Iberian worlds. Anzaldúa points out that Chicanas and Chicanos identify Malinche as:

> A synthesis of the old world and the new, of the religion and culture of the two races in our psyche, the conquerors and the conquered...She mediated between the Spanish and Indian cultures and between Chicanos and the white world. She...is the symbol of ethnic identity and of the tolerance for ambiguity that...people who cross cultures...possess. (29)

Accordingly, Malinche synthesizes Judeo-Christian and Mesoamerican worlds by crossing between them. Malinche demonstrates the tension of this rhetorical interchangeability by weaving within and between the opposing discourses of the Conquest. It should be emphasized that Malinche's intermediation is key to reading resistance, even if such struggles are hidden under a guise of compliance. Her quadri-lingual rhetorics in motion not only served to save her own life, but the lives of her own people among the Maya.

Baca Frames her as a powerful subversive Rhetor who plays the Spanish for the sake of the idians because she has ultimat agency of language.

Malinche is a symbolic intermediary between divergent worlds. The
Maya language contrasts with Nahuatl that in turn counters Spanish.
Far from suggesting a cultural utopia, these relations are fraught with
tension. Strategic oppositions and reversals between these languages
help Chicana and Chicano subjectivity to disengage from the hierarchical dichotomy of conversion by legitimizing its alternatives.
This tactic is akin to Gloria Anzaldúa's call for a "massive uprooting
of dualistic thinking in the individual and collective consciousness"
(102). By refusing to designate Spanish and Roman Catholic theological perspectives as the only truth, Malinche's rhetorical performance
rejects conceiving Mesoamerican spirituality as deviant, barbarian, and
insufficient. Asserting pre-Columbian spiritualities as enduring and
equally suitable frames of reference effectively interrupts and resists the
triumphant narrative of subjugation. The linguistic weaving demonstrates Mesoamerica's strategic intertwining of Catholicism without the
hierarchical logic of conversion. In sum, the significant presence and
intervention of Malinche symbolically produces an interruption in the
dominant macro-narrative of conquest and erasure.

Thus, Malinche endures today not because of naïve devotion to some
positivist reconstruction of "authentic" Mesoamerican subjectivities but
because she continues to hold meaning as colonial relations of power shift
across space and time. Malinche plays an important role in the formation
of communal and individual subjectivity on both sides of the U.S.-Mexico
border. Malinche's decolonial rhetorics in motion can unfold at different
levels. The simultaneous embracing of and resistance to macro-narratives
can be understood in the context of present-day struggles against the
exclusion and erasure of Mexican-origin cultures within Rhetoric and
Composition studies, pedagogies, and historiographies.

Rethinking rhetoric history, however, is not that of the projects of
postmoderns or neo-Marxists or Eurocentric feminisms, as such critics continue to center European modernity as their organizing system. Instead, Mesoamerican "subalternized" representations posit new
articulations of our time that provide not only much-needed historiographical correctives, but political expressions better suited to current
material realities for both the so-called First and Third Worlds. In place
of the uni-linear developmental "from ancient Athens to America,"
Malinche's rhetorics in motion invoke a hermeneutic reconstruction of
temporal and spatial correlations, in which it becomes possible to perceive multiple histories and memories coexisting, without assumptions
that all civilizations follow a single Western trajectory. A pluralization
of rhetoric that accounts for pan-Mexican collectives can help scholars

and practitioners move toward other conceptions, other possibilities, and other cultural narratives about rhetorical practices. Malinche's *Nepantlisma* pushes us away from a monoglossic, dominant conception of rhetoric and instead point us toward a plurality of knowledges and histories across the Americas.

Of particular interest to Rhetoric and Composition is the performance of coexisting and conflicting rhetorics in a single discursive event. Chontol Maya juxtaposed with Aztec Nahuatl and Iberian Castilian reflect competing rationalities and histories; a linguistic palimpsest of divergent traditions and ideologies where a Mesoamerican Cosmos and Ibero-Christian world converge. More than hybrid expressions of cultural dichotomies, Malinche's translations are fractured enunciations in response to colonial relations of power that disfigure the Mesoamerican world as a mere periphery to a "civilized" Western center. These rhetorics in motion work to destabilize the idea of a single overarching hegemonic discourse as a naturalized and valorized element of communication while calling into question the integrity of clear and secure linguistic barriers. *Nepantlisma* can be seen as a regenerative force, as an antithesis of colonialism and of the very principles, categories of thought, and argumentative logics used to justify progress and civilization while denying and erasing other forms of knowledge. Moreover, Malinche's translations help to open up an interesting problem in the global history of modernity: how to think about the history of power in an age when capital and the governing institutions of modernity increasingly develop a global reach.

Conclusion

I have proposed that *Nepantlisma*, Malinche's rhetorics in motion, interrupts and revises the colonial logic of translation and conversion. This rhetorical tactic speaks to the subjugated covertly in order to critique dominant cultures. This transcript is embedded within the larger historical narrative of Christian conversion and Tenochtitlan's defeat under the Spanish Cross and Crown. The strategy I have adapted from Gloria Anzaldúa's *Borderlands/La Frontera: The New Mestiza* accounts for how rhetorical oppositions and reversals between Mesoamerica and Spain work to disrupt the hierarchies of power between them. By inventing and adapting between cultural paradigms, Malinche enacts possibilities beyond them. *Nepantlisma* rearticulates Western rhetoric without the baggage of cultural betrayal or assimilation.

Malinche as subversive rhetorician works toward decolonial inventions, that is, toward fracturing the naturalization of the two spaces in which the dominant system functions: on the one hand, the rhetoric of modernity, and, on the other hand, the opposing forces, which in the name of tradition (e.g., "cultural rhetorics") remains within the same logic of the system. Rhetoric and Composition studies maintains the imaginary of Western civilization as a pristine development from ancient Athens to "America," where the bases of modernity were laid out. In contrast, Malinche's conceptualization is not rooted in Hellenism, Christendom, Eurocentrism, Manifest Destiny, Orientalism, or other colonial horizons. Malintzin underlies a spatial articulation of power rather than a linear succession of events across the planet. The rhetorical potentials of translation—not only between languages but also between cultural and epistemological categories—as well as the interrelations between symbolic production, power systems, and cultural adaptation are at the heart of this project.

The fusions and crossings between opposing cultural worlds are dramatically symbolized through Malintzin's translations. Her conflicting and contrastive translations and movements are enacted within colonial structures of power in order to resist and displace the dominant narratives of conversion and assimilation. Malinche's rhetorics resist these narratives by fusing and embellishing their own historical memories. This is by definition a product of the ongoing fusions and fissures between the historical memories of Spanish-Iberian, Mesoamerican, Mexican, Chicana, Chicano, and United States cultures. Today, *Nepantlisma* is not a matter of archaic survival but of ongoing rhetorical strategies in motion, strategies of interrupting and revising macro-narratives of domination as they endure today. Perhaps *Nepantlisma*, then, can reemerge as an intellectual project devoted to the task of revisiting, remembering, and interrogating Rhetoric and Composition's colonial history and its continuous colonizing of bodies and minds—those of students, graduate students, and faculty alike. Malinche's decolonial rhetorics in motion register their presence by interrupting enduring macro-narratives, by forcing them into contradictions and making them speak in a plurality of tongues.

Notes

1. Leon-Portilla.
2. See Baca, Draher, and Gómez-Peña.
3. See Berlin, Blair, Brooks, Schiappa, and Vitanza for a few examples of a much larger debate.

Bibliography

Anzaldúa, Gloria. *Borderlands/La Frontera: The New Mestiza*. San Francisco: Aunt Lute Books, 1987.

Baca, Damián. *Mestiz@ Scripts, Digital Migrations, and the Territories of Writing*. New York: Palgrave Macmillan, 2008.

Berlin, James, Susan Jarratt, John Schilb, and Victor Vitanza. "Historiography and the Histories of Rhetorics II: Revisionary Histories and Ethics." *PRE/TEXT* 11 (1990): 169–287.

Blair, Carole, and Mary L. Kahl. "Introduction: Revising the History of Rhetorical Theory." *Western Journal of Speech Communication* 54 (1990): 148–59.

Brooks, Kevin. "Reviewing and Redescribing 'The Politics of Historiography': Octalog I, 1988." *Rhetoric Review* 16.01 (Fall 1997): 6–21.

Cantares Mexicanos: Songs of the Aztecs. Translated by John Bierhorst. Palo Alto, CA: Stanford University Press, 1985.

Gaspar de Alba, Alicia. "Malinchista, A Myth Revisited." Beggar on the Córdoba Bridge. Here Times a Woman: Chicana Poetry. Tempe: Bilingual Press, 1989. 16–17.

Schiappa, Edward. "The Historiography of Rhetoric: Conflicts and Their Implications." *The Writing Instructor* 8 (1988): 15–22.

Vitanza, Victor. *Writing Histories of Rhetoric*. Carbondale: Southern Illinois University Press, 1994.

CHAPTER NINE

In Search of the Invisible World: Uncovering Mesoamerican Rhetoric in Contemporary Mexico

TRACY BRANDENBURG

Contemporary Zapotec poet, Víctor de la Cruz, laments that he composes his poetry on paper. Even writing in his native Zapotec, the poet finds it impossible to authentically represent his language when writing on paper. In his poem "Who are we? What is our name?" de la Cruz refers to pre-Hispanic times where he envisions writing as more expansive, where its surfaces could be found in nature, songs, and adornments.[1] The poet's anguish implies that to write is to relive the violence of the colonial project that not only imprisoned the indigenous peoples' word with the letter, but severed its ties to the senses and the sacred. When the Spanish brought the alphabet to the New World, the civilizations of Mesoamerica had been practicing their own systems of writing for centuries. Mesoamerican writing implied more than the letter; indeed, with the exception of the Maya, an alphabet was not involved at all. "To write" was also "to paint" and its surfaces could be found on stone, animal skins, or screen "books" or codices.[2]

In the case of central Mexico, the geographic area we will focus on in this chapter, the Spanish friars who were entrusted with the task of converting the indigenous populations found that the Mesoamericans had different kinds of books, among which, Elizabeth Hill Boone points out, were a class of texts considered most dangerous to the project of evangelization.[3] These books, Boone explains, were the divinatory books, the ones that spoke of the "invisible world" or "the world of divine or spirit beings, supernaturals and cosmic forces."[4]

They were consulted for all aspects of life and were "books of fate."[5] For this reason, they were also among the first books to be burned by the Spanish.[6]

Contemporary historical reflections generally concur that the writing/painting of the Mesoamerican peoples was eventually usurped by the Spanish project that systematically sought to colonize their language, writing, and souls.[7] The evidence to support this is indeed compelling. James Lockhart pinpoints the end of the seventeenth century as the time when the pictorial completely disappeared from Nahua writing. In the 1530s centers in Mexico City and Tlaxcala had begun to instruct the Nahuas on how to write their own language alphabetically, and by the 1540s numerous alphabetic texts in Nahuatl could be found.[8] While Lockhart suggests that the pictographic tradition continued to some extent, "and the two methods supported each other" after the conquest, he states that the pictorial eventually gave way to the alphabetic: "Ultimately, however, they competed, and the alphabetic method took over more and more of the functions of communication, to the point that the pictorial component became unnecessary and fell by the wayside."[9] Walter Mignolo adds yet more evidence to this account by illustrating that the colonial project was infused with the philosophy of the Spanish grammarian, Antonio Nebrija, and his belief that to conquer implied to civilize and that this could be accomplished by disseminating alphabetic writing and Castilian.[10] The eventual result of this, writes Mignolo, was "the fading out of every writing system except the alphabetic."[11] With so much overwhelming evidence to support the belief that there was indeed a passage from the pictorial to the alphabetic, this would hardly seem a topic that needs to be revisited, yet that is precisely what this chapter will attempt to do.

My own work on this topic began with a trip to Oaxaca, Mexico to meet with a Zapotec artist who had founded an art school in the rural village of Santa Ana de Zegache. He called his school The Center for Visual Thought, and as it turns out the artists were farmers—children and adults—the meeting place a tree. And the actual center? "It's here," the artist said, as he pointed to his heart.[12] The artist, Nicéforo Urbieta, had begun a personal journey to discover whether the Zapotec people of today were thinking and communicating as they did in pre-Hispanic times. His question has now inspired my own investigation as I continue to inquire whether the passage from the pictorial to the alphabetic was completed centuries ago, or whether the two sign systems continue to compete today. What I have found through fieldwork with Urbieta and the artists of the Center for Visual Thought is that revisiting history through its legacy in the present day rather than through records from the past provides an opportunity to examine image-making today and to discover that imagistic production, rhetoric, and reception challenge the notion that Mesoamerican writing was completely abandoned for the alphabet. Indeed, I would suggest that the battle for souls persists and that the image, that is, the writing of the Mesoamerican peoples, continues to be used.[13]

What I would also like to propose in this work is that the Mesoamerican valorization of duality, concealment, and metaphor in writing/painting lends itself to a mode of visual rhetoric that may go unrecognized to those of us steeped in Western literacy. This may be the reason why scholars do not recognize that the image is alive and well in contemporary Mexico. The central example I will discuss is the story of a portrait that was commissioned of Nicéforo Urbieta and that was presented to Pope John Paul II in 2002 when he came to Mexico to beatify two Zapotec martyrs and to canonize Juan Diego Cuauhtlatoatzin. I will discuss the hidden layers of meaning in this painting, how it embraces Mesoamerican rhetoric, and how it ultimately was perceived as a threat by the Catholic church.

Why on Paper?

"Why write on paper?" asks Víctor de la Cruz. Instead, he offers leaves, sky, and song. That of which he speaks, I dare say, is not merely poetic but speaks instead of a writing that is connected to the cosmos and the sacred. It also defies all Western notions of writing, for writing today is most commonly believed to be "graphically recorded language."[14] The fact that Mesoamerican writing, with the exception of the Maya, did not employ an alphabet has always made it difficult for scholars to consider the codices legitimate writing at all.[15] The pervasiveness of writing as recorded speech is evident in the recent response to the discovery of an Olmec tablet in Veracruz, Mexico, supposedly the earliest known writing in the Western Hemisphere. William Saturno, anthropologist and expert on Mesoamerican writing, says of the tablet, "That's full-blown, legitimate text—written symbol taking the place of spoken word."[16] But when the early Spaniards described Mesoamerican texts they did not talk about recorded speech, but rather the image, which the friars quickly learned was how they read and wrote, and was therefore the most effective way to communicate with them.[17]

The Image Today

Before describing some similar present-day images, let me briefly summarize my earlier work where I shared my journey to the Center for Visual Thought to meet Nicéforo Urbieta and the artists of this special school.[18] Urbieta spent six years in maximum security prison during Mexico's "dirty war." During this time he continued to be dedicated to his then-Marxist beliefs and undertook an artistic project to help him synthesize his readings of *Das Kapital*. His plan was to put all of the first volume of *Das Kapital* into graphic form so as to have an easier way of understanding it. On this he worked for one year, spending day and night making glyphs, codes, and graphic symbols, putting all of these onto two pieces of paper. At the time he did not make a connection with this project and the writing of his pre-Hispanic ancestors, but when he finished and stood back to gaze upon his work, he marveled at what he had created: Pre-Hispanic codices.

At this point he began to realize that this system of writing—which we recall is not even considered true writing—is actually exceptionally advanced as it allows the reader to take in everything at once and to capture "the explosion of thought."[19] This connection with the past made Urbieta wonder whether the same people and mode of thought and communication that created this system was still alive today. So after his release from jail, he went back to his Zapotec village to find out what remained of ancient Zapotec culture and communication. He began by meeting with members of his hometown; they discussed the economic hardships of the pueblo as well as how to preserve their Zapotec language and culture. Someone in the group proposed they do something with their hands while they speak as the custom in the community is to work while visiting with friends and neighbors: "while my mouth speaks my hands work."[20] On one occasion, Urbieta brought clay to the group and to his amazement, while the group spoke, extraordinarily beautiful and complex sculptures were produced. Urbieta saw this as a confirmation of what he had suspected, that for indigenous communities orality and images continued as dominant forms of communication. For Urbieta, the image is similar to that of the poet, de la Cruz, in that it includes all of the senses in which culture and meaning is shared; Urbieta cites not only these sculptures, but also the sounds, colors, and food of the yearly fiestas in which meaning is made and ancient traditions are shared.

Barbara Mundy, in her study of the maps made by Mesoamericans in central Mexico in 1580, describes an environment where "cultural communication was dominated by images."[21] But in several hundred years, according to Lockhart and Mignolo, this would no longer be the case, as the alphabet would supposedly reign supreme. How then could Urbieta's findings be true, that nonalphabetic communication was still dominant? Mundy observes that friars did not actually erase the image but used it for their own purposes. She points out that in New Spain mendicant friars embraced the image as a means to educate and convert the Amerindians. The friars themselves did not necessarily have the artistic skills to work in an imagistic medium, so they recruited indigenous artists to make Christian iconography.[22] And so, while the Mesoamerican pictorial texts were banned, the imagistic medium continued: "Friars sought to replace not only the image with the text but the indigenous image with the Christian one."[23] In Mundy's findings, there was an interruption regarding the *content* of the image; but the *medium* most important to the indigenous people—their method of reading and writing—was still very much alive.

Mesoamerican Rhetoric: The Flower and the Song

The great Aztec poet Nezahualcoyotl (1402–1472) anguished over finding a symbol that would live forever. The solution he would find in poetry itself, what the Aztecs called "the flower and the song:" "At last my heart knows it. I hear a song, I contemplate a flower...May they never fade."[24] According to Davíd Carrasco, the Nahua poet-philosophers or *tlamatinime* ("those who know something") responded to their anxiety over the illusory and temporal nature of the human experience by devising a method to transcend the mortal world and connect with the gods: "The main technique was the creation of *in xochitl, in cuicatl,* or the flowers and songs, artistic expressions in the forms of words, songs, and paintings that connected the human personality, referred to as 'face and heart,' with the divine."[25] Carrasco explains that the rhetoric they developed mirrored the Nahuatl philosophy of duality. The Nahuas believed their creator, Ometeotl, was a deity of two, also known as Tonantzin, Totahtzin, or "Our Mother," "Our Father." Reality was constructed of dualities that could be found everywhere: "male/female, hot/cold, left/right, underworld/celestial world, above/below, darkness/light, rain/drought, death/life."[26] The rhetoric the *tlamatinime* developed embraced this dual reality by means of the *difrasismo,* or two entities expressed together to form a single concept; for example, "in atl, in tepetl = water and hill = town; in xochitl, in cuicatl = flower and song, = poetry or truth."[27] Poetry and art were indeed powerful, explains Carrasco, for to express oneself in flower and song—that is in the verbal and visual arts—was to be imbued with the sacred: "the human personality became linked to the divine duality above."[28]

Boone understands the graphic image to be parallel to the *nahuallatolli* or "speech of the sorcerers" that was used by the diviners to communicate with and about the supernatural world.[29] It was not a language intended to clarify or be readily accessible, but it "was a rich and complex manner of speaking, one that approached meaning obliquely and through metaphor."[30] The intention, Boone explains, was "to obscure and hide rather than clarify," and to reveal "by its indirectness the fuller qualities of an essence."[31] She explains how "water," for instance, was expressed as "she of the jade skirt," "her blouse is jade," "the mistress of jade."[32] The important thing to note is that the metaphor both reveals the fundamental nature of the term it describes—its color—for example, yet does so by means of a rhetoric that simultaneously conceals the item itself. The ability to obscure meaning would prove to be useful, I believe, in the war of images that was about to come.

The War of Images

Mundy describes the Spanish battle to win indigenous souls as "a war fought with images."[33] The author explains that while the friars of New Spain continued the tradition of using the image as a means to evangelize, and did so with the aid of indigenous artists, they hoped that in controlling the images the native people produced they could control them politically and ideologically.[34] Replacing Mesoamerican images with Christian ones did not, of course, lead to an easy conquest of the souls of the local people. The Dominican friar Diego Durán expressed his frustration over how the indigenous people pretended to be faithful to the church but held on to their pre-Hispanic rituals and beliefs, "feigning that the rejoicing is made to God, when their object is the idol."[35] Sahagún remarked in the same vein: "They easily accepted as god the god of the Spaniards, but not in order to leave their ancient ones, and this they hid during the catechism when they were baptized."[36] The struggle would be played out in a visual realm as the Spanish friars sought to destroy the pagan gods by annihilating their images and idols and replacing them with Christian ones. Serge Gruzinski explains that the movement to convert the indigenous population began in 1525 with the Franciscans: "It opened with the systematic and irreversible destruction of sanctuaries and idols: the war of images was intensifying."[37]

Whereas many scholars believe that pictographic writing, with its concealments and ambiguities, is an artifact of the past, I would like to present an example of a contemporary pictorial text that displays many of the features of the divinatory books I have discussed earlier. I believe that the visual techniques employed in this text are meant to obscure meaning in a way that opens up the possibility that hidden messages and an "invisible world" could exist today. The story I will relate is that of Pope John Paul II's final trip to Mexico where he came to beatify two Zapotec martyrs and to canonize Juan Diego, to whom many faithful believe the Virgin of Guadalupe appeared. For this event, a painting of the martyrs was commissioned of Nicéforo Urbieta, and later reproduced in various items such as scapulars, posters, and candles. In recounting the commission of the painting of the martyrs of Cajonos, I highlight how this contemporary painting was controlled and censored and thus mirrors the colonial context Mundy described was taking place in 1580 in central Mexico. As such it implies that the ancient form of writing, the pictorial, continues to be both relevant and threatening.

The Papal Visit

In July of 2002 Pope John Paul II visited Mexico where he beatified two Zapotec martyrs, Juan Bautista and Jacinto de los Ángeles, and canonized Juan Diego Cuauhtlatoatzin, the Chichimeca Indian said to have been visited by the Virgin of Guadalupe. Juan Bautista and Jacinto de los Ángeles were *fiscales* (local indigenous assistants to priests) from San Francisco Cajonos, Oaxaca who are said to have been murdered by Zapotec townspeople in September of 1700 as revenge for their having reported to parish priests that an "idolotrous" gathering would be taking place.[38]

In honor of the Pope's visit, Nicéforo Urbieta was asked to paint a portrait of the Zapotec martyrs, a copy of which would be presented to the Pope at the Basilica in Mexico City.[39] The process Urbieta underwent in the creation of this painting strongly resembles Mundy's account of how Mesoamericans were monitored and controlled when asked to make Christian iconography. In the time period about which Mundy writes, sixty years after the conquest, most Christian images were being made by native locals.[40] And though the friars were attempting to oversee this process, the viceregal government was concerned that the indigenous peoples making the images actually had too much control over their art.[41] The viceroys, thus, called for a formal means to observe the images being made: "Within San José de los Naturales was an examination center for native painters, and in 1552 Viceroy don Luis de Velasco commanded that no native be allowed to paint religious images without first being examined in San José."[42]

The fear that native painters might infuse the Catholic image with their own symbols is visible in a modern context with the case of Urbieta's commission. Urbieta was invited by a priest to paint the portrait of Juan Bautista and Jacinto de los Ángeles that would be used in the celebration of their beatification. His preliminary sketch, he explained to me, produced syncretistic symbols: a dove and a snake, that held both pre-Hispanic as well as Christian meanings. The archbishop and priests requested weekly meetings with Urbieta to monitor his work, and at these gatherings the idea of syncretism and symbols was immediately vetoed by the church. Week after week they met with the artist to discuss and critique his progress. The archbishop and his council were very specific about how the martyrs should be represented; Urbieta explained that they insisted on every detail: "Their faces should look like this, their expressions like this, the signature should be here..."[43] Urbieta felt more like an instrument than an artist: "They practically did the painting themselves. I was just the paintbrush."[44] Ultimately the archbishop and priests were satisfied with the final result and the portrait was revealed in a public gathering with the media present.

The painting appears to be fairly straightforward: two Zapotec men in humble clothing each holding a cross, thus showing their allegiance to the Catholic church. The artist, however, when interviewed by the media, revealed another layer of meaning to the painting. Urbieta first explained that in the cathedral in Oaxaca, where the painting was to be displayed, there were already two Christian icons that could be interpreted as pre-Hispanic ones. One was the black Christ of Esquipulus, whom he interpreted as the dark Lord Tezcatlipoca. Also in the cathedral was the cross of Quetzalcoatl, a pre-Hispanic cross that some believe was left by one of Christ's apostles, while others view as a pre-Hispanic symbol of Quetzalcoatl. What Urbieta accomplished in his painting, he explained, was to unite the two deities, Tezcatlipoca and Quetzalcoatl, already present in the cathedral, but not joined together. This he did in the portrait of Juan and Jacinto, who he explained represented the union of Tezcatlipoca and Quetzalcoatl. These two deities formed a duality in the Mesoamerican pantheon, and while they often had an antagonistic relationship, joined to create heaven and earth by seizing the earth monster and dividing it into half.[45] In an interview, Urbieta unravels the layers of meaning in his painting:

> The square, symbol of the universe, is in the portrait. The color of jade, that is the symbol of life, the water of the harvest. The scapular of Monte Albán—each one of the men portrayed has one—one has the color red in his cross. The other the color black in his cross—Quetzalcoatl and Tezcatlipoca. And well, the symbol of duality, the two, because of the fact that it was going to be in the cathedral where there already was a symbol of the black Christ, the Señor del Rayo, the black Christ of Esquipulus, they call him, and that is the symbol of Tezcatlipoca, who is the black Lord. There already was the symbol of the cross of Quetzalcoatl in the chapel where the Martyrs of Cajonos are. Now, the only thing that was missing was the symbol of duality to make it complete.[46]

In essence, Urbieta managed to represent two realities, a technique Mundy discovered in her own studies of the *Relaciones Geográficas*, the maps made by indigenous peoples of New Spain at the request of the Spanish crown. Mundy wondered whether the Mesoamericans were representing space according to their own reality or whether they were trying to please the Spanish audience for whom they were making the maps. She believes that most of the maps convey both influences—their true feelings and reality along with what the Spanish Catholic king would like to see. Mundy writes, "In short, the native colonial artist's work was colored by his (or her) 'double consciousness,' as he (or she) painted for the local community as well as for a shadowy, but powerful Spanish patron."[47]

Indeed it would appear that Urbieta was attempting the same: to conceal an indigenous belief or reality while providing the Catholic church with one that is acceptable. Meaning is clearly layered in Urbieta's painting, which brings us back to the divinatory books that spoke of the "invisible world" and did so through highly cryptic vocabulary where meaning was often masked and required a diviner to interpret it.

Let us now examine this graphic vocabulary and investigate whether its abstruse and hidden features are both relevant and present in contemporary Mexico. One characteristic of the divinatory codices is that they always feature an image of a supernatural being that is physically identifiable by such characteristics as clothing, facial paint, and the like.[48] Urbieta's painting features two supernaturals, though they are only physically identified by their symbolic colors, red and black. In other words, that the Zapotec martyrs represent Mesoamerican supernaturals in the Urbieta painting is not readily evident. In the case of the divinatory codices, Boone emphasizes that understanding these ancient books was difficult for the ancient reader as well as for the modern one. She explains, "The difficulty for the modern reader, as for the pre-conquest diviner, is first to identify the images and then to recognize their intended meaning."[49] Indeed, in the case of the ancient codices, only a trained priest or diviner could interpret the mysteries of these texts. In the case of the Urbieta's painting, we require his interpretation and explanation as the Mesoamerican message and symbolism remains almost completely concealed beneath the Christian images.

Graphic signs that identify locations are an important element of the divinatory codices.[50] In the case of the supernatural beings in the divinatory codices, meaning is derived from the association the supernaturals have with each other as well as the spatial context in which they are located. Boone explains, "The elements composing the scene jointly participate in the creation of meaning, for the message is not merely the presence of a certain supernatural or being but of some entity doing or having done it to a specific thing, and occasionally it is important that the action take place in a specific kind of location."[51] In the case of Urbieta's painting, the artist was not permitted to include any symbols, actions, or identifiable locations, so it is my belief that he extended his "codices" by including the entire cathedral in Oaxaca as his backdrop.

In other words, the location of where the painting was to be displayed, the cathedral in Oaxaca, is significant as it forms part of the narrative and contributes to the layers of meaning in the work. The painting of the Martyrs of Cajonos reveals the ancient technique of "the flower and the song," the verbal and visual arts that sought to invoke the divine duality of the cosmos by means of a graphic and visual representation of duality. The red and the black are not only the artist's nod to both deities, but also to the metaphor of writing (a reference to the red and black ink used to make the codices) and to the greater transcendent goal of the flower and song. Urbieta says, "And now the two are there—the red and the black. How many poets around Nezahualcoyotl talked about the color red and black, the symbol of wisdom, the wisdom to harmonize chaos and order.[52]

Unveiling the Painting

The artist revealed his portrait in a public ceremony where he "divined" or interpreted the Mesoamerican narrative concealed in the image of the Zapotec martyrs. This portion of his explanation was neither revealed in the print media, nor did it appear on the local TV news, both of which had interviewed him. In addition, the two promised subsequent interviews with Urbieta that were to take place at the Basilica in Mexico City and later in Oaxaca were cancelled. As to why the Mesoamerican reading of his painting was excluded in the media became more clear when the artist and I stumbled upon an altered version of his painting. While shopping together at a market in Oaxaca, we stopped in a small store where I noticed religious candles that displayed Urbieta's painting. On closer examination, however, the image was not quite the one Urbieta had made. The red and the black circles—the smallest nod to the deities Quetzalcoatl and Tezcatlipoca—had been erased. In their place were not the two crosses with the red and black centers, but now a single cross in a traditional Spanish Baroque style (see figure 9.1). That the red and the black—the ancient metaphor for Mesoamerican writing—had been erased is, I believe, symbolic of a larger attempt to win an ongoing battle for images, writing, and souls. At the same time, it also mirrors the colonial project that Gruzinski describes as having two phases: "According to the chronicles it was carried out by way of a simple and precise scenario that would often be replayed. A scenario in two acts, linking annihilation and substitution; the idols first were broken (by the Indians and/or by the Spanish), then the conquerors replaced them with Christian images."[53] I would like to suggest that the alteration of the painting that censures the Mesoamerican layer of meaning points to a desire to control both ideology and image, despite the fact that we are told that dangerous books ceased in their production centuries ago.

Let us now turn to another example of how the church continues to wage a war through images. This case is also related to the Papal visit of 2002. The canonization of Juan Diego Cuauhtlatoatzin was of enormous significance to indigenous people everywhere, as Juan Diego was the first indigenous Roman Catholic saint. But the portrait of Juan Diego that the church chose to represent on posters, stamps, and the like was "a light-skinned, full bearded man who looks more like one of the sword-wielding Spanish conquistadors who subjugated the Aztec empire."[54] Thus the two images, that of Juan Diego and Urbieta's portrait of Juan Bautista and Jacinto de los Ángeles that were widely

Figure 9.1   Paper wrapper for a candle.
Source: Photograph by Meltem K. Cervantes.

distributed to the public were ultimately controlled by a Catholic church that appears to continue to exert a message of dominance by means of the image.

In order for Urbieta to present the "double consciousness" that Mundy described, he had to utilize ancient techniques that both concealed and revealed Mesoamerican cosmology. That is, through duality, supernaturals, metaphor, and location. And so, to return to the quest of Nezahualcoyotl—did he find a symbol that would last? Nezahualcoyotl and the *tlamatinime* developed not merely a symbol that would last, the flower and the song, but a rhetoric that by design could survive and resist by means of its power to conceal meaning. That this art is still monitored, altered, and viewed as threatening points to the persistence of the pictorial rhetoric of Mesoamerican art and the "invisible world" it continues to protect.

Notes

I want to express my deepest thanks to Damián Baca, Giovanna Pompele, Meltem K. Cervantes, Víctor de la Cruz, Marc Brudzinski, and Martha Few. Their contributions strengthened this chapter enormously. I especially want to thank Nicéforo Urbieta, for continuing to believe that the wonders of the ancient past live among us today.

1. De la Cruz, 80–83. Unless otherwise specified, all translations from Spanish are my own.

2. León-Portilla and Shorris, *In the Language of Kings*, 25–26. Leon-Portilla stresses that Mesoamerican literature had a performative element as well and was often recited in public spaces, such as feasts and involved both music and dance.

3. Boone, *Cycles of Time*, 5.

4. Ibid., 2.

5. Ibid.

6. Ibid., 5.

7. For a history of literacy in New Spain, particularly the passage from the pictorial to the alphabetic, see Mignolo (1995); Lockhart (1992).

8. Lockhart, 330.

9. Ibid., 331.

10. Mignolo, 41.

11. Ibid., 66.

12. Nicéforo Urbieta, Interview by author, 1999.

13. Serge Gruzinski suggests that the battle for political and religious hegemony, which took place in the imagistic realm, may indeed be ongoing: "The gigantic enterprise of Westernization that swooped down upon the American continent became in part a war of images that perpetuated itself for centuries and—according to all indications—may not even be over today." Gruzinski, 2.

14. Elizabeth Hill Boone, "Introduction: Writing and Recording Knowledge," in *Writing without Words*, 6.

15. This point is made by Elizabeth Hill Boone who provides a detailed analysis on why Mesoamerican writing has not been considered "true writing." See, "Introduction: Writing and Recording Knowledge."

16. Andrew Bridges, "Stone Writing Earliest Seen in Americas," Associated Press, Discovery Channel, http://dsc.discovery.com/news/2006/09/14stonewriting_arc.html (accessed August 1, 2008).

17. "In New Spain, the mendicant friars celebrated the image as the way to reach and to teach New Spain's native peoples." Mundy, 84.

18. Brandenburg (Fall 2003).

19. Matus, 20.

20. Adelaida Salvador Martínez, Interview by author, Santa Ana de Zegache, Oaxaca, Mexico, 1999.

21. Mundy, 84.

22. Ibid.

23. Ibid.

24. León-Portilla, *Fifteen Poets of the Aztec World*, 82.

25. Carrasco, 80. Bold in the original.

26. Carrasco, 81.

27. Ibid.

28. Ibid.

29. Boone, *Cycles of Time*, 4.

30. Ibid.

31. Ibid.

32. Ibid.

33. Mundy, 85.

34. Ibid., 84.

35. Leon-Portilla, *Endangered Cultures*, 61.
36. Ibid.
37. Gruzinski, 61.
38. For an excellent discussion of the Cajonos Rebellion and its aftermath, see Yannakakis (2008).
39. Urbieta, Interview by author, Oaxaca, Mexico, 2003.
40. Mundy, 85.
41. Ibid., 86.
42. Ibid.
43. Urbieta, *Interview by author*, 2003.
44. Ibid.
45. León-Portilla, *In the Language of Kings*, 18.
46. Urbieta, Interview by author, Oaxaca, Mexico, 2003.
47. Mundy, 72.
48. Boone, *Cycles of Time*, 40.
49. Ibid., 35.
50. Ibid., 34.
51. Ibid., 61.
52. Urbieta, Interview by author, Oaxaca, Mexico, 2003.
53. Gruzinski, *Image*, 31.
54. Richard Boudreaux, "Latin America's Indigenous Saint Stirs Anger, Pride," *Los Angeles Times*, July 30, 2002.

Bibliography

Boone, Elizabeth Hill. *Cycles of Time and Meaning in the Mexican Books of Fate.* Austin: University of Texas Press, 2007.

———. "Introduction: Writing and Recorded Knowledge." In *Writing without Words*, edited by Elizabeth Hill Boone and Walter D. Mignolo, 3–26. Durham, NC: Duke University Press, 1994.

Brandenburg, Tracy. "Journey to the Centre of Visual Thought." *Revista Canadiense de Estudios Hispánicos* 28, no.2 (Fall 2003): 159–72.

Carrasco, Davíd. *Religions of Mesoamerica: Cosmovision and Ceremonial Centers.* San Francisco: Harper and Row, 1990.

De la Cruz, Víctor. *En torno a las islas del mar océano.* Oaxaca: H. Ayuntamiento Popular de Juchitán, 1983.

Gruzinski, Serge. *Images at War: Mexico from Columbus to Blade Runner (1492–2019).* Translated by Heather MacLean. Durham, NC: Duke University Press, 2001.

Lockhart, James. *The Nahuas after the Conquest: A Social and Cultural History of the Indians of Central Mexico, Sixteenth through Eighteenth Centuries.* Stanford: Stanford University Press, 1992.

León-Portilla Miguel, and Earl Shorris. *Endangered Cultures.* Translated by Julie Goodson-Lawe. Dallas: Southern Methodist University Press, 1990.

———. *Fifteen Poets of the Aztec World.* Norman: University of Oklahoma Press, 1992.

———. *In the Language of Kings: An Anthology of Mesoamerican Literature—Pre-Colombian to the Present.* New York: W.W.Norton, 2001.

Matus, Macario. "La batalla plástica de Nicéforo Urbieta." *Brecha: sociedad y cultura* 9 (1998): 20–23.

Mignolo, Walter D. *The Darker Side of the Renaissance: Literacy, Territoriality, and Colonialization.* Ann Arbor: University of Michigan Press, 1995.

Mundy, Barbara E. *The Mapping of New Spain: Indigenous Cartography and the Maps of the Relaciones Geográficas.* Chicago: University of Chicago Press, 1996.

Yannakakis, Yanna. *The Art of Being In-between: Native Intermediaries, Indian Identity, and Local rule in Colonial Oaxaca.* Durham, NC: Duke University Press, 2008.

CHAPTER TEN

"When They Awaken": Indigeneity, Miscegenation, and Anticolonial Visuality

DYLAN A. T. MINER

Colonialism did not dream of wasting its time in denying the existence of one national culture after another. Therefore the reply of the colonized people will be straight away continental in its breadth.
—Frantz Fanon, *Les damnés de la terre*

My people will sleep for 100 years, and when they awake, it will be the artists who give them back their spirit.
—Louis Riel, Michif Revolutionary hanged by the Canadian Government in 1885

Allow me to begin this chapter by prefacing it with two parallel yet divergent citations. Over the course of the past year, these two epistemic manifestos have become foundational within my body of current work as I struggle to theorize about and through Indigenous, Latina/o, and anticolonial visual culture. These important and paradigmatic formulations, spoken nearly a century apart, demonstrate the diversity and continuity between and among various radical intellectuals in the Western Hemisphere. Together, they create a sytagmatic order to the otherwise anarchic nature of colonial and imperial (i.e., hegemonic) visual domination.

The two preceding citations serve as the epistemological and theoretical framework for this chapter. The former epigraph was written by renowned psychologist and anticolonial freedom fighter Frantz Fanon, while the latter comes from aboriginal "prophet" and Michif[1] revolutionary martyr Louis Riel. These observations, uttered nearly a century apart, speak to the liberatory potential of artistic practice, while simultaneously recognizing the continentality and diversity that these anticolonial practices must embody. I find it not the least bit odd that I began writing this chapter while living in New Mexico and developed it while teaching a course in Oaxaca, Mexico. Both of these spaces remain utterly resistant to the European colonial visuality mandated by the continued presence of settler populations and associated political regimes. Contemporary Native and mixedblood artists in both locations have used anticolonial visual language to challenge the system in which we all find ourselves.

The former words were uttered by Louis Riel, an infamous Michif (or Métis) dignitary who played a primary role in two successive anticolonial insurrections in the Dominion of Canada. These insurrections were fought against Euro-Canadian domination as it expanded westward onto the plains and prairies. For his role in these anticolonial movements against the Dominion, he was hanged. On the eve of his demise, Riel acknowledged the power and capacity for artists to transform contemporary society in a cogent and robust fashion. According to Riel, "My people will sleep for 100 years, and when they awake, it will be the artists who give them back their spirit." The Dominion of Canada assassinated Riel in 1885, but his prophetic words are no more appropriate than they are today, just over a century after their initial utterance. The renewed importance of revolutionary Indigenous modernism associated with this sort of engaged partisanship cannot be understated.

Moreover, Frantz Fanon's writings, particularly his text *Les damnés de la terre* (*The Wretched of the Earth*), serve as an outline not only for the horrific implications of (neo-) colonial society, but they also articulate several of the modes that a sustainable anticolonialism must embody. Acknowledging the continentality and reciprocity that must emerge to counter the unending burden of colonial control, Fanon maintains that since "Colonialism did not dream of wasting its time in denying the existence of one national culture after another...the reply of the colonized people will be straight away continental in its breadth."[2] In the Western Hemisphere, the landmass commonly and inappropriately labeled the New World, we are now well into the sixth century of European colonial expansion, control, and settlement. By looking across political and geographical borders, we may begin to illuminate perspectives previously denied.

This chapter will investigate the way that visual (in some ways "art historical") practices of Indigenous projects are always entwined in multiple discursive fields. Therefore, as I will assert, Indigenous visual practices transgress the limitations of disciplinary knowledge and the coloniality of biological racism through a particular anticolonial visual language. By focusing on visual culture, I will critically analyze the discourses of *mestizaje* (*métissage* in the Francophonie) and indigeneity, while critically looking at the efficacy of using racializing discourses to discuss cultural practices. Although migrating throughout the environs of Turtle Island (or Ixachilan as the Nahua evoke), I will pay particular attention to the cultural practices of detribalized Native communities, particularly Chicanas/os and Métis.

As I hope to lay bare, the very colonial process of imperial expansion is one tied to European modes of modernity, modernism, and modernization. I pursue David Craven's position that these three interrelated concepts have been used inappropriately as collective synonyms and that "they *have always existed only in assymetrical and unsettled relation to each other*."[3] Moreover, Craven also asserts that modernism, as a cultural manifestation, was first applied in Nicaragua (not France) by poet laureate Rubén Darío. Resurrecting this buried history will begin to rectify the colonizing forces of Eurocentrism.

Following the writings of Perry Anderson and Marshall Berman, Craven demonstrates that "*modernism* designates the minority artistic tendencies in opposition to, yet also tied to, the official high culture of the West."[4] Conceptualizing modernism(s) within this framework, I will briefly theorize modernist visual culture before looking at Chicana/o and Métis practices.

West: The Colonial (Visual) Project

Although I find it paramount to assert that anticolonialism and its cultural manifestations must never avow the effortless unearthing of extinct or previously destroyed customs, they do, however, engage in a complex dialectic of modernity, its antithesis, and its eventual disavowal. As Fanon so profoundly maintains, colonized citizen-subjects must fully assert themselves through an engaged partisanship that has historically been aligned with modernism and its utopian desire for a better future. As Nikos Papastergiadis clarifies in a special issue of *Theory, Culture & Society*:

> The story of modernism can no longer be told exclusively as a historical survey of linear progress, or as the subsequent cultural effect of socioeconomic changes. To try to explain modernism in purely formal terms, or to assume that modernity is exclusively driven by the social and political agenda, is to miss the point. Modernism is always in a state of critical dialogue with modernity. With hindsight we can see that the dialogue shifted and oscillated between the different locales. Parallel, and in some cases, counter forms of modernism, were developed by artists in places like Latin America and Australia.[5]

I would extrapolate that Indigenous artists in these locations were (and continue to be) particularly engaged in these modernist practices. A contemporary Native visuality is inherently modern in orientation. Following the lead of Diné (Navajo) art critic Shanna Ketchum Heap-of-Birds, I will develop a theoretical framework within which to position modern (and contemporary) art by American Indian and mixedblood artists. While anthropologists commonly analyze "traditional" artistic practices, this project investigates artists working within modernist and contemporary visual idioms and therefore places particular importance on the dialectic between "tradition" and "modernity." In opposition to the (outmoded) maxim that Western visual culture is purely "art for art's sake," I intend to explicate why the production of modern and contemporary art is fundamental to vibrant and sustainable Indigenous sovereignty.

The colonial project, or rather colonialism's tentacle-like encroachment on all things Indigenous, has manifest in a variety of both tangible and nontangible processes since Columbus and his minions first arrived in the so-called New World. For more than a half millennium, European-based lifeways have been the benchmark against which all others are measured. And in comparison to the fictitious grandeur of Europe and its settlements, Natives have never been able to compete. Although the explicit character of past colonialisms no longer exist as they once did, the horrific practices associated with these projects have become more and more elaborate and intricate, usually masked under the guise of development or globalization. In many ways, modernity and coloniality are inverted representatives of another. Walter Mignolo writes that coloniality is the site of enunciation that reveals and denounces the blindness of the narrative of modernity from the perspective of modernity itself, and it is at the same time the platform of pluriversality, of diverse projects coming from the experience of local histories touched by western expansion (as the Word Social Forum demonstrates); thus coloniality is not a new abstract universal (Marxism is imbedded in modernity, good but shortsighted), but the place where diversality as a universal project can be thought out; where the question of languages and knowledges becomes crucial (Arabic, Chinese, Aymara, Bengali, etc) as the site of the pluriversal—that is, the "traditional" that the "modern" is rolling over and ruling out.[6]

For Mignolo, modernity and coloniality are interrelated and interconnected projects that reciprocally inscribe one another in a dialectic and dialogic fashion.

With the confrontation and imposition of settler cultural traditions, Native cultural practices ruptured from their organic trajectory. However, this rupture, occurring at differing times in varied climates, has not been complete. In fact, a global investigation of colonialism/modernism reveals that it can and never will fully envelope Native peoples, no matter how hard it tries. Still, some epistemic gashes run deeper than others, while some of these cuts are merely surface wounds. Tsalagi literary critic Daniel Heath Justice argues in "Go Away, Water!," Native American tribal groups in the northeastern United States faced a much harsher biological and cultural "cleansing" than did tribal groups in other parts of the continent.[7] As such, the psychological wounds run much deeper in those eastern tribal communities where traditional language and cultural practices are held intact, although most likely hidden under European spiritual and cultural nomenclature. Nonetheless, the effects of colonialism are expansive and must not be ignored. As Frantz Fanon lays bear, colonialism was adamant about destroying Indigenous ways of being on a continental scale and therefore aboriginal response must likewise be continental.

While settler-Indigenous relations have not always been confrontational, the very nature of colonialism is a barbarous and savage one. It de-humanizes both the colonizer and the colonized in a vicious dialectic process. Through the course of colonization, settlers must transform the Indigenous people, as sentient and tangible human beings, into abstract objects. As anticolonial intellectual Aimé Césaire argues

Between colonizer and colonized there is room only for forced
labor, intimidation, pressure, the police, taxation, theft, rape, com-
pulsory crops, contempt, mistrust, arrogance, self-complacency,
swinishness, brainless elites, degraded masses.

No human contact, but relations of domination and submis-
sion which turn the colonizing man into a class-room monitor,
an army sergeant, a prison guard, a slave driver, and the indigenous man into an instrument of production...colonization =
"thing-ification."[8]

For Césaire, colonialism bifurcates. By its very nature, colonialism
forces the complex realities of human existence into an easily codifi-
able system of opposites. The Native response to this colonial "thing-
ification" is what interests me in this chapter. Although there were
anticolonial resistance movements before the arrival of European settlers (think about the multifaceted resistance to Mexican hegemony
in Central Mexico), the twentieth century has seen these anticolonial
insurrections catch fire like never before. This wildfire was spread by
fanning the flames of colonial dissent, particularly in the late-1950s and
1960s, which initiated a new level of anticolonial struggle on a multi-
plicity of fronts in Africa, Asia, and the Americas. By 1968, this anticolonial wildfire engulfed the entire world, including the First World.

East: A Sustained Anticolonial Visuality

During this period, third and fourth world intellectuals, joined in
solidarity by a handful of revolutionary white colleagues and allies,
produced scholarship that was both intellectually stimulating and
politically engaged. Figures such as Césaire, Fanon, Albert Memmi,
Jean-Paul Sartre, are but a few of the intellectuals who directly confronted the colonial project, particularly as it was manifest in Africa. For
Indigenous North Americans, figures such as Vine Deloria, Howard
Adams, and others were engaged in similar projects. Osage literary
critic and American Indian Movement historian Robert Warrior places
this period (1963–1971) as one where Native intellectuals were heavily
involved in dialogical praxis that produced a uniquely (although not
isolated) Indigenous discourse.[9] Although many periodizations place
these years outside of modernism, I believe that when we re-envision
and redefine modernism along the lines of Craven and Papastergiadis,
the canonical and hegemonic periodization breaks down.

Sadly, through government repression and changing social climates, the radical intellectual partisanship of the 1950s and 1960s was pacified during the 1970s and later transformed into the postmodern and post-structural ambiguity of the 1980s, 1990s, and 2000s. The community-centered nature of 1960s activism and intellectualism (which I believe could be called modernist) have given way to scholarship more interested in asserting academic credentials than challenging Indigenous oppression. In many ways, radical indigenism and anticolonialism were co-opted by the amorphous capitalist project, which turned its thinkers into academic functionaries. This co-optation strategy, although not necessarily intentional, follows the trajectory of a critique of globalizing knowledge put forth by Marxist scholar and cultural studies foundational voice Stuart Hall. As Hall notes, the conciliatory power of capitalism enables any and all oppositional projects to be co-opted and redirected into a capitalist model. Hall asserts "that in order to maintain its global position, capital has had to negotiate, has had to incorporate and partly reflect the differences it was trying to overcome."[10] This means that while Indigenous cultural and epistemological systems were being systematically destroyed, capitalism began to incorporate the resistant voices of Indigenous struggle. As Michif intellectual Howard Adams posits, this cooptation of Native leadership has been going on for sometime and is itself colonial in nature.[11]

Tsalagi (Cherokee) political scientist Jeff Corntassell names the totalizing and globalizing colonial and capitalist projects as a complex manifestation of *imperial shape-shifting*. He writes that

> Through indigenous eyes, globalization reflects a deepening, hastening and stretching of an already-existing empire; it is merely the latest permutation of imperialism. Shape-shifting colonial powers continue to invent new methods of domination in order to erase indigenous histories and senses of place.[12]

Since time-immemorial, activists, intellectuals, and artists, have struggled to confront the colonial shape-shifter. At times we have been successful, while other struggles have proven futile. Nonetheless, the expanding processes of globalization have made resistance all the more difficult. Although unable and unwilling to answer the following rhetorical question, I nonetheless find it helpful to ask if an anti-postmodern turn (could this be a continued modernism?) be used to combat these unending global capitulations?

Although anticolonial and partisan scholarship has diminished during the twenty-first century, the affects of colonialism continue indefinitely. The most obvious authority of colonialism may be seen in the epidemic loss of Indigenous languages, seen on a global-scale. Of equal importance (at least in terms of my argument), running parallel to the extinction of Indigenous languages, is the extinction of uniquely aboriginal forms of visuality.

The reciprocity between visuality, modernity, and imperialism runs deep. As Nicholas Mirzoeff demonstrates,

> Thomas Carlyle coined both "visuality" and the verb "visualizing" in a series of writings between 1837 and 1841 designed to create a spiritual antidote to modernity that was nonetheless strongly supportive of imperialism. The terms followed from his sense of his work as embodying the "eye of history."[13]

Although the concept of visuality is usually evoked within contemporary scholarship to demonstrate an ideological move away from the disciplinary constraints of "art history," as Mirzoeff demonstrates, even the concept of visuality is one tied to European (particularly British) imperial expansion and European society's engagement with modernity. According to Craven, this engagement with modernity is one of the hallmarks of modernism.

Mirzoeff, nonetheless, posits two forms of oppositional visuality that may be evoked to counter imperial and hegemonic visual culture. He calls these unique forms *inverse visuality* and *veiled visuality*, in an indirect nod to W. E. B. DuBois's application of the veil in his construction of *double consciousness*. Mirzoeff writes that

> Inverse visuality is any moment of visual experience in which the subjectivity of the viewer is called into question by the density or opacity of what he or she sees. These flickering, excessive, hyper-real, overlaid, pixelated, disjunctive and distracting moments are spectral dust in the eyes of visuality that cause it to blink and become momentarily unsighted. Veiled visuality performs a similar function by dividing visuality into two by means of the veil that is both visible and invisible at once.[14]

I would like to expand this thinking into an anticolonial and postcontact Indigenous vsiuality. This form of visuality is by its very nature going to be divided into two, much like veiled visuality, since by its very nature colonialism bifurcates society into two opposing fields. In response, anticolonialism (including a sustained anticolonial modernism) will, as Walter Mignolo so eloquently states, emerge not in binaries, but rather from these very dichotomies.[15]

So what I am presenting is not simply the production of binary thinking (or seeing), but rather an Indigenous form of vision that emerges from this dichotomous structure. While I prefer to address these concepts as anticolonial and Indigenous, Mignolo prefers the notions of border gnoseology or border gnosis to name the very processes of anticolonial indigenisms emerging from colonizing systems of control. But how do we begin to understand these anticolonial and Indigenous ways of seeing?

At this point, let us momentarily digress so that we may define exactly how I am using visuality, since there are at least two competing definitions of the term. In this chapter, I am defining *visuality* as a discursively and ideologically mediated process, which although *tied to modes to vision*, is distinguished from the more pseudoscientific notion of *vision*. For Anglo-American art critic Hal Foster,

> The difference between [vision and visuality] signals a difference within the visual—between the mechanism of sight and its historical techniques, between the datum of vision and its discursive determinations—a difference, many difference, among how we see, how we are able, allowed or made to see, and how we see this seeing or the unseen therein.[16]

Unlike vision, which presupposes an apolitical and common mode of seeing, visuality recognizes the complexities and different ways of looking. In many ways, this follows ideas outlined in John Berger's important art historical text *Ways of Seeing*. In this short pedagogical manuscript, which originally began as a BBC television series, Berger maintains that there are multiple ways of seeing, but these modes are contained by structural limitations. He writes, "It is seeing which established our place in the surrounding world; we explain the world with words, but words can never undo the fact that we are surrounded by it. The relation between what we see and what we know is never settled."[17] By understanding visuality and (post)modernity, we begin to scratch the metaphoric surface and will hopefully recognize the *situatedness of seeing*.

For Native peoples, colonial vision always places the aboriginal within the gaze of the settler. The Indigenous subject functions merely as the object of vision, almost exclusively belonging to the settlers. To fully combat this legacy of oppression, one must invert this process and reinsert the Native as visionary and as the subject with the ability to partake in visual power. Of course, this process or concept that I am advocating is nothing new. For at least a generation now art historians, particularly those writing from feminist and postcolonial positions, have recognized the power of the gaze to objectify. Laura Mulvey's seminal essay "Visual Pleasure and Narrative Cinema" introduced the model of the gaze as symptomatic of asymmetrical power relations by hypothesizing what she terms the "male gaze."[18]

What differentiates my approach from those theorized in the past is that I believe that we are obliged to initiate an understanding of Native visual culture from a uniquely aboriginal critical theory that combines both academic and tribal ways of the knowing. I must be clear, however, that I am not advocating a continued ghetto-ization of Indigenous contemporary art or that only Native critics may theorize aboriginal visual studies. Inversely, as Tsalagi art historian Aaron Fry writes when discussing Tewa (San Ildefonso Pueblo) art, we must incorporate local epistemologies into the analysis of the global. To dismiss or ignore local texts (either written, oral, visual, or performative) would be to misrepresent that particular work. Fry advocates "that local knowledge must be engaged as an interpretive or analytical methodology, what we might call an ethnotheoretical or indigenous epistemological approach to the creation of art historical explanations."[19] To fully comprehend any creative expression, one must contextualize its production within correct cultural parameters. This, of course, becomes extremely complex when addressing modern and contemporary art that (falsely) proposes a global cosmopolitan positionality.

In her ground-breaking essay "Native American Cosmopolitan Modernism(s)," Shanna Ketchum (now Shanna Ketchum Heap-of-Birds) notes the absence of Indigenous theory within published postcolonial and postmodern thought (and I would extrapolate her arguments as to apply to modernist discourses, as well). Ketchum writes that

> The articulation of Native American experiences abroad or even in their own homeland has not been adequately addressed by postcolonial theory and postmodernism. The anti-colonial struggle that modernity entreats has always been exercised by Native Americans across time and space or, in short, in history.[20]

What Ketchum does, particularly in relation to modernist and contemporary Indigenous art-making practices, is insert Native ways of thinking and doing in dialogue with the ideas issued by other contemporary thinkers such as Edward Said, Terry Eagleton, Walter Benjamin, Michel Foucault, James Clifford, Rasheed Araeen, Homi Bhabha, Stuart Hall, and so on. After all, as Ketchum presents, why can't Native intellectuals such as Andrea Smith or Gerald McMaster intellectually engage with these more recognized and canonical voices? Sadly, these voices have been too frequently destroyed, denied, or disavowed from larger dialogues.

One way of destroying Indigenous visuality and Indigenous modernisms may be tied to the demolition of aboriginal texts. Although predating modernity by many centuries, Daniel Heath Justice points to the destruction of Maya and other Mesoamerican libraries as the course of action used by *illiteracy campaigns*. He writes that "Empire contains within it the insistence on the erasure of the indigenous populations, through overt destruction or co-optation; indeed, the very memory of an unbroken Native presence is often furiously repressed by the colonizers."[21] It should come as no surprise that both the Cuban and Sandinista revolutions initiated Frierian *literacy campaigns* as the core revolutionary pedagogy. Reading and learning to see is paramount to a re-humanization process.

One of the ways that Indigenous memory has been destroyed is by attacking and rendering void the manner that Native people have used vision within their visual and performative cultures, but it also denies them active participation into mainstream visual discourse. In tandem with the Spanish *conquistadores'* physical destruction of aboriginal texts was the de-legitimization of Mesoamerican visuality and performative modes associated with seeing. Before contact, the Mixtec and Nahua codices, for instance, were not simply meant to be read in static European fashion, in which the knowledge was physically embodied in the text. Rather Mesoamerican texts were meant to function as mnemonic devices that served as the foundation for *tlacuilome* (scribe) performances. These texts did not necessarily contain knowledge in the European sense, but the knowledge emerged through the dialogic space activated by ceremonial performance.

So when the colonial regime embarked on the destruction of all non-Christian (and therefore demonic) texts, Indigenous knowledge was attacked on multiple fronts. Not only did aboriginal literature loose its primary written texts, the reciprocity between seeing and being was simultaneously ruptured. It is from the cultural ashes of these oppressive acts that anticolonial visuality has emerged. And in many ways, it has continued to be modernist in scope.

Although most Native peoples have tribal creation stories that enunciate who they are as a people, sharing a common history and cosmology. Mixedblood narratives of collective mixed-Indigenous ethnogenesis have commonly been excluded from the canon of Indigenous story-telling. In much of Latin America, for instance, the collective national identity of each respective nation-state is tied to the initial sexual relations between Natives and settlers. Mexicans frequently tell the story of Malintzin (also known as La Malinche or Doña Marina), the Indigenous slave who was given as a "gift" to Hernán Cortés. Because of her multilingual fluency, including her facility to quickly learn European languages, Malintzin served as a translator for Cortés and associated Spanish military forces within the parameters of colonial society. While she had few options to do otherwise, traditional misogynist historiography has labeled her a traitor to her people, selling them out through her interpretive serves.

Under the control of Spanish patriarchy, Malintzin bore children with Cortés. For the "imagined" Mexican community, these children have commonly signified the birth of the first "*mexicano.*" Their "bi-racial" stature denotes that they physically embodied the bicultural *mestizaje* that has come to symbolize modern Mexican nationalism. However, while privileging the biological intermingling of two distinct cultural groups, the role of the Indigenous women is commonly seen as one subordinate to settler society. In many ways, and this will be developed later in this chapter, discourses on the mestiza/o served to de-Indianize while ignoring the historic specificity of the situation.

North: Halfbreed Visual Theory

To combat colonialism, activists have forged a particular visual language that directly confronts the various colonial projects, including colonial visuality. The two resistant forms of visuality presented by Mirzoeff are important in that they offer an alternative to imperial and hegemonic notions of visual culture. Part and parcel to the destruction of Indigenous lifeways was (and continue to be) the demolition of Indigenous visuality. As Fanon so astutely recognized, colonialism is a continental or global project and therefore its disavowal must also be continental or global in scale. As previously cited, Frantz Fanon recognized that

Colonialism did not dream of wasting its time in denying the existence of one national culture after another. Therefore the reply of the colonized people will be straight away continental in its breadth.[22]

But before a true continentality may emerge, we must first begin to disembowel colonialism and recognize the liberatory potential embodied in Indigenous ways of knowing and seeing, as well as how these engage in (post)modern ways of being. In fact, although we must never idealize the precolonial past, Cesaire is correct in his assessment that many (although not all) aboriginal communities persist in an anticolonial, mutually supportive, and autonomous fashion. In *Discourse on Colonialism*, Cesaire asserts that precolonial communities

were communal societies, never societies of the many for the few.
They were societies that were not only ante-capitalist, as has been said, but also *anti-capitalist*.
They were democratic societies, always.
They were cooperative societies, fraternal societies.[23]

Indigenous forms of seeing may allow us to visualize a new world or re-envision the trajectory of the present clusterfuck in which we find our selves. Although the struggles and efforts have become quite trendy, the multiethnic aboriginal resistance of the *Ejército Zapatista de Liberación Nacional* (EZLN) or Zapatista movement is but one example of the production of a sustained anticolonial visuality. EZLN practices must not be ignored, as they have engaged in modernist and postmodernist visual legacies in a way that does not deny the importance of modernist utopian projects, but weaves them into contemporary aboriginal lifeways.

But what exactly does anticolonial visuality mean? And how do we produce it in a sustainable fashion? As Chickasaw scholar Amanda Cobb demonstrates, decolonization and sovereignty are parallel although not analogous concepts. She writes that "Tribal sovereignty existed before colonization and does (or will depending on your point of view) exist after colonization. Sovereignty is *the going on* of life—the living."[24] To produce a sustainable anticolonial visuality, participants must have the ability to see in a manner that is (although not entirely autonomous) free from colonial constraints. Since sovereignty is one such manifestation of a people's collective ability to self-determine, it can be seen as one of the benchmarks of anticolonialism. However as has been frequently pointed out, the sovereignty of First Nations, American Indians, and Métis peoples in North America is always constrained by the parameters of European-based settler regimes. So the question remains: can an anticolonial or Indigenous visuality exist within the parameters of modern (albeit diminished) nation-states?

Although the crux of this chapter is prefaced on the production and thinking through anticolonial and Indigenous modernisms, up to this point in my chapter I have not actually discussed a particular image or object within discourse. As irritating as this strategy may have been for those of you trained as art historians, its application is nevertheless intentional. Without visual allocation, I hope to have commenced formulation (or critique) of a thorough and nuanced discussion on how to think about and through these concepts. Since these methodologies are in many ways operating from (but not within) traditional art historical and rhetorical paradigms, their application and usage is extremely complex. By leaving an absence of visual assignment, I hope to allow each and every one of us, as well as fellow travelers inside and outside of the academy, to continue theorizing these concepts and engage these alternative modernisms, be they Indigenous modernisms, anticolonial modernisms, or any and all of their postmodern and antimodern manifestations. At this point, however, I shall engage some specificity to begin to flesh out my argument. The Michif ideally serve on this end.

As a distinct aboriginal nation, the Michif people are usually defined as the descendents of First Nations mothers and white (usually Francophone) *voyageurs*. Their homeland is predominantly located in the Canadian provinces, but Michif peoples have historically lived throughout the Great Lakes and across the Canada-U.S. border. Unlike most aboriginal people whose collective identity and memory predates colonization, the Michif are unique in claiming their origins in the early capitalist economies of the fur-trade. As a mixedblood people, the Michif are in many ways a postcontact (although not postcolonial) Native people. However, identifying as Métis (or Michif or Halfbreed) does not assert assimilation into Euro-Canadian society. Unlike *mestiza/o* identities in Latin American that aim to de-Indianize mixedblood identities, Michif identities are centered in an aboriginal way of being. Although little is written comparing Mexican *mestizaje* with Canadian *métissage*, I am of the opinion that they in fact serve different needs. In Mexico, *mestizaje* was about the assimilation into European society, while Canadian *métissage* served primarily to indigenize the mixedblood population.

Nonetheless, the ethnogenesis of the Michif as a uniquely identifiable people is difficult to pinpoint, as Native and voyageur relations often existed outside the written histories of Anglo- and Franco-Canada.

Defining who is Métis has likewise become a complex endeavor in Canada, particularly since the rewriting of the Canadian constitution with the 1982 Constitution Act. Following decades of aboriginal political struggles, this important act bestowed Aboriginal Status on the Michif. Sadly, this has resulted in numerous court-cases legislating who is allowed to be "Métis" under Canadian law. Although Native identities have little to do with European legal structures, these discourses have nonetheless colonized Native ontology and have altered its way of being.

Understanding Michif identity in the United States is even more complex, as Métis histories have been systematically written out of our collective memory. As fur-trade historian Jennifer S. H. Brown writes in "Métis, Halfbreeds, and Other Real People,"

> "Métis" is not an ethnic term well known in American history. It is far more familiar to Canadians, many thousands of whom (particularly in the prairie provinces) identify themselves as Métis, that is, of mixed Aboriginal-European descent. The Métis, however, were never simply confined to Canada; many more thousands of people who could identify themselves as Métis by ancestry live on the American side of the Forty-ninth Parallel.[25]

As a U.S.-born Michif with roots in the Métis communities of Red River, Manitoba, Slave Lake, Alberta and Penetanguishine, Ontario, asserting an aboriginal identity in the United States becomes difficult in a society where blood quantum remains the legal bar to which Native identities are still held. Acknowledging the colonial nature of using blood quantum to legislate aboriginal identity, Louis Riel is quoted as questioning: "Why should we concern ourselves about what degree of mixture we possess of European or Indian blood? If we have ever so little of either gratitude or filial love, would we not be proud to say 'We are Mètis!'?"[26] Even though Riel was adamant about going beyond notions of racial purity, its psychological affects still persist for contemporary Native people. Michif feelings of inadequacy are not isolated to those of us in the United States, rather the issue of belonging is one that transcends borders and is shared by countless other Michif, even those living in the Métis Nation Homeland of western Canada.

This is documented by Cathy Richardson, a Michif Counselor living in British Columbia, who understands the psychological pathologies among the Métis in relation to identity and social well-being. She has found that regardless of phenotype or cultural heritage, most Michif individuals feel a sense of inequality, as they are taught to identify as neither settler, nor Native. Citing one of her participants, Richardson writes, "prejudice is such an evil thing, and as Metis we often get it from both sides of the blanket. A feeling of never belonging haunts me."[27] Although a "hybrid" sense of permanent in-betweenness is one that permeates Michif social being, I believe that visually and rhetorically we continue to expand our own indigeneity in the face of constant and unending pressure to cease being Native.

In the same way that our identities emerge because of colonial economic expansion, so too did Michif cultural practices descend from colonial era social relations. It is well documented that floral beadwork, one of the hallmarks of Michif visual expression, was introduced to Native communities through Catholic missions (particularly the Grey nuns) as they expanded westward across the St. Lawrence River, into the Great Lakes and onto the prairies of North America. Although "traditional" geometric designs were used by Native peoples until the 1840s, floral patterning was introduced by Francophone nuns and flower beadwork became an increasingly flamboyant Michif cultural expression. The direct relationship between visuality and identity is one that comes to the fore when the Sioux began calling the Michif the "Flower Beadwork People," connecting the cultural practice of beading with Michif community identity. In this particular instance, the Michif visual language was one that was indistinguishable from their collective indigeneity (and ontology) and served at the core of how they resisted continued colonial control. It is not inconsequential that in addition to being called the flower beadwork people, the Cree used the term *Otepemisiwak*, meaning the people without bosses, to refer to the Michif. An egalitarian and anarchist mode of living separated the Michif from their European kin, while the absence of a chief system distinguished them from many First Nations. This resistance to state control functions at both the political and epistemological levels, not to mention its rhetorical application. Operating without leaders is ontologically Michif.

Even though commencing through the colonial processes of Europe, Michif epistemologies (including visualities and rhetorics) are ones that cannot be reduced to the simple mimicry of settler practices. In fact, what is so exciting about Michif cultural expressions are the ways with which they re-articulate common French Canadian, Anglo-Canadian, and First Nations visual culture into uniquely Michif manifestations. In his seminal essay, "In Search of Métis Art," Ted J. Brasser highlights the ineffectiveness of museum curators to properly label "Métis art." When discussing the writing of George P. Murdock, he writes that problems arise when we try to distinguish métis art from that of neighbouring—and related—tribal groups. Literature about the widespread and culturally far-from-homogenous bands of Cree is lumped together under one headings by Murdock and the same is true for the Ojibwa and Assiniboine-Stoney...Obviously we will not be able to define Red River métis art until we know what their Indian neighbours were producing in the early nineteenth century.[28]

Although Brasser is accurate in his assessment that museums (and other academic institutions) do not know how to identify Michif material culture, he is nonetheless shortsighted in his search to differentiate the Michif from their Indigenous neighbors, with whom they frequently shared kin relations. It must be asserted that Michif visuality must not be extracted from First Nations (Cree, Assiniboine, Anishinabe) histories, but rather it needs to be inserted and intertwined with them. Although Michif histories and creative culture may problematize European notions of purity, their visuality is couched within aboriginal ways of seeing and being in the world.

Since the Métis are commonly dismissed as inauthentic *halfbreeds*, neither settler nor aboriginal, Michif visual culture, such as flower beadwork serves as the site for authentic psychological reclamation. In effect, Native visual culture (whatever that may actually be) allows Michif cultural producers to salvage and re-inscribe the derogatory and racist appellation "halfbreed" as a space of resistance to European colonial visuality. Therefore, self-identification as Métis, Michif, or Halfbreed is paramount to proper psychological healing. This healing and survivance, to use the language of Gerald Vizenor, is the basis for Indigenous visuality.[29] Métis intellectual Howard Adams argues that

> To the whites of Canada, "Métis" means a light-coloured Indian. In Canadian history, "halfbreed" refers specifically to the group of people who are part Indian and part white. These halfbreed people did not have a choice as to whether they would be Indians or whites or in-between; society defined them as members of native society and it still does today. Halfbreed was the original name used by white traders in the early fur-trading years, but it has become unacceptable to mainstream society. To whites, half-breed became a vulgar expression for mixed blood—which seems to be a more polite term...to say I was Métis might have been less insulting to some, though many would not have known the

meaning of the term...However, Halfbreed to me was a powerful word. (2002, np)

This rhetorical strategy of reclaiming colonial and European derogatory language is highlighted in the work of Maori intellectual Linda
Tuhiwai Smith. For Smith, "claiming" is the very first project, followed by the likes of activities such as "celebrating survival," "revital-
izing," "reframing," and "naming," among others.[30]

This anticolonial reclamation, another one of Smith's Indigenous
projects, is also connected to the writing of Maria Campbell. In her
autobiographical novel *Halfbreed*, she describes her life journey of struggle and survivance. For both Campbell and Adams, to be a Halfbreed
was to claim one's indigeneity, while reclaiming the racist language
emerging from settler colonialism. Even though contemporary Euro-
Canadians feel uncomfortable with the appellation (which of course
emerges from Euro-Canadian society), Adams and Campbell intentionally used this term as to not allow the erasure of the horrific historical trauma to Native peoples. This same process of linguistic resistance
to the expunging of Native oppression runs true for Campbell. How
different would these ideas be if they simply used the name *Métis*? For
both Campbell and Adams, to be a halfbreed was (and is) to reclaims
one's humanity.

Taiaiake Alfred, a Kanien'kehaka (Mohawk) intellectual, believes
that "[t]he imposition of labels and definitions of identity on indigenous people has been a central feature of the colonization process from
the start."[31] By applying the commonly vulgar appellation *Halfbreed* to
her successful autobiography, Métis intellectuals are active in reclaiming colonial language from an Aboriginal perspective. Alongside the
reclamation of colonizing usage of European languages is the retention
and maintenance of Indigenous epistemologies, worldviews, and most
importantly ways of seeing.

Elsewhere, I have posited that the work of Maria Campbell, renowned
author of the autobiographical tome *Halfbreed*, serves in the literary
development of what I call Halfbreed Theory.[32] Akin to, yet divergent
from, Chicana lesbian feminist Gloría Anzaldúa's "mestiza consciousness," Halfbreed Theory is rooted in Indigenous ways of knowing, yet
incorporates Western knowledge systems into its practice. It is, after
all, halfbreed.

In many ways, as citizens of the (continuing) colonial environment,
Native thinkers and cultural workers cannot escape the incorporation
of settler knowledge into our own. In *Empires, Ruins, + Networks*, art

historians Scott McQuire and Nikos Papastergiadis maintain that 'To consider the place of art today is not a matter of imagining alternative places that exist outside capitalism or beyond the reaches of colonialism, for these structures have already claimed a space within us.'[33]

Halfbreed Visual Theory does just that: acknowledges the role of colonization within Michif visuality, while asserting itself as wholly Indigenous. Since at least the seventeenth century, but particularly during the nineteenth and twentieth centuries, Michif cultural expressions were ones that accepted colonialism's inherent role, yet disavowed its ability to be fully circumscribed by it. Flower beadwork, as a visual and rhetorical strategy, is a practice that is now considered "traditional" for many Native peoples in North America. Its acquiescence into these communities was not always so acceptable, yet functioned as a site of contestation. Through visual dialogue and confrontation, Michif visual culture became what it is today. What we see through Indigenous cultural expansion is the eventual discursive (and visual) changes that allow for the incorporation of external visual languages, without diminishing the aboriginality of Native culture. Even though racially "impure" halfbreeds, Halfbreed visuality is entirely Indigenous and anticolonial in its ability to resist capitalist exploitation.

South: Chicana/o Visuality, Class versus Nation

Much like the Michif who are seen as deplorable halfbreeds, Chicanas/os were likewise forcefully detribalized and de-legitimized at the hands of Spanish and Anglo-American forces. In response, Chicana/o visuality maintains a "hybrid" Nativeness even after colonization. Chicana/o aesthetic theory and visuality are based on parallel constructions of *rasquachismo* and *domesticana*, theories evoked by Tomás Ybarra-Frausto and Amalia Mesa-Bains respectively. Accordingly, Chicana/o visuality, as a mestizo visual form, maintains a working-class aesthetics.

As part of this section, I will present a reciprocal critique of the conceptualization of class-based cultural practices. Alongside this cogent and corresponding argumentation will be my preliminary analysis of Chicana/o identity as working-class identity, while bursting the very notion of class-based aesthetics in the first place. Moreover, I will foreground my work by positioning Chicanas/os as both a "nation" and class of detribalized Indigenous workers. By investigating Chicana/o cultural production, particularly during the civil rights era, this re-analysis of class and nationhood are inescapable and ones that have not been adequately addressed within the field. Although I hope to de-mystify the cultural implications of class, I remain unconvinced whether Chicanas/os, as both an Indigenous people (read "nation") and as a class, already an untenable contradiction, do in fact produce class-based aesthetics or if these are instead a "national" form.

Allow me to begin by highlighting *rasquachismo*, a concept organically developing from within the Chicana/o community, which was subsequently applied to the visual arts by Tomás Ybarra-Frausto in his 1991 essay "Rasquachismo: A Chicano Sensibility." In this evocation, Ybarra-Frausto cements the way with which impoverished *mexicanas/os* were able to create a vibrant and sustainable culture amidst continued Anglo-American colonization.

As Ybarra-Frausto posits, *rasquachismo* seeks "to subvert and turn the ruling paradigm on its head."[34] As a force of resistance, *rasquachismo* allows the subversion and transcendence of hegemonic and colonial structures as they have played out along the U.S.-Mexico borderlands and among the global diaspora of Chicana/o-Mexicana/o people. Although I see the importance and utility of this construct, it appears that rasquachismo is couched in terms of prolonged otherness that permeates all social relations. In his extensive explication of rasquachismo, Ybarra-Frausto begins his essay by explaining that "One is never rasquache, it is always someone else, someone of a lower status, who is judged to be outside the demarcators of approved taste and decorum."[35] Here, Ybarra-Frausto presents the relational argument that identities are simply lived in opposition to what one is not, even within the same "ethnic" or "class" community. Accordingly, Chicanas/os never self-identify as rasquache, rather this category is placed upon one's peers (presumably of a lower social standing).

Furthermore, Ybarra-Frausto maintains that

> Social class demarcates rasquache, which is a working-class sensibility (a lived reality) only recently appropriated as an aesthetic program of the [Chicana/o] professional class...Rasquachismo is brash and hybrid, sending shudders through the ranks of the elite who seek solace in less exuberant, more muted, and purer tradition.[36]

In this instance, Ybarra-Frausto collapses class, as an economic relationship to capital (particularly the ownership of one's own labor), into the cultural expressions of the "Chicana/o working-class."

In his essay critical of the effects of rasquachismo, Ramón García confronts Ybarra-Frausto's aesthetic category for its appropriation of a working-class aesthetic by what he calls the "middle-class intelligentsia," very similar to Ybarra-Frausto's own "professional class."[37] Although García's argument follows a logical mode of critique, and I am drawn to their applicability, I must comment that Ybarra-Frausto and García are both shortsighted (although they are in no ways the only ones) to articulate the construct of a "working-class" aesthetic in opposition to either the middle or professional classes. Let me briefly outline *domesticana*, in many ways a uniquely feminist and woman-centered version of rasquachismo, as to pull this theoretical framework into the debate.

Amalia Mesa-Bains, a clinical psychologist, artist, and director of visual and public art at CSU-MB, articulates domesticana as the "sensibility of Chicana rasquache." For Mesa-Bains, "the day-to-day experience of working-class Chicanas is replete with the practices within the domestic space."[38] As she presents it, domesticana allows Chicanas (as women) an articulate space to respond to the class, race, and gender restraints of patriarchal, racist, and capitalist society in North America. As such, domesticana focuses on familial histories and ephemeral domestic practices as the sites that are both reflective as well as constructive of working-class ideology. As such, domesticana not only reflects the gendered, classes, raced, and sexualized ideologies of the Chicana/o community, but also allows for their reconstruction and rewriting. In many ways, both domesticana and rasquachismo are important aesthetic categories that help classify and categorize Chicana/o cultural practices, respectively.

At this moment, let me pose a series of question, questions that serve as the undercurrent of this chapter, though they are questions that I am neither able to articulate fully nor that I am able to answer adequately. Therefore I ask them both rhetorically as well as in wait of eventual responses. Can we truly have working-class aesthetics? Do classes produce their own forms of visuality and ways of seeing, or rather are aesthetics tied to "national" communities?

While binary structures have been re-evaluated and subsequently dismantled as epistemological systems, I believe that class nonetheless needs to maintain some semblance of a dialectic structure. According to Teresa L. Ebert and Mas'ud Zavarzadeh,

> the myth of the middle class is invented to obscure the fact that "we" (black and white, man and woman, gay and straight, etc.)

are all wage-workers, and, therefore, "we" are "all equal here" because, as Marx puts it, "middle and transitional levels of social differences 'always conceal the boundaries' of classes."[39]

Although I doubt that Ebert and Zavarzadeh would condense the social realities that differentiate among the various sectors of the working class (or better yet, working classes), they nonetheless are adamant that capitalism inherently creates a life-world where humans are bifurcated between owners and workers. Those of us who continue to work as wage-laborers, no matter how "middle class" we may think we are, are actually just privileged workers who have assimilated the hegemonic ideology of the "professional class." Class is not about cultural practice, but it is a series of social relations based on one's placement within the capitalist economy.

Unfortunately, the discursive and ideological practices of the hegemony commonly position class, not as the relational nature that it is, but rather as certain life-style attributes that emerge from economic status. Along this problematic trajectory, if you have a mortgage, you are middle class; if you rent, you are working class. They expand outward to engage in a series of consumptive cultural practices, none of which relate directly to one's unique class identity. Although most radical intellectuals associate their academic labor as working-class activity, dominant discursive practices most definitely differ from our own complex articulation of class politics. Sadly, both domesticana and rasquachismo segregate artists and intellectuals from a larger working-class base. Both of these paradigms position the artist or cultural worker as external to the working class.

This reductive class analysis, of course, solely diminishes the economic (i.e., class) relations of contemporary society by turning to the cultural practices that are at the "essence" of one's own class standing. That is to say, instead of acknowledging that one engages in certain cultural and social practices as a response to class, they become the tangible expressions of class. In turn, intellectuals analyze the cultural expressions organically emerging from the working class, not as bourgeois outsiders appropriating cultural practices to which they are not connected (as Ybarra-Frausto and García, and in some ways Mesa-Bains maintain), but as members of that class, however obliquely related. Since, as I will show, Chicanas/os are all working class, a discussion of Chicana/o working-class aesthetics is both tautological and illogical. Allow me to articulate my proposition that Chicanas/os are a class, before countering this by situating Chicanas/os as a nation.

The Chicana/o, as a "hybrid-racial-cultural" type (meaning mestiza/o or mixedblood) has been at the core of Mexican-American collective memory and cultural practice since at least the late-1960s. A brief examination of *movimiento* cultural texts quickly reveals a focus on the Chicana/o body as mestiza/o, having roots in both Spanish and Indigenous life-ways. If we turn to the frequently cited *Plan Espiritual de Aztlán*, a poetic and polemic manifesto of national liberation written by Alurista in 1969, this point is quickly revealed. In this document, *mestizaje*, class struggle, and national liberation are all merged in a seamless and liberatory fashion. Despite this, one of the failures of mestiza/o discourse, and this is true about the plan, is that it dismisses the compound and dynamic disposition of identity and subsumes this into stagnant and a priori biological objects! Instead, Native intellectual Jack Forbes argues that Chicanas/os are "de-Indianized" Indians, to borrow from the vocabulary of anthropologist Guillermo Bonfil Batalla.[40]

Forbes maintains that "the so-called 'mestizos' of Anishinabe-waki [the Americas] are nothing more nor less than proletarianized Anishinabe [Indians]...whether the proletarianized detribalized mass is of pure Anishinabe or mixed descent is inconsequential."[41] Following this logic, if Chicanas/os are a class, that is to say, if they are de-tribalized and proletarianized Indians, they may produce particular cultural expressions, but these practices are not class-relations, but rather effects of their class relationships. It makes sense, then, that rasquachismo and domesticana are not "working class" Chicana/o aesthetic theories; rather, they are simply community-based (or I would argue "national") strategies that have been employed by Indigenous people as counterdiscursive modes of resistance to hegemony. There is nothing either essentially working-class or Chicana/o about how domesticana and rasquachismo are enacted; instead, they are purely strategic expressions of an "ethnic" group. But as Ashcroft, Griffiths, and Tiffin argue "the term 'ethnicity'...only achieves wide currency when...'national' groups find themselves as minorities within a larger national groupings, as occurs in the aftermath of colonization."[42] For me then, the question becomes: Are Chicanas/os a class or a nation or both? And if we choose to think of them one-way or another, how does this shift our mode of analysis and potential political strategies?

As colonized and original inhabitants who have subsequently peopled North America through kin-based diaspora, it is helpful to think of Chicanas/os, not as an ethnic community, but as a nation. By doing so we are brought to a re-envisioning of Chicana/o cultural and social history by acknowledging the importance of "national" theories of aesthetics within this history. Although early activist-intellectuals wrote from the position that Chicanas/os were a nation during the 1960s–1970s, the death of the internal-colony model and the academic assimilation of post-structural ambiguity have marginalized most intellectual labor that continues to evoke nation and nationalism within Chicana/o Studies. Instead, Chicanas/os, like many colonized "nations," get inappropriately labeled as an ethnic or minority group and therefore eternally inferior to dominant modes of being.

If we begin to see Chicanas/os as a nation (and better yet an Indigenous nation), then it is quite feasible that there are specific national allegories that emerge from art and culture of the Chicana/o nation. These national allegories, as Fredric Jameson aptly labels them, serve at the core of my research.[43] To date, however, Chicana/o cultural studies have failed to adequately create a framework to analyze Chicana/o cultural practice as national in form. Instead, we have aesthetic paradigms that use class as a cipher for nation, as is the case with both rasquachismo and domesticana. As discussions of national liberation lost currency in the 1970s and 1980s, so too did its application by "legitimate" intellectuals activists. What emerged instead was an incomplete paradigm that evokes class as a cultural category. This trajectory, as can be seen through my radical rhetoric, must be redirected.

Allow me leave you with the following words from Chicano poet Andrés Montoya:

> And where, raza, are our heroes?
> The heroes of Aztlán?
> What became of that great nation
> We were going to build?[44]

With the demise of our present economy and the collective disavowal of capitalism, not to mention shifting demographics in the United States, I propose that a sustained re-analysis of Aztlán as an Indigenous working-class nation and Chicana/o history in general are very much in order.

Skyworld(s): Artists as Warriors

In the end, artists form the core of whom and what may be done to challenge the continued legacy of visual colonization. The words of

Louis Riel, so prophetic in their enunciation, serve to demonstrate how important the work of the Indigenous cultural worker remains today. Chicana/o and Michif artists, like all citizens of the world, are left with a difficult decision when attempting to decipher what to sustain and what to change. Regardless of their intentions, visual artists form the core of any resistance to colonialism. If this insurrection has any sustainable future, we must all recognize its potential. Now that we have awoken, it is the artists who bear our spirit.

Notes

1. In this chapter I prefer to use the nomenclature Michif to refer to the specific tribal group commonly known as the Métis. At times, however I will also apply the terms Métis and Halfbreed. These words each have a distinct and important rhetorical function. Michif is the name that many Michif-speaking Métis use to self-identify. As such, its power lies in its origins within the community. Halfbreed is used by many radical Métis as the means to reclaim the racist language used by Anglo-Canadian. By continuing to evoke this term, Native rhetors have been able to make certain that Euro-Canadians do not forget their own racist past. Finally, Métis is the most commonly used. In recent times, however, the label Métis, Metis, or métis may be used to label any person of mixed aboriginal-European ancestry. As such, it has been destilled of any particular Native context.
2. Fanon, 212.
3. Craven, 27. Original italics.
4. Ibid.
5. Papastergiadis, 467.
6. Walter Mignolo in an e-mail communication with Arturo Escobar. Escobar, 218.
7. Justice, 147–68.
8. Cesaire, 42.
9. Warrior, 4.
10. Hall, 182.
11. Adams, *Tortured People*.
12. Corntassell, 36.
13. Mirzoeff, 55.
14. Ibid., 70.
15. Mignolo, *Local Histories/Global Designs*.
16. Foster, ix.
17. Berger, 7.
18. Mulvey, 44–52.
19. Fry, 47.
20. Ketchum, 359.
21. Justice, 155.
22. Fanon, 212.
23. Cesaire, 44.
24. Cobb, 115–32.
25. Brown, "Métis, Halfbreeds, and Other Real People," 19.
26. Brown, *Strangers In Blood*, 219.
27. Richardson, 60.
28. Brasser, 222.

194   *Dylan A. T. Miner*

29. Vizenor, *Survivance*.
30. Smith, *Decolonizing Methodologies*.
31. Alfred, 84.
32. Forthcoming in Jolene Armstrong, ed., *Maria Campbell: Essays on Her Works* (Toronto: Guernica Editions).
33. McQuire and Papastergiadis, 7.
34. Ybarra-Frausto, 155.
35. Ibid.
36. Ibid., 156.
37. García, 211–23.
38. Mesa-Bains, 158.
39. Ebert and Zavarzadeh, 89.
40. Batalla, *México Profundo*.
41. Jack Forbes, unpublished manuscript, 25.
42. Ashcroft, Griffiths, and Tiffin, 81.
43. Jameson, 65–88.
44. Montoya, 15–17.

Bibliography

Adams, Howard. *Tortured People: The Politics of Colonization*, revised ed. Penicton, BC: Theytus, 1999.
Alfred, Taiaiake. *Peace, Power, Righteousness: An Indigenous Manifesto*. New York: Oxford University Press, 1999.
Armstrong, Jolene, ed. *Maria Campbell: Essays on Her Works*. Toronto: Guernica Editions, forthcoming.
Ashcroft, Bill, Gareth Griffiths, and Helen Tiffin. *Post-Colonial Studies: The Key Concepts*. New York: Routledge, 2001.
Berger, John. *Ways of Seeing*. New York: Penguin, 1977.
Bonfil Batalla, Guillermo. *México Profundo: Reclaiming a Civilization*. Austin: University of Texas Press, 1996.
Brasser, Ted J. "In Search of Métis Art." In *The New Peoples: Being and Becoming Métis in North America*, edited by Jacqueline Peterson and Jennifer S. H. Brown, 221–30. Minneapolis: Minnesota Historical Society, 2001.
Brown, Jennifer S. H. "Métis, Halfbreeds, and Other Real People: Challenging Cultures and Categories." *The History Teacher* 27, no. 1 (1993): 19–26.
———. *Strangers in Blood: Furtrade Families in Indian Country*. Vancouver: University of British Columbia, 1985.
Cesaire, Aimé. *Discourse on Colonialism*. New York: Monthly Review, 2001.
Cobb, Amanda. "Understanding Tribal Sovereignty: Definitions, Conceptualizations, and Interpretation." *American Studies* (Fall 2005): 115–32.
Corntassell, Jeff. "To Be Ungovernable." *New Socialist* 58 (September/October 2006): 35–37.
Craven, David. "Latin American Origins of 'Alternative Modernism.'" *The Third Text Reader on Art, Culture and Theory*. New York: Continuum, 2002. 24–34.
Ebert, Teresa and Ma'sud Zavarzadeh. *Class in Culture*. Boulder, CO: Paradigm, 2007.
Escobar, Arturo. "Beyond the Third World: Imperial Globality, Global Coloniality and Anti-globalisation Social Movements." *Third World Quarterly* 25, no. 1 (2004): 207–30.
Fanon, Frantz. *Wretched of the Earth*. New York: Grove, 1963. 212.
Foster, Hal. *Vision and Visuality*. Seattle: Bay Press, 1988.

Fry, Aaron. "Local Knowledge and Art Historical Methodology: A New Perspective on Awa Tsireh and the San Ildefonso Easel Painting Movement." *Hemisphere: Visual Cultures of the Americas* 1 (Spring 2008): 46–61.

García, Ramón. "Against Rasquache: Chicano Camp and the Politics of Identity in Los Angeles." In *The Chicana/o Cultural Studies Reader*, edited by Angie Chabram-Dernersesian, 211–23. New York: Routledge, 2006.

Hall, Stuart. "The Local and the Global: Globalization and Ethnicity." In *Dangerous Liasons: Gender, Nation, and Postcolonial Perspectives*, edited by Anne McClintock, Aamir Mufti, and Ella Shohat, 173–87. Minneapolis: University of Minnesota Press, 1997.

Jameson, Fredric. "Third-World Literature in the Era of Multinational Capitalism." *Social Text* 15 (1986): 65–88.

Justice, Daniel Heath. "'Go Away, Water!': Kinship Criticism and the Decolonization Imperative." In *Reasoning Together: The Native Critics Collective*, edited by Janice Accose, Lisa Brooks, Tol Foster, 147–68. Norman: University of Oklahoma Press, 2008.

Ketchum, Shann. "Native American Cosmopolitan Modernism(s): A Re-Articulation through Time and Space." *Third Text* 19, no. 4 (July 2005): 357–64.

McQuire, Scott and Nikos Papastergiadis, eds. *Empires, Ruins, and Networks: The Transcultural Agenda*. London: Rivers Oram, 2005.

Mesa-Bains, Amalia. "*Domesticana*: The Sensibility of Chicana Rasquache." In *Distant Relations: Chicano, Irish, Mexican Art and Critical Writings*, edited by Trisha Ziff, ed, 156–63. New York: Smart Art.

Mignolo, Walter. *Local Histories/Global Designs: Coloniality, Subaltern Knowledges, and Border Thinking*. Princeton, NJ: Princeton University Press, 2000.

Mirzoeff, Nicholas. "On Visuality," *Journal of Visual Culture* 5 (2006): 53–79.

Montoya, Andrés. "Locura." *The Iceworker Sings and Other Poems*. Tempe, AZ: Bilingual Review, 1999. 15–17.

Mulvey, Laura. "Visual Pleasure and Narrative Cinema." In *The Feminism and Visual Culture Reader*, edited by Amelia Jones, 44–52. New York: Routledge, 2002.

Papastergiadis, Nikos. "Modernism and Contemporary Art." *Theory, Culture & Society* 22, nos. 2–3 (2007): 466–69.

Richardson, Cathy. "Metis identity Creation and Tactical Responses to Opression and Racism." *Variegations* 2 (2006): 56–71.

Tuhiwai Smith, Linda. *Decolonizing Methodologies: Research and Indigenous Peoples*. London: Zed, 1999.

Vizenor, Gerald. *Survivance: Narratives of Native Presence*. Lincoln: University of Nebraska Press, 2008.

Warrior, Robert Allan. *Tribal Secrets: Recovering American Indian Intellectual Traditions*. Minneapolis: University of Minnesota Press, 1994.

Ybarra-Frausto, Tomás. "Rasquachismo: A Chicano Sensibility." In *Chicano Art: Resistance and Affirmation*, edited by Richard Griswold del Castillo, Teresa McKenna, Yvonne Yarbro-Bejarano, 155–62. Los Angeles: Wight Art Gallery, 1995.

CHAPTER ELEVEN

Spirit Glyphs: Reimagining Art and Artist in the Work of Chicana Tlamatinime

LAURA E. PÉREZ

Fruto del diálogo sostenido con su propio corazón, que ha rumi-
nado, por así decir, el legado espiritual del mundo náhuatl, el artista
comenzará a transformarse en un yoltéotl, "corazón endiosado," o
mejor, movilidad y dinamismo humano orientados por un especie
de inspiración divina.

Fruit of the dialogue sustained with his/her own heart, that has
ruminated, so to speak, the spiritual legacy of the Náhuatl world,
the artist will begin to transform him/herself into a yoltéotl, "a
deified heart," or better, human mobility and dynamism oriented
by a kind of a divine inspiration. [my translation]
—Miguel León-Portilla, *Los antiguos mexicanos
a través de sus crónicas y cantares*

But what, or who, can emerge intact from such traumatic crossings, in response to the passionate call of the originary language,
figured by the drum? Only the black trickster....
—Henry Louis Gates, Jr., *The Signifying Monkey*

The journey of this writing is as much a journey into the past as
it is into the future, a resurrection of the ancient in order to construct the modern. It is a place where prophecy and past meet and
speak to each other.
—Cherríe Moraga, *The Last Generation*

Making Spirit Opposition

It seems that what individuals and groups perceive and represent as the spiritual—that having to do with the s/Spirit(s)—is a socially and politically significant field of differences and contention, as well as of resonances, crossings, and even hybridization.[1] Culturally specific notions of the spiritual circulate unevenly and with different political meaning in the United States. Thus, though we might perhaps be able to generalize the notion of the spiritual sufficiently to speak cross-culturally within and outside of the United States, doing so within Euro-dominated discourse runs the risk of collapsing cultural differences with respect to conception, experience, and representation of the same. The notion of the spiritual that I wish to discuss here as it is invoked and represented in contemporary Chicana writing and visual art derives its inspiration primarily, though not exclusively, from Mesoamerican, other American Indian, and African perceptions of belief, concept, and experience: that there is an essential spiritual nature, and thus an interconnectedness, of all beings, human and nonhuman. Interestingly, this view is also present in less dominant versions of Christianity (e.g., gnosticism) and Judaism (e.g., Kabbala), even as it is among the beliefs that are ascribed significant cultural difference in dominant Euroamerican thought and projected onto people such as U.S. Latina/os, African Americans, and third world populations more generally, as well as onto the rural or "uneducated."

Beliefs and practices consciously making reference to the s/Spirit as the common life force within and between all beings are largely marginalized from serious intellectual discourse as superstition, folk belief, or New Age delusion, when they are not relegated to the socially controlled spaces of the orientalist study of "primitive animism" or of "respectable" religion within dominant culture. Even in invoking the spiritual as a field articulated through cultural differences, and in so doing attempting to displace dominant Christian notions of the spiritual while addressing the fear of politically regressive essentialisms, to speak about the s/Spirit and the spiritual in U.S. culture is risky business that raises anxieties of different sorts.[2] Yet the very discomfort that attends talk of the spiritual outside of authorized and institutionalized spaces (i.e., churches, certain disciplines, old and new Eurocentric ideological and theory orthodoxies) alerts us to a tender zone constituted by the (dis)encounters of culturally different and politically significant beliefs and practices.

To speak of the spiritual with respect to the cultural practices of politically disempowered communities, particularly the work of women, is perhaps even more fraught with dangers. Given this loaded landscape, the invocation of the spiritual in the work of contemporary Chicana writers and visual artists, as a part of an oppositional politics, is especially provocative and ambitious, for, as Ana Castillo writes,

> our long-range objective in understanding ourselves, integrating our fragmented identities, truly believing in the wisdom of our ancient knowledge is to bring the rest of humanity to the fold. That is, today, we grapple with our need to thoroughly understand who we are—gifted human beings—and to believe in our gifts, talents, our worthiness and beauty, while having to survive within the constructs of a world antithetical to our intuition and knowledge regarding life's meaning. Our vision must encompass sufficient confidence that dominant society will eventually give credence to our ways, if the world is to survive. Who in this world of the glorification of material wealth, whiteness, and phallic worship would consider *us* holders of knowledge that could transform this world into a place where the quality of life for all living things on this planet is the utmost priority; where we are all engaged in a life process that is meaningful from birth to death, where we accept death as organic to life, where death does not come to us in the form of one more violent and unjust act committed against our right to live? (148–49)

The linkages within imperialist and racist thinking between the spiritual, the female, and peoples of color are what make the conditions for talking about women, particularly women of color, and the spiritual especially difficult. For, as Marianna Torgovnick writes, "[b]it by bit, thread by thread, the West has woven a tapestry in which the primitive, the oceanic, and the feminine have been banished to the margins in order to protect—or so the logic went—the primacy of civilization, masculinity, and the autonomous self" (212). Regardless of intention, then, it might seem that connections made between the spiritual and women of color finally reproduce dominant narratives about these as the inferior opposites to the rational, Christian, Western European, and male.

The stakes involved in the struggle over these narratives are not small. With respect to the ascription of the magical to Indians in the Putumayo region of Colombia, Michael Taussig has commented: "This

magical attraction of the Indian is not only a cunningly wrought colonial *objet d'art*; it is also a refurbished and revitalized one. It is not just
primitivism but third-world modernism, a neocolonial reworking of
primitivism" (*Shamanism* 172). Nonetheless, the necessity of addressing
the politics of spirituality from the perspective of the "Indian" other of
Eurocentric cultures, and/or of claiming one's belittled spiritual worldview, is crucial to many, particularly if it is a personally and socially
empowering one, and especially if it is so for women.[3] From the viewpoint of many Chicana artists whose work is consciously structured
through references to the spiritual, the struggle for the valorization of
worldviews that dominant cultures imagine as non-Western, and thus
other, is a decolonizing one not only for the colonized, but also for the
colonizer, as the quote from Castillo suggests. Unlike the institutionalized religions that have colluded with patriarchy and class-exploitation,
the spiritualities constructed in contemporary Chicana writing and art
express egalitarian worldviews that are inseparable from questions of
social justice, with respect to class, gender, sexuality, culture, "race,"[4]
and environmental welfare.

Thus, if imperialist and neocolonial states trivialize the spiritual in
politically consequential maneuvers even as they exploit and manipulate belief in the spirit world in performances that Taussig has elsewhere called "the magic of the state,"[5] the "spirit work" of Chicana
writers and artists suggests that the trivialization and privatization of
spiritual belief that is socially empowering to the exploited is, perhaps, the most powerful sleight of hand of all. A politics of spirituality that views human and nonhuman as an interrelated web of
sacred life force is inimical to ideologies of essential difference that
justify subjugation, exploitation, and abuse of "racially" different
peoples and other animate and inanimate life forms. Following Avery
Gordon's recent observations about the political and social significance of the ghostly traces that remain of people, events, and things,
we might speak of the ghostly status of egalitarian forms of spirituality in U.S. culture, whose traces ultimately call for our engagement
and transformation.[6]

Conjuring and reimagining traditions of spiritual belief upon
whose cultural differences discourses of civilization and modernization have justified subjugation and devaluation are conscious acts of
healing the cultural *susto*, that is, the "frightening" of spirit from one's
body-mind in the colonial and neocolonial ordeals, that results in the
"in-between" state of *nepantla*, the postconquest condition of cultural
fragmentation and social indeterminacy.[7] Put in perhaps more familiar

terms, such identification works toward the reintegration of the psyche fragmented by the internalization of loathing of the native self, which Franz Fanon described so vitally for a decolonizing practice in *Black Skin, White Masks*. Braving differing degrees of cultural discontinuity with Amerindian traditions, and opposing a history of gendered vilification and attempted destruction of the "pagan" Indian, African, and Asian philosophical and spiritual worldviews, many contemporary Chicana writers and artists seek to remember, reimagine, and redeploy ideas and practices culled from these as critiques of and alternatives to male-dominated, Christian, Eurocentric, capitalist, and imperialist cultures. Citing the work of Paula Gunn Allen and Gloria Anzaldúa, Norma Alarcón writes:

> For many writers the point is not so much to recover a lost "utopia" nor the "true" essence of our being, although, of course, there are those who long for the "lost origins," as well as those who feel a profound spiritual kinship with the "lost"—a spirituality whose resistant political implications must not be underestimated, but refocused for feminist change. The most relevant point in the present is to understand how a pivotal indigenous portion of the mestiza past may represent a collective female experience as well as "the mark of the Beast" within us—the maligned and abused indigenous woman. By invoking the "dark Beast" within and without, which many have forced us to deny, the cultural and psychic dismemberment that is linked to imperialist and sexist practices is brought into focus. (251)

From this perspective, Chicana writers and artists such as Ester Hernández, Santa Barraza, Yreina D. Cervántez, Patricia González, Celia Rodríguez, Amalia Mesa-Bains, Gloria Anzaldúa, Cherríe Moraga, Pattsi Valdez, Frances Salomé España, Sandra Cisneros, Ana Castillo, Rosa Martha Villarreal, and Kathleen Alcalá engage in what is in fact *curandera* (healer) work: reclaiming and reformulating spiritual worldviews that are empowering to them as women, and that in that same gesture reimage what the social role of art and the artist might be.[8] In this spirit work, Chicana writers and artists interrupt the reproduction of gendered, raced, and sexed politics of spirituality and of art. From a perspective of concern for social, global, and environmental justice, this kind of writing and art rejects politically disempowering European and Euroamerican narratives of the socially useless (i.e., economically unproductive), and thus marginal role of the writer/

artist (see Bürger), and the commodification of art as signifier of cultural capital (see Bourdieu).

In numerous ways that include the invocation and reworking of pre-Columbian Mesoamerican notions of art and art making represented in glyphs, codices, and the figures of the *tlacuilo* (glyphmaker) and the *tlamatini* (sage, decoder of the glyphs), the Chicana artists and writers mentioned earlier are "spirit tongues" of a metadiscourse of art whose social role is more broadly conceived and engaged than that of hegemonic cultures. These writers and artists structure their work like the painter-scribes of Mesoamerica, particularly those of the immediate aftermath of the Spanish invasion, in that the glyphs they trace, like those painted by the Nahua *tlacuilo*, are signs that always point beyond the sign system itself to that which cannot be figured by it. Chicana work inscribing culturally different and politically oppositional views of art and spirituality points beyond Euro-dominated languages and worldviews to the necessity of a more complex hermeneutics, one that is cross-cultural, interdisciplinary, and beyond sexist and heterosexist myopias. Thus, many Chicana artists and writers reenvision culturally potent symbols of gendered, raced, and sexed spirituality, such as the Virgin Mary/*Virgen de Guadalupe* or demonized female Nahua deities such as Coatlicue, into "pre-" or postgendered, powerful and empowering images. They give voice to alternative spiritualities through works referencing beliefs culled from various and diasporic third world cultures circulating in the United States, and/or through creating very personal expressions of spirituality and sanctity, in writing, painting, altar and *caja* installations, performance, video, and other forms.

What is particularly relevant and unique to the "spirit glyphs" of the Chicanas named, and others like them today—particularly given the accelerated and transnational human and nonhuman ravaging by a seemingly omnipotent machine of insatiable greed—is their mapping of pathways beyond the alienation and disempowerment of nepantlism, indeed *back*, though not to some mythical Eden, sign of a hierarchical, jealous, punitive, and male God, but rather to some essential sense of personal wholeness, communal interdependence, purpose, and meaningfulness in the social, global, and cosmic web(s). The conscious identification with politically marginalized and differently spiritual knowledges that bicultural Chicana/os hold alongside many other peoples is hardly nostalgic or reproductive of detrimental racialist essentialisms as progressives fear: it is part of a broader attempt to decisively interrupt the dream of capitalist and imperialist civilizations and see *más allá*, beyond the present structurings of personal, communal, global, and cosmic relations that benefit crucially from our exile from the field of spiritual discourse.

'Membering the Spirit

The politics of the spiritual for some Chicana/os is linked to a politics of memory, as has repeatedly been theorized by artists and thinkers of communities resisting the melting pot's selective dissolution of cultural difference. But unless this be understood as a politically paralyzing nostalgia, and in the face of the cultural discontinuities that characterize much of Chicana/o culture, this is a tactic of remembering that has been understood in the work of the women mentioned earlier, as a reimagining and thus, as a reformulating of beliefs and practices. It is perhaps more precisely a politics of the will to remember: to maintain in one's consciousness, to recall, and to reintegrate a spiritual worldview about the interconnectedness of life, even if it is fragmented, circulating, as its pieces have, through colonial and neocolonial relations. Amalia Mesa-Bains, art critic and scholar, perhaps best known for her altar-installations, considers that

> It is through memory that we construct the bridge between the past and the present, the old and the new. The spiritual memory reflected in the works of contemporary Latino artists is a memory of absence constructed from losses endured in the destructive project of colonialism and its aftermath. This redemptive memory claims a broken reality that is made whole in the retelling. In this context, contemporary art is more than a mirror of history and belief, it is a construction of ideology. Art becomes a social imagination through which essential worldviews and identities are constructed, reproduced, and even redefined. Memory becomes the instrument of redefinition in a politicizing spirituality. (9)

The hybrid spiritualities claimed and practiced in the work of the Chicanas named earlier are, paradoxically, decolonizing cultural appropriations, in part, because the traditions or contemporary practices from American Indian, U.S. Latino, Latin American, and African diasporic cultures from which they draw in their writing and art are politically oppositional to (neo)colonizing cultural and religious systems, but also because some of these traditions have not been altogether interrupted in the memory or practices of Chicana/o culture itself.[9] Cross-cultural

borrowing and refashioning of this kind, a kind of "minority"/Third
World postnational cultural environment from which culturally kin-
dred *forms* are recycled[10] from (neo)colonizations' "waste," attempts to
give expression to what is perceived at heart to be a common worldview. That worldview focuses upon the spiritual nature of all being,
and thus its interconnectedness. It is a view ultimately at odds with the
reigning capitalist culture of extreme exploitation of the planet and
human beings, hierarchically ordered according to degrees of difference with respect to the dominant.

For Gloria Anzaldúa, in her culturally acupunctural[11] *Borderlands/La
Frontera*, a "new mestiza" spirituality is inclusive and affirming of her
multiple positionings as a feminist Chicana lesbian writer. The spiritual
worldview, like the aesthetic of the book, "seems an assemblage, a mon-
tage, a beaded work with several letimotifs and with a central core, now
appearing, now disappearing in a crazy dance" (66) of diverse American
Indian, African, and African diaspora beliefs and practices, recoded
patriarchal Christian and Aztec symbols (e.g., *Virgen de Guadalupe* and
Coatlicue), and culturally relevant translations of archetypal psychology (expressed in her formulation of "the Coatlicue state"). Similarly,
in the face of traditional, patriarchal Catholicism, Ana Castillo speaks
of the right to craft spiritual practices from any traditions that make us
"feel better, that is, stronger willed and self-confident" (147), including
elements from that same belief system. While, in his essay in *Ceremony
of Memory*, Tomás Ybarra-Frausto observes:

> Creative reorganization of traditional religious systems from
> Indigenous and African religions continue in a dynamic pro-
> cess throughout the Spanish-speaking world. Within the United
> States, artists accentuating spiritual domains re-examine, reinter-
> pret and redefine ancestral religious forms with multiple impulses;
> as counterparts to socio-political commentary, as symbolic and
> iconographic systems united to autobiographical exploration or
> as primal icons that illuminate and foreground social conditions.
> Contemporary artists reworking spiritual canons augment their
> power and beauty. New forms of spirituality reverberate with the
> presence and potency of an ancient living ethos expanded with
> modern signification. (12)

Whether remembered through surviving traditional practices or rei-
magined and fused together from chosen traditions, invoking the spiritual in Chicana writing and art is a politically significant, socially

transformative, and psychically healing practice. In considering the work of women such as Kathleen Alcalá, Gloria Anzaldúa, Santa Barraza, Ana Castillo, Yreina D. Cervántez, Sandra Cisneros, Frances Salomé España, Diane Gamboa, Ester Hernández, Amalia Mesa-Bains, Celia Rodríguez, Patricia Rodríguez, Patssi Valdez, and Rosa Martha Villarreal, to name a few among a much larger group of writers and artists, we are pushed even further beyond the increasingly familiar, if still relevant, observations about the survival, resistance, opposition, and transformative powers of the socially abject other. For what also calls for reckoning in the work of these and other Chicana *tlamatinime*, as they are redefining this word, is the very question of the spiritual, understood as the sacred and interconnected nature of self and world, and the empowering effects of that belief/knowledge. In their work, the reality of a politically significant, socially and materially embodied s/Spirit is consciously remembered within it, which we are called to witness and act on, alongside other historically specific and related issues of "race," gender, sexuality, and class.

Spirit Tongues: Glyphs, Codices, and Tlamatinime

Chicana/o art practices in general are historically rooted in the 1960s reclamation of the spiritual within the Chicana/o Movement, as evidenced in nation-forming practices such as the manifesto, "*El Plan Espiritual de Aztlán*," poetry like that of Alurista, the spiritual mitos of Teatro Campesino, writings such as Rudolfo Anaya's novel, *Bless Me, Ultima*, and countless pre-Columbian-themed murals and other visual art. The birth of Chicana/o consciousness through the reclamation and reimagining of the colonially despised Indian self and beliefs is well known in Chicana/o art and scholarship.[12] The work of Miguel León-Portilla, whose important body of scholarship recuperating the literary and philosophical brilliance of the pre-Columbian Nahua peoples can be read as part of the Mexican postrevolutionary project of rehabilitating the Indian legacy of a mestizo national identity in construction has been particularly significant in Chicana/o attempts to integrate the indigenous.[13] His studies of the philosophy and artistic traditions of the Nahua peoples, and his translations of pre- and postconquest codices recording Nahua belief and practices, greatly influenced Chicana/os in books such as his *Aztec Thought and Culture* (1956, Spanish; 1963, English translation) and *Los antiguos mexicanos a través de sus crónicas y cantares* (1961).[14] Distinguishing between the new tradition of the imperialist

Aztecs who burned codices of conquered peoples, rewrote histories, and appropriated cultures and the older, Toltec tradition which they had displaced, and to which they were related, León-Portilla writes,

> Alejados de la visión místico-guerrera de Tlacaél, fueron estos tlamatinime nahuas quienes elaboraron una concepción hondamente poética acerca del mundo, del hombre y de la divinidad.... Valiéndose de una metáfora, de las muchas que posee la rica lengua náhuatl, afirmaron en incontables ocasiones que tal vez la única manera posible de decir palabras verdaderas en la tierra era por el camino de la poesía y el arte que son "flor y canto".... La poesía y el arte en general, "flores y cantos", son para los tlamatinime, expresión oculta y velada que con las alas del símbolo y la metáfora puede llevar al hombre a balbucir, proyectándolo más allá de sí mismo, lo que en forma misteriosa, lo acerca tal vez a su raíz. Parecen afirmar que la verdadera poesía implica un modo peculiar del conocimiento, fruto de auténtica experiencia interior, o si se prefiere, resultado de una intuición. (*Los antiguos* 124–26)

> Removed from the mystico-warrior vision of Tlacaél, it was these Nahua *tlamatinime* who elaborated a deeply poetic conception of the world, [hu]man, and divinity.... Relying upon one of the many metaphors that the rich Náhuatl language possesses, they affirmed on innumerable occasions that perhaps the only possible way to speak truthful words on earth was through the path of poetry and art, which are "flower and song." ... Poetry and art, in general, "flowers and songs," are for the *tlamatinime*, occult and veiled expressions that with the wings of symbol and metaphor can lead a [hu]man to stutter, projecting him/her beyond the self, which in mysterious form, brings him/her closer perhaps to his/her root. They appear to affirm that true poetry implies a peculiar mode of knowledge, fruit of an authentic interior experience, or if one prefers, the result of an intuition. [My translation]

Walter Mignolo has recently pointed to the significant cultural misperceptions that are present in postconquest translations of historically and culturally specific pre-Columbian material practices into the equally specific, European sixteenth-century concepts "*libro*" and "book." In his view,

> the Spanish and the Mexica had not only different material ways of encoding and transmitting knowledge but also—as is

natural—different concepts of the activities of reading and writing. The Mexicas put the accent on the act of observing and telling out loud the stories of what they were looking at (movements of the sky or the black and the red ink). The Spanish stressed reading the word rather than reading the world, and made the letter the anchor of knowledge and understanding. Contemplating and recounting what was on the painting (*amoxtli*) was not enough, from the point of view of the Spanish concept of reading, writing, and the book, to ensure correct and reliable knowledge. (253)

With respect to the distinction between the *tlacuilo* ("*escritores*"/ "scribes") and *tlamatinime* ("*sabios*"/"wise men"), also sometimes erased in translation, he writes:

Was the *tlamatini* also a *tlacuilo*? Apparently not. Those who had the wisdom of the word were those who could "look" at the sky or at the painted books and interpret them, to tell stories based on their discerning of the signs. The oral narrative of the wise men seems to have had a social function as well as a rank superior to the *tlacuilo*, who was placed by Sahagún among those who were skilled craftsmen. (252)

While the crucial question of cultural differences Mignolo is mindful of does not seem to have been lost on writers like Anzaldúa and Moraga or artists like those in the antiquincentary *The Chicano Codices Show: Encountering Art of the Americas* (1992), interestingly, they have appropriated these concepts in ways that suggest the return of what may have been lost in Eurocentric translations. More often than not, they conflate *tlacuilo* and *tlamatinime* in their reimagining of both the writer and artist as glyph-makers; that is, as makers of signs that signify beyond themselves, to significations that are spiritually and politically interdependent and simultaneous, and that hold ancient, alternative knowledges with respect to dominant forms. Chicana artists' collapse of glyph-makers and their sagely readers, the *tlamatinime*, operates through their perception of both through the metaphor of the divinely attuned artist as a "Toltec," wise beyond technical mastery, to a deep sense of the sacred purpose of her or his material practices, and therefore able to move those who behold the work along in the life-long process of "making face, making soul."[15] The Toltec or artist is in this way engaged in teaching and healing, in the sense of mediating greater spiritual growth and well-being of the beholder.[16] Thus, the question raised by Chicana/o writing and art is the reverse of that posed by Mignolo: was the *tlacuilo* perhaps not also a *tlamatini*? And a corollary: within the spiritual worldview of Nahuatl culture that crucially informed "art" practices, did not the social role of the artist exceed that of merely glyph-maker? León-Portilla's translations suggest that guiding the work of conscientious *tlacuilo* and *tlamatini* was concern for the ultimate meaning of their life's work. In this perception, the worthy *tlacuilo*, the "good" glyph-maker, must by necessity also be a spiritually guided sage. Conversely, the codices suggest that the *tlamatini* was also a *tlacuilo*, schooled in the painting of glyphs, like other select members of society.[17]

When writers and artists refer to themselves as *tlamatini* and to their work as glyphs or codices of our own times, like Anzaldúa in *Borderlands*, the artists in *The Chicano Codices* show, and Moraga in "Codex Xeri," they are reimagining art and artist along broader social parameters, for in themselves glyphs, codices, and the words *"tlacuilo"* and *"tlamatini"* are signs that point beyond modern, Eurocentric cultural conceptions of art and artist. They point to different systems of reading visual signs, that is, to different ways of knowing, and even more, to the insufficiency of one system of signs (visual, oral, performative) to convey meaning and "truths" fully. Old and new glyphs point to necessary semiotic counterparts. They call for broader cultural readings, such as those constituted in the *tlamatini's* performance of decipherment, that take into account the space and occasion, as well as the knowledge specifically coded in the pictographs or ideograms.[18] Glyphs rooted in Mesoamerican worldviews are signs meant to point beyond themselves to that which is outside of verbal and visual language, including the realm of the spiritual. Art and writing by the Chicana women mentioned attempts to access the codices on some or all of these registers, as signs of alternative spiritual and material knowledges and practices.

New scholarship, such as the collection in which Mignolo's article appears, criticizes Eurocentric histories of writing that culminate in alphabetical systems, and has begun to consider the difference of Native American writing systems more positively, and to consider its implications for modern Western ways of knowing. In the estimation of Gordon Brotherston, for example, *"tlacuilloli*, that which is produced with a brush-pen by the painter-scribe.... integrat[es] into one holistic statement what for us are the separate concepts of letter, picture, and arithmetic, [Mesoamerican iconic script] positively flouts received Western notions of writing" (50). Even more suggestively, philosopher and magician David Abram observes: "the glyphs which constitute the bulk of these ancient scripts [Chinese and Mesoamerican] continually remind the reading body of its inherence in a more-than-human field of meanings. As signatures not only of the human form but of other animals, trees, sun, moon, and landforms, they continually refer our senses beyond the strictly human sphere" (6).

Most precortesian *amoxtli* (painted, screenfold "books") were destroyed during the Spanish Conquest in a devastation that has been compared to the burning of the library in Alexandria.[19] Most of the codices that are held in the West were written postconquest. Schooled in both their traditional Nahuatl culture and the Renaissance culture of written and visual representation in which the missionaries wished them to record their traditional knowledges (see Gruzinski), newly Hispanized "scribes" wrote/painted amidst the devastation and transformation of their cultures and their identities, indeed of their art and social function, in the postconquest state of *nepantla*. However, if the processes of colonialism in Mesoamerica involved the cultural and psychic alienation of the native self through the Catholic Church's "deployment of the penitential system, with its sacramental confession, and most importantly, its imposition of self-forming tactics of intro-spection," as Klor de Alva argues in "Contar vidas [Telling Lives]" (74), then the rebirth, so to speak, of the Chicana *tlamatinime*, the keepers and imaginers of the kinds of native knowledges persecuted by the institutions of exploitative power, maps pathways beyond nepantlism, through "confessions" that like that of their Nahua ancestors, may also be read as testimonies of the failure of European governments and religions to fully displace native culture and belief systems and reconstitute their subjectivity through colonization.

Beyond the Susto of Nepantla: Culture Cures

Chicana writing and art hybridizes the different cultural meanings and functions of preconquest "books," or *amoxtli* (as imagined and understood through scholars like León-Portilla), postconquest codices, and contemporary books and art work. As in the stylistically hybrid works of the first-generation, postconquest codices described by Serge Gruzinski, in Chicana writing and art we see the complex rework-ings of the technologies and belief systems of the imposed dominat-ing culture and the parallel inscription of alternative knowledges and practices.[20] What follows are sightings of the different ways in which *la cultura cura* (culture cures) in contemporary "spirit glyphs" of Chicana writing and visual art practices.

In Anzaldúa's *Borderlands*, image and written or spoken word are inseparably linked, as image and spoken word are in the functioning of the Mesoamerican glyph (pictograph/ideogram). In a chapter titled "*Tlilli, Tlapalli*/The Path of the Red and Black Ink," she writes that "[t]o write, to be a writer, I have to trust and believe in myself as a speaker, as a voice for the images," and that when writing, "it feels like I'm creating my own face, my own heart—a Náhuatl concept. My soul makes itself through the creative act" (73). "The stress of living with cultural ambiguity" also allows her, as a "mestiza writer," to be a "*nahual*, an agent of transformation, able to modify and shape primordial energy and therefore able to change herself and others into turkey, coyote, tree, or human" (74). From Anzaldúa's cultural perspective, writing is an image-making practice, that as such can indeed shape and transform what we imagine, are able to perceive, and are able to give material embodiment. Understood, therefore, is the great responsibility and sacredness of the very real and consequential "transformative power" wielded by the image-makers, which literally "makes face, makes soul" in a reading process understood to be part of a larger performance. Following Robert Plant Armstrong's study of the cultural difference and "power of affecting presence" of African masks and statues, Anzaldúa speaks of her work as "invoked art," a being imbued with spiritual presence and power, unlike art that concerns itself primarily with aesthetic and technical virtuosity:

> My "stories" are acts encapsulated in time, "enacted" every time they are spoken aloud or read silently. I like to think of them as performances and not as inert and "dead" objects (as the aesthetics of Western culture think [*sic*] of art works). Instead, the work has an identity; it is a "who" or a "what" and contains the presences of persons, that is, incarnations of gods or ancestors or natural and cosmic powers. The work manifests the same needs as a person, it needs to be "fed," *la tengo que bañar y vestir.*
>
> When invoked in rite, the object/event is "present"; that is, "enacted," it is both a physical thing and the power that infuses it. It is metaphysical in that it "spins its energies between gods and humans" and its task is to move the gods. This type of work dedicates itself to managing the universe and its energies.... Invoked art is communal and speaks of everyday life. It is dedicated to the validation of humans; that is, it makes people hopeful, happy,

secure, and it can have negative effects as well, which propel one towards a search for validation. (67)

Anzaldúa understands the image-making process not only through the sacred and shamanic aspects of the *tlamatinime/tlacuilo*'s path of writing and wisdom that the red and black inks signify, but also through James Hillman's archetypal psychology in *Re-Visioning Psychology*, from whom she also selectively draws in conceptualizing identity as multiple, and in reimagining the role of art and artist. In an interesting resonance with Mesoamerican thought, for example, Hillman writes, "Because our psychic stuff is images, image-making is a *via regia*, a royal road to soul-making. The making of soul-stuff calls for dreaming, fantasying, imagining.... [T]o be in touch with soul means to live in sensuous connection with fantasy. To be in soul is to experience the fantasy in all realities and the basic reality of fantasy" (23). Like Hillman's, Anzaldúa's interest in the image is both as sign of the language of the soul and as mediator of the growth of the soul or soul-making.

Her truly important book may itself be thought of as a glyph pointing beyond the cultural and psychological location of *nepantla* by seeing that "in between" space *al revés*, in reverse: as powerful, indeed, as emblematic of the nature of being and meaning. Her perception of the greater meaning of the resonances in different kinds of experiences of marginalization (e.g., geographical, cultural, psychological, spiritual, and sexual borderlands) is a politically significant re-envisioning of interrelated cultural discourses of history, location, and identity that produce hierarchical orderings of difference. As the title of the book suggests, the borderlands are not invoked as yet another valuable, but peripheral, resource in the center's production of meaning. Rather, "borderlands" becomes a sign of the centrality of the marginalized, the mutable, and the unarticulated in the construction of fuller, and not merely partial and self-reflecting, knowledges and identities. Thus, through the glyph of the borderlands, Anzaldúa points away from too literal an identification with the signs of individual and collective identities, toward ways of knowing that allow for the complexity of that which exceeds language and which, crucially, allows us to re-envision other versions of self and reality. To this end, she also returns to the center of our vision the importance of marginalized ways of knowing through our spirits. "*La facultad*," for example, and other forms of "inner knowledge," affirm the "divine within" (50), as well as the "supernatural" (49) or "the spirit world" (38), and represent alternative forms of perception ("seeing" 39, 42, 45) and "other mode[s] of consciousness" (37), and thus, other epistemologies and paths of knowledge (37, 42) than the rational as it is understood and privileged in Euroamerican and European dominant cultures.[21]

The widely circulating *Woman Hollering Creek and Other Stories* by Sandra Cisneros, offers another interesting refiguration of the glyph. The story "Little Miracles, Kept Promises," itself functions as an ex-voto, the visual and written sign left by the faithful as material testimony of the miraculous, that is, of the presence and intervention of spiritual power.[22] The story is thus made up of the different testimonies of faith in the spiritual, as represented by various saints, including the mestiza *Virgen de Guadalupe*, long since redefined by Chicanas through the Mesoamerican goddess Tonantzin, an aspect of Coatlicue.[23] One such testimony is crafted by Chayo, disaffected from Catholicism, and particularly from its oppression of women through the image and discourse of "Mary the mild." She writes a letter to the Virgin of Guadalupe, bearing witness to the huge *milagrito* (little miracle) of a newfound and empowering faith:

> I don't know how it all fell in place. How I finally understood who you are.... When I could see you in all your facets, all at once the Buddha, the Tao, the true Messiah, Yahweh, Allah, the Heart of the Sky, the Heart of the Earth, the Lord of the Near and Far, the Spirit, the Light, the Universe, I could love you, and, finally, learn to love me. (128)

The recuperation of a spirituality empowering to women not being one of the usually celebrated miracles in Latin American and U.S. Latina/o communities where *mestizo*-identity sways toward the Eurocentric, Chayo cannot choose from the common stock of human-body part and animal medallions referring to the afflicted and now healed self or property, but must create her own image or *milagrito* to accompany her letter of gratitude. Thus, in an eloquent and feminist glyph, Chayo offers her braid of hair, symbol of her body's gendering and racialization, in a sacrifice that understandably leaves her "heart buoyant" (125).

"Codex Xeri," published originally in *The Chicano Codices: Encountering Art of the Americas* and then in *The Last Generation: Prose & Poetry*, offers another important re-articulation of pre-Columbian notions of art and art making. Cherríe Moraga specifically identifies herself and these two writings with the last generation of conquest-era *tlamatinime* that not only witnessed the subjugation of their world, but more positively, that succeeded in transmitting their worldviews through the codices they left, as her work exemplifies. In the Introduction to *The Last Generation*, Moraga figures her writing as prayer, codex, prophecy, "a resurrection of the ancient in order to construct the modern," as picture book, as "queer mixture of glyphs," and as writing that responds to the political urgency of the times. For her, the prophetic, seeing with the mystical third eye (137), is the politically significant heart of writing and art making, particularly in the present times where selfishness, violence, and greed could make this the planet's last generation. Thus, she writes:

> As a Latina artist I can choose to contribute to the development of a docile generation of would-be Republican "Hispanics" loyal to the United States, or to the creation of a force of "disloyal" americanos who subscribe to a multicultural, multilingual, radical re-structuring of América. Revolution is not only won by numbers, but by visionaries, and if artists aren't visionaries, then we have no business doing what we do. (56)

Like Anzaldúa, her invocation of the *tlamatinime*, glyphs, and codices, is not a nostalgic inscription of cultural difference meant as a sign of resistance to cultural imperialism, but rather through these, Moraga attempts to "disenchant" and re-empower artists through the recognition of the political power of their vision as it is externalized in their work. In "Codex Xeri," which closes both the exhibition catalog and her own book, she states:

> The Chicano scribe remembers, not out of nostalgia but out of hope. She remembers in order to envision. She looks backward in order to look forward to a world founded not on greed, but on respect for the sovereignty of nature....
> As it was for the tlamatinime centuries ago, the scribe's task is to interpret the signs of the time, read the writing on barrio walls, decode the hieroglyphs of street violence, unravel the skewed message of brown-on-brown crime and sister-rape. The Chicano codex is *our* book of revelation. It is the philosopher's stone, serpentine and regenerative. It prescribes our fate and releases us from it. It understands the relationship between darkness and dawn. "*Mira que te has de morir. Mira que no sabes cuándo.*" (190–91)[24]

"Codex Makers" are therefore also *tlamatinime*, whose tasks are to remember, envision, and inscribe their readings of the meaning of the cultural signs of their day in illuminating and transformative ways.

In Frances Salomé España's videos, *El Espejo/The Mirror* (1987), *Anima* (1989), and *The Confessions Trilogy* (1997), which includes *Spitfire*, *Vivir*, and *Nepantla*, a space imbued with spirit is created, or perhaps facilitated, if we follow Andrei Tarkovsky's comparison of his filmic craft to that of "sculpting in time," where the being within the material is allowed to emerge and it is the artist's job to cut away the excess as much as it is to envision the final work's form within the marble (qtd. in Tucker 260). España's video art might be said to record such sightings of spirit.[25] If the colonial and neocolonial photographic/filmic eye historically "steals" or occludes the spirit of American Indian and third world subjects in visual narratives that render them objects in a European discourse of otherness, España's video work operates through the opposite principle. From an experimental poetics, España's film language returns spirit to the tribe,[26] allowing us to perceive spiritual presence and power, and within this culturally transformative framework, illuminates Latina womanhood in its complexity, integrity, and beauty.

The Confessions Trilogy may be read as a series of *vislumbramientos*, as illuminations, rather than received or resolved narratives about Latina women. Images of women, particular gestures, and culturally resonant symbols are slowly, purposefully returned to over and over again, thus constructing meaning in rich, glyph-like fashion as oblique and multiply layered. España's *Trilogy*, like the other two video works mentioned earlier, allows us to look again, to look more carefully, and perhaps as well to perceive more intuitively, with a greater range of intelligences at work than those sanctioned in dominant cultures. The last piece of the trilogy, *Nepantla*, for example, might be more accurately described as a third *acercamiento*, as another and a different approach to the image making of Latinas in relation to *Spitfire* and *Vivir* rather than their resolution. As in the first two videos of the trilogy, in *Nepantla*, a "live" woman and a historically received image of Latina femaleness shadow each other, their identity articulated and disarticulated in a resonant gesture. Here, viewed in slow motion, a Los Angeles-style, punkish Latina dances, chain-clad arms flailing in an image reminiscent of an *ánima en pena*, a shackled female soul amidst the flames of purgatory. The contemporary Latina, however, moves with pleasure on her face as she looks into the camera. In a white, fifties-style party dress, black high-heeled platform sandals, dark makeup, leather belts and chains, she appears a kind of urban angel, at once powerful and vulnerable. Another scene shows her moving away from a white wall on which hangs a black girdle. Through repetition in slow motion and freezing at different moments, that same movement begins to look and read differently. It begins to appear that she is stuck, for "every time" she steps away, she is sucked back into a space where that black girdle is in full view again and increasingly visible (to some readers) as a symbol of bodily and social constrictions. While clearly not concerned with constructing linear narratives or new paradigmatic images of Latina women, España's grounded angel suggests alternative narratives to the culturally loaded and gendered image of a penitent soul represented as female. Perhaps the angelic is subjected to the purgatory of *nepantla* because of a flesh coded sinful in traditionally Christian, male-dominated, Eurocentric cultures.

Yreina Cervántez's *Nepantla* (1995) lithograph triptych, like España's, destabilizes racist and sexist histories of representation that inform the field of visual arts in which she works. She too reinscribes alternative and healing visions of reality that can further the making of face and soul for both minority- and dominant-culture viewers. The first piece introduces nepantlism as the ongoing struggle between two cultural legacies, as revealed in their different ways of seeing: that of an ostensibly universal, European scientific perspective that measures difference in descending order against the standard of European man, and that of American Indian worldviews, represented by several objects symbolic of the spiritual nature of all being, such as a feather, sage, and the Nahua glyph *ollin*, signifying harmoniously balanced differences. The image of a humanoid skeleton on all fours, repeated throughout the lithograph, brings to mind racialist narratives about the unequal evolutionary development of humans and cultures. The pretensions to objectivity of such culturally biased views and their generalization are revealed in the reproduction of a lithograph from *The Annals of San Francisco* (1855), presumably illustrating the "civilized and employed" Indian, the "Partly civilized Indian," and "A Wild Indian," as the caption states. Directly beneath that image, the reproduction of a newspaper clipping reports on California Governor Pete Wilson's anti-immigration politics, accompanied by a photograph of protestors demonstrating against Proposition 187. Floating somewhere between these two images is a passage from León-Portilla's *Endangered Cultures*, which reads:

> The violent attacks against the indigenous religion and traditions, the death of the gods, and the difficulty in accepting the new teachings as true had already affected the people deeply and had brought about, as a consequence, the appearance of nepantlism.

The concept of nepantlism, "to remain in the middle," one of the greatest dangers of culture contact ruled by the desire to impose change, retains its full significance, applicable to any meaningful understanding of similar situations.

Further text from *Endangered Cultures* appears beneath a photograph of student protestors at UCLA, in the lower left hand of the lithograph, as does the Nahua glyph, *ollin*, symbol of balanced dualities:

In an attempt to escape nepantlism, even while amid the dangers that continue to threaten its onset, the Chicanos' response and their aim are to define their identity as a base from which to orient their actions and their interactions, and thus to make their demands heard.

A large portion of the lithograph is occupied by a drawing of the artist's upper body, her face looking directly out at the viewer, and holding up and perhaps out, a sprig of sage, an herb used in many healing ways, including purification ceremonies. Beneath her is the drawing of a feather. Above her, a drawing of a clay mask from about 1000 B.C. unearthed in Tlatlilco, Mexico, one of the oldest records of the perspective (León-Portilla, *La filosofía* fig. 17) of the balanced duality of life and death. Above this image, and rather dwarfed by it, is a perspective schema of the type developed during the Renaissance by artists as an attempt to rationalize the artistic point of view.[27]

Various images representing the artist appear as a composite self-portrait in the second lithograph, *Mi Nepantla*. The most prominent of these is from a computerized photograph of the artist in which her eyes are closed, as if in meditation. On her cheeks she bears glyphs associated with Coyolxauqui, the warrior daughter of Coatlicue, dismembered by her brother, Tezcatlipoca, and re-membered in the figure of the moon. At the level of her brain is a ghostly image from *Nepantla*, here in blue ink, of the skeleton of the less-than-human figure, that, from a racist perspective and her internalization of it, must also represent her. Within the humanoid's view is the word "DECOLONIZATION" against a red field. Alongside the photographic image of the artist's face is the typeset word "Perspective," and, as a kind of mirror image of this, handwritten in Spanish, and underlined in red, "*no es mi perspectiva.*" Incorporating written texts as in the other two pieces, this lithograph contains two poems, "*Como Unión*" (Like Union/I Eat Union) and its culturally different translation, "Come Union," by Los Angeles poet Gloria Enedina Alvárez, as well as a portion from Anzaldúa's *Borderlands* on the new mestiza's tolerance for ambiguity and transformation of contradiction.

Another cultural text whose reproduction signifies contradiction in the self-portrait is an engraving by one of the "fathers" of the rationalization of perspective, Albrecht Dürer (1471–1528), in which a seated European male scientifically draws the reclining figure of a seminude woman through a "window" grid. Cervántez comments ironically on the Eurocentric and male perspective recorded in the lithograph by juxtaposing a photograph of herself with the female nude's head. The word "Nepantla" is handwritten in red, directly beneath the figure of the woman. Below this is another perspective schema occupied by the Nahuatl glyph for the physically and spiritually dead: a bound, veiled *bulto* (bundle). At the lower right border of the lithograph, and pacing out and away from it, is the image of Cervántez's own *nagualito*, or animal/spirit helper, the jaguar. Other images also appear here, among these, the drawing of the artist from the first piece that is repeated with some variations in the other two lithographs, of her looking out at the viewer, sage in hand.

In *Beyond Nepantla*, the image that dominates our view is a circle made by the spiral of the feathered serpent, the glyph of Quetzalcoatl, symbol of both wisdom and the arts, and the unity of the spiritual and the materialized.[28] The symbol of the circle brings to mind Paula Gunn Allen's observations regarding the difference between Christian European and American Indian perspectives in *The Sacred Hoop*:

> Another difference between these two ways of perceiving reality lies in the tendency of the American Indian to view space as spherical and time as cyclical, whereas the non-Indian tends to view space as linear and time as sequential. The circular concept requires all "points" that make up the sphere of being to have a significant identity and function, while the linear model assumes that some "points" are more significant than others. In the one, significance is a necessary factor of being in itself, whereas in the other, significance is a function of placement on an absolute scale that is fixed in time and space. (59)

Other objects representing different Indian cultures also mark this last piece, including an *ollin* glyph and the image in reverse of the artist holding the healing herb. The three "kinds" of Indians referred to in *Nepantla* reappear, ordered according to degrees of Europeanization, but now contextualized from Indian cultural perspectives represented both by the images described and others that dominate the lithograph.

While the effects of colonial histories and continued neocolonial practices are as difficult to erase as the inscriptions on stone made in the lithographic process, Cervántez's work suggests that perhaps what they represent or narrate may be transformed in viewing them from the nonhierarchical, circular perspectives of American Indian and other cultures. Indeed, perception and meaning are constructed in the *Nepantla* series in multiple layers and through the signifying systems of different cultures, in a process that, like that of *Borderlands*, argues for the value of expanding our perspectives, particularly with respect to cultural difference. Finally, perhaps, Cervántez's work operates as an offering, hybridizing or broadening dominant cultural and visual politics under the glyph of balanced dualities.

Más Allá: Cosmic Cruising

The path beyond both nepantlism and Eurocentrism in Cervántez's *Nepantla* series thus appears to be in the reviewing of humanist cultural awareness from a broader perspective of the sacred interconnectedness of all being, here embodied in Amerindian cultures, a reviewing that describes many worldviews, including contemporary nondominant European views and historically earlier ones. Beyond historically specific cultural differences, Ester Hernández also works to restore at the center a perspective of larger consciousness. *Mis Madres* (1986) and *Cosmic Cruise/Paseo Cósmico* (1990) represent American Indian and Latina women at the center of the cosmos. In *Mis Madres*, an American Indian or mestiza Elder holds up the planet in her left hand. She glows, made up of the very stuff of the stars and the cosmos around her. The size and silhouette of her figure convey a sense of sacredness about her that is reinforced by her celestial pigmentation. Hernández's silkscreen inscribes into the cultural consciousness of the beholder the existence and, indeed, the centrality and sacredness of the American Indian, the female, and the Elder.

Cosmic Cruise/Paseo Cósmico embeds a personal history, recounted elsewhere by Amalia Mesa-Bains (The Mexican Fine Arts Center Museum 58), of the artist's mother as the first woman to drive in her agricultural labor camp, and then reinscribes the symbol of this narrative against the cosmos, symbol of time and space realities different from dominant notions of these with respect to our planet. The historically specific memory of the significance of the Chicana female-driven and occupied Model-T in *Cosmic Cruise*, like all of the works referred to thus far in this chapter, might perhaps be read simultaneously as a glyph of the greater spiritual significance of our movements through culturally multiple notions of time-space.

The truly healing work of Chicana *tlamatinime*, such as those I have named earlier in the chapter, or briefly discussed in this last section, indeed redefines the social role of art and artist in more complex, more ambitious, and more politically and spiritually significant ways than are culturally dominant in the United States and other parts of the world. They create culturally hybrid art practices that I have signified through the glyph and codex that are neither about nostalgia nor mere resistance to cultural imperialism, but rather about transforming a familiar present whose reality is destructive to individual, community, and planet. The visionary and prophetic quality of their work is politically and historically significant, as is their returning to our field of vision a politically oppositional spiritual consciousness of the interconnection and meaningfulness of all being.

Notes

1. For, as communications theorist H. L. Goodall, Jr., puts it:

   Spirit, it seems, is best read as a sign that means to be taken as deeper clue.... To move toward the unifying awareness of Spirit in our ordinary, everyday texts; social texts; and communal texts is to grant voice to the creative powers of imagination and interpretation, from which emerges a fuller body for experiential knowing capable of sustaining not only a rhetoric for the ordinary, the ritualized, and the rational, but one ready to embrace a poetics of the extraordinary, the intuited, the felt, and the lived. From this unifying awareness comes the possibility for genuine holistic dialogue, a dialogue capable of learning from the body of experience without denying to Others what has not been bodily experienced for oneself, a dialogue in which the full measure of truth is found only in the quality of our lives. (213)

2. For, as Janice Hocker Rushing puts it: "Spirit was thus revealed by Nietzsche to have died, by Marx as a pretense to maintain political domination by the ruling classes, by Freud as an illusory and neurotic hedge against the finality of death, by feminists as an excuse for male domination, and by poststructuralists as the illusory transcendental signifier" (qtd. in Goodall 212).

3. In Paula Gunn Allen's view,

   We as feminists must be aware of our history on this continent. We need to recognize that the same forces that devastated the gynarchies of Britain and the Continent also devastated the ancient African civilizations, and we must know that those same materialistic, antispiritual forces are presently engaged in wiping out the same gynarchical values, along with the peoples who adhere to them, in Latin America. I am convinced that those wars were and continue to be about the imposition of patriarchal civilization over the holistic, pacifist, and spirit-based gynarchies they supplant. To that end the wars of imperial conquest have not been solely or even mostly waged over the land and its resources, but they have been fought within the bodies, minds, and hearts of the people of the earth for dominion over them. I think this is the reason traditionals say we must remember our origins, our cultures, our histories, our mothers and grandmothers, for without that memory, which implies continuance rather than nostalgia, we are doomed to engulfment by a paradigm that is fundamentally inimical to the vitality, autonomy, and self-empowerment essential for satisfying, high-quality life. (214)

4. As Henry Louis Gates, Jr. states,

    Race, as a meaningful criterion within the biological sciences, has long been recognized to be a fiction. When we speak of "the white race" or "the black race," "the Jewish race" or "the Aryan race," we speak in biological misnomers and, more generally, in metaphors. Nevertheless, our conversations are replete with usages of race which have their sources in the dubious pseudoscience of the eighteenth and nineteenth centuries.... The sense of difference defined in popular usages of the term "race" has both described and inscribed differences of language, belief system, artistic tradition, and gene pool, as well as all sorts of supposedly natural attributes such as rhythm, athletic ability, cerebration, usury, fidelity, and so forth. The relation between "racial character" and these sorts of characteristics has been inscribed through tropes of race, lending the sanction of God, biology, or the natural order to even presumably unbiased descriptions of cultural tendencies and differences. ("Editor's Introduction" 4–5)

5. See Taussig, *The Magic of the State.*

6. "The ghost always registers the actual 'degraded present' in which we are inextricably entangled and the longing for the arrival of a future, entangled certainly, but ripe in the plentitude of nonsacrificial freedoms and exuberant unforeseen pleasures.... [b]ecause ultimately haunting is about how to transform a shadow of a life into an undiminished life" (Gordon 207–8).

7. "The words of a Náhuatl Indian from the middle of the sixteenth century refer to the risks, so closely related to cultural identity, that can present themselves in attempts at inducing acculturation. A Dominican friar, Diego Durán, had reprimanded a native for his behavior, pointing out that it was also in discord with the ancient indigenous customs and morals. The wise old native responded: 'Father, don't be afraid, for we are still *"nepantla"'* [*sic*]—in other words, 'in the middle,' or as he later added, 'we are neutral'" (León-Portilla, *Endangered Cultures* 10).

8. "Perhaps the most prominent contemporary archetypal heroine in Chicana literature is the *curandera/partera* (healer/midwife) who is also the *bruja* (witch). As do most complex symbols, the *curandera/bruja* encodes both positive and negative attributes.... The *curandera* possesses intuitive and cognitive skills, and her connection to and interrelation with the natural world is particularly relevant. She emerges as a powerful figure throughout Chicano writing" (Rebolledo 83). Also interesting to bear in mind with respect to *curanderismo* are the conclusions of a study of Mexican American "folk" healing practices: "Indeed, the study of *curanderismo* questions specific techniques, philosophies, and goals of contemporary dynamic psychotherapy, which may have developed more for their compatibility with the ethos and value system of our own [*sic*] culture than for any well-founded scientific reason" (Kiev 179). Kiev later states, "Finally, there is no evidence that dynamic psychotherapy is of more value than such forms of treatment as *curanderismo*" (183).

9. "Like the ancients, I worship the rain god and the maize goddess, but unlike my father I have recovered their names" (Anzaldúa, *Borderlands* 90).

10. With respect to the discursive power of what she calls "third-degree kitsch" in postmodern art that incorporates religious imagery, Celeste Olalquiagua notes that

    Besides imploding the boundaries of art and reality, the third degree carries out an active transformation of kitsch. Taking religious imagery both for its kitsch value and its signifying and iconic strength, it absorbs the icon in full and recycles it into new meanings. These meanings are related to personal spiritual experiences, recalling users' relationships to first-degree [kitsch] imagery, except that the first-degree images are part of a given cultural heritage and as such they are readily available and their usage is automatic. Third-degree kitsch, on the other hand, appropriates this tradition from "outside," searching for an imagery that will be adequate to its expressive needs.... Instead of appropriation annihilating what it absorbs, the absorbed invades the appropriating system and begins to constitute and transform it....Rather than of active or passive cultures, one can now speak of mutual appropriation. (52–54)

11. From Richard feather Anderson's "Geomancy":
Until recent times every structure was situated with regard for the patterns of biomagnetic energy within the earth's body. Geomancers were employed to maintain the most beneficial flow of ch'i within the veins of the earth's body, variously known as dragon paths or energy ley-lines. It was taboo in earth-centered cultures to sever these vital channels, for the same reason that it is suicidal to cut our own arteries. Where the flow of earth ch'i has stagnated, "earth acupuncture" procedures can be used to stimulate the ch'i. Some earth mysteries researchers believe that the megalithic standing stones of Europe may have functioned as acupuncture needles for the planet. (198)

12. See Klor de Alva, "California Chicano"; Ybarra-Fausto, "Alurista's Poetics"; and Anaya.

13. My thanks to Norma Alarcón for reminding me of the significance of the political climate in which León-Portilla's scholarship arose.

14. See Klor de Alva, "California Chicano." The scholar's translations in *Aztec Thought and Culture* were also quoted in an important anthology, *Aztlán: An Anthology of Mexican American Literature* edited by Valdez and Steiner, in the section "The Toltec (The Artist): He Makes Things Live" (347–53).

15. See León-Portilla, *Los antiguos* 146–54. This is a concept that Anzaldúa appropriates and redefines in the anthology she edited, *Making Face, Making Soul.* "'Making faces' is my metaphor for constructing one's identity. '[U]sted es el modeador [sic] de su carne tanto como el de su alma.' You are the shaper of your flesh as well as of your soul. According to the ancient *nahuas*, one was put on earth to create one's 'face' (body) and 'heart' (soul). To them, the soul was a speaker of words and the body a doer of deeds" (xvi). It is interesting to compare these understandings with that of Roger Lipsey in *An Art of Our Own*:
Oneself as one might be. The reminder of what one has forgotten is a call to action. The spiritual in art offers a transient experience of intensity, of a larger world and larger self. One begins to care again, reawakened to old longings, to remorse, perhaps to new thoughts and feelings, almost always to a clarified sense of direction. This blend of hope and remorse is a sign that one has encountered the spiritual in art....The spiritual in art makes its contribution to the pilgrim's halting progress. It is a resource for those who look beyond, understand that there is work to do, and undertake it. (16)

16. On the Toltec/artist see León-Portilla, *Native Mesoamerican Spirituality* 208; on the *tlamatinime*, see León-Portilla, Los antiguos 62, 123–25; and *Native Mesoamerican Spirituality* 200.

17. As Joyce Markus points out,
The *calmecac* (literally, "row of houses") was a set of priestly residences associated with the temples of Tenochtitlán. Children of nobles were brought here by their parents to receive an education in the priesthood. Chronicles differ on whether children entered the *calmecac* at age four or fifteen. Apparently, some promising commoner children could be enrolled by parents who wanted them to enter the priesthood, but they appear to have been a very small minority. In the Florentine Codex, Sahagún makes clear the association of the *calmecac* with the education of well-born members of the society.

The *calmecac* curriculum apparently included astrology, star lore, divination and the calendars, hieroglyphic writing, and "life's history" *(nemiliz tlacuilolli)*; it is here that future scribes (not to mention priests and diviners) were started on their career trajectory. All nobles, including future rulers, received their education in one of the six or more *calmecac* located in Tenochtitlán. Following some years of education there, all those entering administration, law, or other important governmental positions would share a working knowledge of those subjects, including the use and role of the hieroglyphic writing. (50–51)

18. As Paula Gunn Allen states,

The formal structure of a ceremony is as holistic as the universe it purports to reflect and respond to, for the ceremony contains other forms such as incantation, song (dance), and prayer, and it is itself the central mode of literary expression from which all allied songs and stories derive. The Lakota view all the ceremonies as related to one another in various explicit and implicit ways, as though each were one face of a multifaceted prism. This interlocking of the basic forms has led to much confusion among non-Indian collectors and commentators, and this complexity makes all simplistic treatments of American Indian literature more confusing than helpful. Indeed, the non-Indian tendency to separate things from one another—be they literary forms, species, or persons—causes a great deal of unnecessary difficulty with and misinterpretation of American Indian life and culture. It is reasonable, from an Indian point of view, that all literary forms should be interrelated, given the basic idea of unity and relatedness of all the phenomena of life. Separation of parts into this or that category is not agreeable to American Indians, and the attempt to separate essentially unified phenomena results in distortion. (62)

19. "Thanks to Christian incendiarism and the ravages of time, the once copious libraries of these books are now represented by no more than thirty or so texts" (Brotherston 50).

20. Gruzinski writes,

[T]he effort to unite two cultures (often turning the conquerors' culture to the advantage of the conquered) is probably easiest to detect in the realm of images and pictographs. The creation of a twin system of expression—pictographic and alphabetical—was not merely a sign of compromise or collaboration. It also represented discovery of new formal strategies for preserving two living traditions side by side. At the same time that they mastered Latin and massively adopted writing, painter-writers were preserving and enriching their pictographic heritage. (158–60)

21. For discussions of the spiritual concerns of *Borderlands*, see Ramírez (185–87) and Cáliz-Montoro.

22. Julio Ramos's observations on the ex-voto are useful here:

El género del exvoto se inscribe en una economía de la reciprocidad, del intercambio de dones, y como tal trabaja fundamentalmente la mediación, la articulación entre distintos niveles de órdenes discontinuos....Como si de algún modo la temática del viaje y de sus interrupciones condensara las condiciones mismas de producción del género y su insistente reflexión sobre el límite—límite entre la vida y la muerte del sujeto accidentado—así como sobre la discontinuidad y la mediación entre tiempos y espacios diferenciados. Se trata entonces, en varios sentidos, de una forma que a lo largo de su historia (que por cierto antecede a la colonización de América) registra lúcidamente el devenir de distintas concepciones de la estabilidad y el desequilibrio, de la causalidad y la contingencia, del accidente y la ley, del desastre y de la intervención de las mismas prácticas pictórico-narrativas como modos de contener y reparar la catástrofe. (7–8)

23. See, for example, "From Coatlicue to La Llorona: Literary Myths and Archetypes" in Rebolledo 49–81.

24. "See that you shall die. See that you don't know when." Quoted from Amalia Mesa-Bains's art piece *Codex Amalia*. *Venus Envy*, reproduced in *The Chicano Codices* (15).
25. On España's work, see Fregoso, Noriega, and Huaco-Nuzum. My discussion of España's video art draws upon an earlier version of this portion of the chapter.
26. This is a reading of mine that España found useful in describing her work in "Nepantla'd Out":

    As a woman, and particularly as a Chicano artist, the challenge to articulate perception has hardly ever fallen easily upon me. Making fire is making fire. I seek new parameters within film and electronic media because those that do exist have posed severe creative limitations, borne of a different mood and world view. Trial and disgust in the editing room over industry codes and film capital standards forced me to give it up and speak in my own tongue. The challenge to reposition, begin transition, return spirit to the tribe embraced additional dimensions: adapting film language so that it more accurately articulates my vision—experimenting with approach until the artist's tools interpret form and style in ways more applicable to my own experience, in ways more relevant to me. (177)

27. I borrow the term "perspective schema" from Elkins (9), who cautions,

    Perspective proper, including its many methods and sometimes eccentric disciples, is thought to be a single thing, discovered in one form by Brunelleschi and elaborated upon by later workers. Behind this notion is the idea that perspective began in one place, Florence, and more or less at one time (1413–1435). This sense of a unified origin is one of several unities that play parts in the modern concept of perspective. I suggest not that it is mistaken or that perspective has miscellaneous or exotic origins but rather that this unified origin was not perceived as such in the Renaissance and that Renaissance artists and writers saw many techniques where we see a single discovery. (8)

    Thus, he continues, "An interesting sign of the presence in our scholarship of an informal definition of 'meaningless' perspective unrelated to the passage of time is a particular kind of perspective picture that I will call a *perspective schema*" (9).
28. My thanks to the artist for discussing her series with me and clarifying many of the images, as well as for sharing relevant readings with me.

Bibliography

Abram, David. *The Spell of the Sensuous*. New York: Vintage, 1997.
Alarcón, Norma. "Chicana Feminism: In the Tracks of 'The' Native Woman." *Cultural Studies* 4 (1990): 248–56.
Alcalá, Kathleen. *Spirits of the Ordinary: A Tale of Casas Grandes*. San Francisco: Chronicle, 1997.
Allen, Paula Gunn. *The Sacred Hoop: Recovering the Feminine in American Indian Traditions*. Boston: Beacon, 1986.
Alurista. "El Plan Espiritual de Aztlán." In *Aztlán: Essays on the Chicano Homeland*, edited by Rudolfo A. Anaya and Francisco Lomelí, 1–5. Albuquerque: Academia/El Norte, 1989.
Anaya, Rudolfo A. "Aztlán: A Homeland Without Boundaries." In *Aztlán: Essays on the Chicano Homeland*, edited by Rudolfo A. Anaya and Francisco Lomelí, 230–41. Albuquerque: Academia/El Norte, 1989.
Anderson, Richard feather. "Geomancy." In *The Power of Place: Sacred Ground in Natural and Human Environments*, edited by James A. Swan, 191–200. Illinois: Quest, 1991.
Anzaldúa, Gloria. *Borderlands/La Frontera: The New Mestiza*. San Francisco: Aunt Lute, 1987.

Anzaldúa, Gloria, ed. *Making Face, Making Soul. Haciendo Caras: Creative and Critical Perspectives by Women of Color.* San Francisco: Aunt Lute, 1990.

Armstrong, Robert Plant. *The Powers of Presence: Consciousness, Myth, and Affecting Presence.* Philadelphia: University of Pennsylvania Press, 1981.

Bourdieu, Pierre. *Distinction: A Social Critique of the Judgement of Taste.* 1979. Trans. R. Nice. Cambridge, MA: Harvard University Press, 1984.

Brotherston, Gordon. *Book of the Fourth World: Reading the Native Americas through Their Literature.* New York: Cambridge University Press, 1992.

Bürger, Peter. *Theory of the Avant-Garde.* 1974. Trans. Michael Shaw. Minneapolis: University of Minnesota Press, 1984.

Caliz-Montoro, Carmen. "Poetry Is Not Made of Words: A Study of Aesthetics of the Borderlands in Gloria Anzaldúa and Marlene Nourbese Philip." Diss. University of Toronto Press, 1996.

Castillo, Ana. *Massacre of the Dreamers: Essays on Xicanisma.* Albuquerque: University of New Mexico Press, 1994.

Cervántez, Yreina D. *Nepantla, Mi Nepantla, Beyond Nepantla.* Los Angeles, 1995.

Cisneros, Sandra. *Woman Hollering Creek and Other Stories.* New York: Random House, 1991.

Elkins, James. *The Poetics of Perspective.* Ithaca, NY: Cornell University Press, 1994.

España, Frances Salomé. *Anima.* Alhambra, CA, 1989.

———. *El Espejo/The Mirror.* Alhambra, CA, 1987.

———. *The Confessions Trilogy: Spitfire; Vivir; Nepantla.* Alhambra, CA, 1997.

———. "Nepantla'd Out." *Felix: Journal of Media Arts & Communications* 2, no. 1 (1995): 176–78.

Fanon, Frantz. *Black Skin, White Masks.* 1952. Trans. Charles Lam Markmann. New York: Grove, 1967.

Fregoso, Rosa Linda. *The Bronze Screen: Chicana and Chicano Film Culture.* Minneapolis: University of Minnesota Press, 1993.

Gates, Henry Louis, Jr. "Editor's Introduction: Writing 'Race' and the Difference It Makes." In *"Race," Writing, and Difference,* edited by Henry Louis Gates, Jr., 1–20. Chicago: University of Chicago Press, 1986.

———. *The Signifying Monkey: A Theory of African-American Literary Criticism.* New York: Oxford University Press, 1988.

Goodall, H. L., Jr. *Divine Signs: Connecting Spirit to Community.* Carbondale, IL: Southern Illinois University Press, 1989.

Gordon, Avery F. *Ghostly Matters: Haunting and the Sociological Imagination.* Minneapolis: University of Minnesota Press, 1997.

Gruzinski, Serge. *Painting the Conquest: The Mexican Indians and the European Renaissance.* Trans. Deke Dusinberre. Paris: Flammarion, 1992.

Hernandez, Ester. *Mis Madres.* San Francisco, 1986.

———. *Cosmic Cruise/Paseo Cósmico.* San Francisco, 1990.

Hillman, James. *Re-Visioning Psychology.* 1975. New York: Harper Collins, 1992.

Huaco-Nuzum, Carmen. "(Re)constructing Chicana, Mestiza Representation: Frances Salomé España's Spitfire (1991)." In *The Ethnic Eye. Latino Media Arts,* edited by Chon A. Noriega and Ana A. López, 260–74. Minneapolis: University of Minnesota Press, 1996.

Kiev, M. D., Ari. *Curanderismo: Mexican-American Folk Psychiatry.* New York: Free Press, 1968.

Klor de Alva, J. Jorge. "California Chicano Literature and Pre-Columbian Motifs: Foil and Fetish." In *Confluencia: Revista Hispánica de Cultura y Literatura* 2 (1986): 18–26.

———. "Contar vidas: La autobiografía confesional y la reconstrucción del ser nahua." *Arbor.* 515–16 (1988): 49–78. [*Arbor* is a journal of the Consejo Superior de Investigaciones Científicas in Madrid.]

———. "Telling Lives: Confessional Autobiography and the Reconstruction of the Nahua Self." In *Spiritual Encounters: Interactions between Christianity and Native Religions in Colonial America,* edited by Fernando Cervantes and Nicholas Griffiths. Lincoln: University of Nebraska Press, 1999.

León-Portilla, Miguel. *Aztec Thought and Culture: A Study of the Ancient Náhuatl Mind.* Trans. Jack Emory Davis. Norman: University of Oklahoma Press, 1963.

———. *Endangered Cultures.* 1976. Trans. Julie Goodson-Lawes. Dallas: Southern Methodist University Press, 1990.

———. *La filosofía náhuatl estudiada en sus fuentes.* 1956. Mexico: Universidad Nacional Autónoma de México, 1993.

———. *Los antiguos mexicanos a través de sus crónicas y cantares.* 1961. Mexico: Fondo de Cultura Económica, 1988.

———, ed. *Native Mesoamerican Spirituality: Ancient Myths, Discourses, Stories, Doctrines, Hymns, Poems from the Aztec, Yucatec, Quiché-Maya and Other Sacred Traditions.* Trans. Miguel León-Portilla, J. O. Arthur Anderson, Charles E. Dibble, and Munro S. Edmonson. Ramsey, NJ: Paulist Press, 1980.

Lipsey, Roger. *An Art of Our Own: The Spiritual in Twentieth Century Art.* Boston: Shambhala, 1988.

Marcus, Joyce. *Mesoamerican Writing Systems: Propaganda, Myth, and History in Four Ancient Civilizations.* Princeton, NJ: Princeton University Press, 1992.

Mesa-Bains, Amalia. "Curatorial Statement." *Ceremony of Spirit: Nature and Memory in Contemporary Latino Art,* 9–17. San Francisco: The Mexican Museum, 1993.

The Mexican Fine Arts Center Museum. *Art of the Other Mexico: Sources and Meanings.* Chicago: Mexican Fine Arts Center Museum, 1993.

The Mexican Museum. *The Chicano Codices: Encountering Art of the Americas.* Curated by Marcos Sánchez-Tranquilino. San Francisco: Mexican Museum, 1992.

Mignolo, Walter D. "Signs and Their Transmission: The Question of the Book in the New World." In *Writing Without Words,* edited by Elizabeth Hill Boone and Walter D. Mignolo, 220–70. Durham: Duke University Press, 1994.

Moraga, Cherríe. *The Last Generation: Prose and Poetry.* Boston: South End, 1993.

Noriega, Chon A. "Talking Heads, Body Politic: The Plural Self of Chicano Experimental Video." In *Resolutions: Contemporary Video Practices,* edited by Michael Renov and Erika Suderberg, 207–28. Minneapolis: University of Minnesota Press, 1996.

Pérez, Laura E. "Sightings of the Spirit: Frances Salomé España's Possessed Video Work." National Association of Chicana and Chicano Studies. Spokane, WA. March 22, 1996.

Ramírez, Arthur. Rev. of *Borderlands/La Frontera: The New Mestiza,* by Gloria Anzáldua. *Americas Review* 15.3 (Fall/Winter 1989): 185–87.

Ramos, Julio. "Memorial de un accidente: contingencia y tecnología en los exvotos de la Virgen de Quinche." Keynote address. New York University and Columbia University Graduate Student Conference. New York, February 1, 1997.

Rebolledo, Tey Diana. *Women Singing in the Snow: A Cultural Analysis of Chicana Literature.* Tucson: University of Arizona Press, 1995.

Taussig, Michael. *The Magic of the State.* New York: Routledge, 1997.

———. *Shamanism, Colonialism, and the Wild Man: A Study in Terror and Healing.* Chicago: University of Chicago Press, 1987.

Torgovnick, Marianna. *Primitive Passions: Men, Women, and the Quest for Ecstasy.* New York: Knopf, 1997.

Tucker, Michael. *Dreaming with Open Eyes: The Shamanic Spirit in Twentieth Century Art and Culture.* London: Harper Collins, 1992.

Valdez, Luis and Stan Steiner, eds. *Aztlán: An Anthology of Mexican American Literature.* New York: Vintage, 1972.

Villarreal, Rosa Martha. *Doctora Magdalena: Novella.* Berkeley: TQS, 1995.

Ybarra-Frausto, Tomás. "Alurista's Poetics: The Oral, the Bilingual, the Pre-Columbian." In *Modern Chicano Writers: A Collection of Critical Essays,* edited by Joseph Sommers and Tomás Ybarra-Frausto, 117–32. Englewood Cliffs, NJ: Prentice Hall, 1979.

———. "Cultural Context." In *Ceremony of Memory: New Expressions in Spirituality among Contemporary Hispanic Artists,* edited by Amalia Mesa-Bains. 9–13. Santa Fe: Center for Contemporary Arts of Santa Fe, 1988.

CHAPTER TWELVE

Los Puentes Stories: The Rhetorical Realities of Electronic Literacy Sponsors and Gateways on the U.S.-Mexico Border from 1920 to 2001

JOHN SCENTERS-ZAPICO

From stories and data on literacy, literacy access, and border education gathered over the last four years by surveying and interviewing some of the 118 Latino/a participants[1] from the borderlands of the United States and Mexico, I became aware of two important issues: gateways and sponsors are complex rhetorical variables shaping how people here learn to become electronically literate. In addition, traditional formulations of gateway and sponsor are not as clear-cut or rhetorically considered and are in need of some expansion. This chapter begins to shed light on how these Latinos/as, born between 1920 and 2001, learned and had access—or not—to electronic literacy sponsors and gateways over the last seventy-nine years both in and around the Mexico-U.S. borderlands.

Research Background

This research began in 2004 with a nineteen-page survey asking participants a broad range of quantitative and qualitative questions about their experiences learning to traditionally read, write, and work with newer electronic literacies[2] in English and Spanish, in Mexico and the United States. Occasionally a follow-up interview took place and approximately 10 percent of the participants were in an undergraduate or graduate course with me. The chapter shares the results from the participants' responses, focusing on their replies about gateways and sponsors.[3] Other literacy research in the field has studied samples of oral story-based components, what is sometimes called new narrative research, focusing "specifically on lives and lived experience" (Casey 211), on traditional literacy learning (Brandt, *Literacy in American Lives*), on electronic literacy story-based narratives (Selfe and Hawisher, *Literate Lives*), on traditional and electronic literacy narratives on the U.S.-Mexico border (Scenters-Zapico, *Generaciones*), and on African American women as "non-normative subjects in non-normative arenas" (Jones-Royster and Simpkins *Calling Cards*; also see Jones-Royster and Williams). While this chapter draws from the oral stories my participants shared, it nevertheless attempts to intertwine polyphony of voices through the revelation of the summative data from the study. In this regard, I see this chapter as a hybrid, experimental ethnographic "fleshing in" of data that when brought together reveals a more robust rhetorical image of sponsorships and gateways on this international border. The disclosure of statistics on significant numbers of sponsors and gateways has not been published in any research to date. The following section describes and lists the rationale for participant selection.

Population and Movement Patterns

Three participant movement patterns emerged early in the survey and interview process of this study:

1. El Paso born and raised,
2. El Paso born, moved to Juárez or another location in Mexico, usually at a young age, and often end up back in El Paso, and
3. Mexico born, most often in Juárez, then frequently moved to El Paso, and infrequently returned to Mexico.

These patterns in each *generación*[4] were significant enough that I then focused on making sure the participants represented the three patterns so that the data would reflect the array of border cultures, bilingualism, education, economics, politics, and family life. The end result was 118 representative participants of the three movement patterns born from 1920 to 2001.

From participants' movements from one country to another, they displayed diverse cultural, linguistic, and educational influences. Rosaldo hints at some of these, observing "cultural assimilation, often going under the name of acculturation, has to do with fluency, both in the linguistic sense and in the broader sense of the skills required to succeed in the majority group's formal institutions and informal social situations" (1). These participants' stories and data reflect polyphonous assimilations. A popular song by Facundo Cabral suggests, *"No soy de aqui, ni soy de alla."*[5] The implication of the song is that many of these participants have strong cultural traits from the American side, the Mexican side, and the gray area of not feeling a part in either culture. These identities, linguistic backgrounds, and cultural know-hows have created diverse forms of rhetorical sponsorship and gateway experiences.

Participants of Literacy and Their Movements

I brought together participants of literacy whose movements reflect one of the three movement patterns, and whose date of birth represents a range of *generaciones* and consequently experiences.

In the following section, I review recent discussions of literacies to situate the impact that such definitions have on participants' lives, and consequently the rhetorical practices that sponsors and gateways partake in fostering and preventing the acquisition of literacy.

What Are Literacies Anyway?

Literacy, even if used in the singular, has come to be a concept as rhetorically tangled as any in public, academic, and governmental realms. I begin this section by reviewing some of the ways literacy and its counterpart—illiteracy—are characterized. I believe it is important to view the ever-broadening literacy landscape in order to examine developing notions of electronic literacy. I conclude the section pointing out that although it is difficult to come up with a concrete definition of traditional and electronic literacies, it is essential to embrace an idea of the multifarious meanings of it in order to understand the roles of sponsors and gateways of literacy, which I will take up in the following sections.

Literacy has a direct and dichotomous counterpart, illiteracy. The prefix here, "ill," as in ill-legal, and ill-begot implies that literacy's counterpart is sick, unrecognized, or poorly conceived, and the opposites are healthy. Health as literacy is the norm, the expected, and "ill" is outside of the prescribed range, so "ill" needs some sort of treatment in order to be healthy/normal (again). This is the way various academic and governmental entities understand literacy. Often when organizations treat the illiterate with a semi-benevolent approach we see them prepared to doctor those who are ill to literacy health; that is, they identify the problem, and take action to bring the ill to health. The malevolent side to this is that those who are classified as illiterate are not considered for "healthy" jobs or opportunities in their communities. Such a common view and approach to healing (abnormal) illiteracy to (normal) literacy is clearly a Foucaultian idea:

> As Rockhill (168) has argued, literacy has become an emblem of normality, illiteracy a sign of individual and social dis-ease. Whether or not one is officially literate in a standard national language becomes a fundamental criterion of worth and standing. In Foucault's sense, literacy becomes a crucial part of a normalizing power, whereby deviations from the norms are defined as deficiencies and disabilities, as medical problems. (Collins 10)

This examination and approach to "treatment" manifests itself incessantly in the news and many state and governmental approaches to "solving" once and for all the illiteracy sicknesses. An example that regularly appears in the *El Paso Times* is the head librarian's agenda to "fix" literacy:

> The average scores of those who did not finish high school fell into the Below Basic category, while 41 percent of adults with graduate school educations scored Proficient. The study also found [National Center for Educational Statistics] that the average weekly wage of those who scored Below Basic was $432 per week while those who fell into the Proficient range earned on average $972.

Literacy pays!

While these findings may not surprise anyone, they add credence to what educators and librarians have been saying for years—literacy stands at the heart of economic and social development (Brey-Casiano).

Brey-Casiano lays out her "simple" two-step approach to healing this problem: "How do we do this? Step One is to accept the fact that literacy is one of the most important factors affecting the economic and social development of El Paso. The second step is to pool our resources to make certain everyone in the city recognizes the importance of literacy and works to improve our standing" (7B).

A few months later the El Paso Library Public Relations Coordinator, Jack Galindo, uses another set of literacy statistics from another study to make the same pitch, "[A]ccording to the latest study by the National Institute for Literacy, a federal agency that serves as a national resource on literacy, about 34 percent of El Pasoans ages 16 and older were level 1 readers, the lowest of a five-level literacy scale" (Fonce-Olivas 3B). The logic is to cure illiteracy and from this achieve not only better literacy health but wages as well.

Brandt looks at literacy as an empowering mechanism, one that allows certain rights, such as money and access to information. "Literate skills," she stresses, "as a resource, which, like wealth or education or trade skill or social connections, is pursued for the opportunities and protections that it potentially grants its seekers. As a resource, literacy has potential value for gaining power or pleasure, and accruing information, civil rights, education, spirituality, status, or money" ("Literacy Learning" 3). From her research she also argues that literacy was a goal others, such as employers, wanted to push on their employees in order to better their companies' competitiveness. In this sense literacy is a two way street of opportunity and exploitation.

Lankshear and O'Connor separate literacy into three dimensions, ones that avoid most statistical and quantitative views. The operational, cultural, and critical are defined as follows:

> The *operational* dimension involves being able to read and write within a range of contexts in an adequate and appropriate manner employing print and electronic media. The *cultural* dimension involves understanding texts and information in relation to the contexts—real-life practices—in which they are produced, received, and used. Without the cultural dimension, language users are unable to understand what makes particular ways of reading and writing appropriate or inappropriate, adequate or inadequate in a given situation or setting. The *critical* dimension involves being able to innovate, transform, improve, and add value to social practices and the literacies associated with them. It marks the difference between merely being *socialized* into sets of skills, values, beliefs, and procedures and being able to make *judgments* about them from a perspective that identifies them for what they are (and are not) and recognizes alternative possibilities. (33)

Florio-Ruane and McVee also have three touch points to characterizing literacy:

1. variety of school subjects, such as reading, writing, speaking, and listening,
2. private intellectual achievements, and
3. observable community practices essential to cultural and social identity.

Importantly, Florio-Ruane and McVee, heeding Barton's research (1994), further suggest that literacies should be studied within an ecology considering cultural, social, historical, and psychological factors (80). Roberts takes notions of literacy onto the rhetorical and political battlefield: "a more productive line of inquiry would be to consider how literacy has been constructed, shaped and discussed, by whom, when, where, and why.... The struggle over definition, some claim, is more than a merely intellectual tussle; rather, the battle is a thoroughly *political* one" (414). From this political arena (which assumes a loser who will end up "ill"), he, too, arrives at three approaches to characterize and study literacy: (1) Quantitative, (2) Qualitative, and (3) Pluralist (Roberts 414). While the first two are fairly self-explanatory, the last is more in tune with many current academic notions of literacy. The pluralist approach considers literacy as the now often heard "literacies" or "multiple modes of literacy," and includes subheadings such as

1. Survival literacy (see Cassidy and Shanahan),
2. Social literacy (see Diehm),
3. Cultural literacy (see Hirsch xiii),
4. Basic literacy,
5. Functional literacy,
6. Higher-order literacy, and
7. Critical literacy (see Shor 189).

Last, Roberts suggests that these latter takes on literacy focus less on "'literacy itself' to literacy as practiced, developed, conceived, expressed, or manifested on this context, or that discursive setting, or that situation—in these ways, at this time, along these lines, and so on. That is, a move is made toward what might be termed *"particularist constructs"* (420). In the end, he seems to side with theorists such as Street (1984), Lankshear and Lawler (1987), Giroux (1987), Gee (1993), and McLaren (1988), who suggest discussions about "literacy are always historically situated and socially formed" (Roberts 424).

This discussion brings out the complexity and array of issues involved in characterizing traditional literacy and serves as a useful platform for discussing electronic literacy because it carries many of the same challenges, and creates others. Definitions of traditional and electronic literacy are part of the same sociocultural problem. Let me situate this point into the perception of El Paso's literacy. According to national standards, El Paso has a low level of literacy, or conversely stated it has a high level of illiteracy. While the definition of literacy and standards as they have been applied to El Paso have been complicated by Scenters-Zapico because of its bilingualism and its multicultural relationship with its 500 year Mexican sister city, Juárez (*Generaciones*), the typical ranking and consequent perception of the El Paso population, nevertheless, have been crippling. Selfe and Hawisher note the national ill-effect such generic rankings have on minority populations: "The people labeled as 'illiterate' in connection with technology—as expected—are those with the least power to effect a change in this system. They come from families who attend the poorest schools in this country and they attend schools with the highest populations of students of color" ("Technology and Literacy" 427). The common threads are people of color, being poor, and being illiterate. The stakes are high for having a ranked literate population, and the rhetorical constructs of such rankings are—and I shout this—outdated!

In turn, the oft-cited report "Getting America's Students Ready for the 21st Century" defines technological literacy as "computer skills and the ability to use computers and other technology to improve learning, productivity and performance" and being able to use these technologies "has become as fundamental to a person's ability to navigate through society as traditional skills like reading, writing and arithmetic" (5). Roberts teases out these developing ideas about the connections among traditional and electronic literacy:

Speaking and comprehending the language of computing is an important part of "computer literacy", as is facility with various software packages and some knowledge of networking functions. In this reworked conception of literacy, processes of "reading" and "writing" are *reconfigured,* rather than eliminated, as people negotiate new modes of literate activity in postindustrial society. Hitherto accepted views of "literacy" and "the literate person" are not abandoned, but *modified,* in tandem with transformations in social life and the nature of work under contemporary capitalism. (427)

The discussions of electronic literacy also can include other names given to it, such as media literacy, information literacy, and so on. While some of these names have specific disciplinary definitions, the overarching focus, I believe, is on how we use and learn technology for communicative, rhetorical, and meaning-making endeavors.

The often-missing component in discussions of literacies is how and where real people, that is, the actual situated practitioners of diverse literacies, effectively practice, learn, and use literacies to communicate. In my research, since it reflects situated individuals' stories and responses, I came to call those who shared their stories and experiences with me "participants of literacy" (*Generaciones*). These participants, in turn, sketched complex patterns showing the ecological[6] dependence of others, and their ecological habitats: the gateways where participants and sponsors meet. In the next section, I complicate notions of sponsorship and discuss examples of how it is practiced on the border.

The Rhetoric of Direct and Indirect Sponsors of Literacy

The use of "sponsors of literacy" has been described in several revealing ways. Brandt's *Literacy in American Lives*, among several of her writings, interprets sponsors and sponsorship as primarily a top-down, profit-based initiative: "Sponsors are a tangible reminder that literacy learning throughout history has always required permission, sanction, assistance, coercion, or, at minimum, contact with existing trade routes" (166–67).[7] Here Brandt intertwines literacy places (gateways) and what we might term literacy events. A little later she suggests sponsors are concrete individuals: "Intuitively, *sponsors* seemed a fitting term for the figures who turned up most typically in people's memories of literacy learning: older relatives, teachers, priests, supervisors, military officers, editors, influential authors. Sponsors, as we ordinarily think of them, are powerful figures who bankroll events or smooth the way for initiates" (Brandt "Sponsors" 167).[8]

It is clear that sponsorship is a complex, rhetorical process essential to literacy learning. From the responses that the participants shared in this research I found it useful, if not necessary, to divide sponsors of literacy into three primary divisions: direct, indirect, and self. In turn these became even more concrete based on participant responses.

Direct and indirect sponsors are equally important in developing literacies. I would like to stress that reading the chart, like participant experiences, is a-linear. One approach to using it is to examine all the possible influences direct and indirect sponsors can have in participants' lives.

Elena Suárez was born in 1940 in Mexico, and served as a computer lab monitor at a school in El Paso, despite knowing very little about computers. Without her serving as a volunteer, the lab most likely would not be open and there would be no electronic literacy access to the lab for students. By the same token, Elena Suárez's electronic literacy incompetence often is viewed by students negatively since she cannot help them with their developing electronic literacies. In this regard she is unable to provide the ostensibly more significant direct sponsorship. However, the students who benefited from Mrs. Suarez's monitoring the lab, according to the sponsorship data, often ended up sponsoring their peers and were sponsored by them. Alicia Rodriguez's daughter (B: 1949, El Paso) encouraged her to go to technical school to learn electronic literacies in order to land a better job. In each case the sponsorship of either type can enact important changes in people's lives.

Direct and indirect sponsorship has divisions and connections to each other, and this complicated attribute became more prevalent once I examined the responses the participants shared. Brandt's historical characterization of literacy sponsorship is useful because with it we discover the significant role that others, especially family, play in developing literacy (*Literacy* 149). My realization from the participant surveys is that sponsors of literacy are significant individuals in participants' lives, who serve as gatekeepers in three meaningful ways:

1. Physically: These sponsors can be as diverse as a parent or teacher to someone else's grandparent or employer. The roles they take can also be varied, from allowing access to a computer at home to serving as a monitor in a computer lab, despite not knowing a thing about electronic literacies.
2. Financially: At a primary level this is what a sponsor feels he/she can afford for him/herself or someone else. A more subtle angle is what a sponsor deems is a worthy investment, or what an employer believes employees need in the workplace to be competitive or functional (*Generaciones*). A subcategory of financial sponsorship

is Technology Economic Motivator/Motivated (TEM); here a sponsor encourages another or is encouraged to learn new electronic literacies for generally some underlying economic reason.

3. Psychologically: Because one individual's words or actions can cause a lifetime of positive or negative effects on an individual, this is by far the most complex subcategory. These psychological effects I have labeled Micro-Tear Zones.

Because they move outside of what we associate with an external sponsor's actions and become more internalized for participants. These micro-tear zones often surfaced in participants' reflections, and range from how a participant in a specific context shows patience in explaining to a new user how to use a piece of technology or software to someone telling a learner, "good job, bad job" or "you're hopeless." Parents do this by criticizing their children's "smarts," their future roles in the world (e.g., too lazy), and sexist views toward women's and men's roles in society, to name a few. Victoria Montoya (b. 1922 El Paso), for example, was discouraged by her father from continuing with her education after high school, despite having a better academic record than her male siblings. A positive psychological experience MTZ occurred with Gabriela Valdez (b. 1982 Juárez).[9] As she was learning English in El Paso she had her class laughing when she said, "*ya finishiamos*," in order to indicate the lesson was done, in *Spanglish*. Her reflection was positive, even humorous for her. However, for many students this could, and most likely would, have the opposite effect (*Generaciones*).

In all their varying roles and manifestations, sponsors are rhetorically influential figures in the literacy learning process, from overt to covert. In the next section, I list the results from thirteen electronic literacy sponsor questions, and summarize the data from all thirteen questions. While we cannot visibly see sponsors in action, they do leave fingerprints of the influences they have had on the selected 118 participants and in this way help to reveal the paths that participants on the border have had through multiple *generaciones*.

Some surprising results about sponsors came to light from this data. First, overwhelmingly participants self-sponsored. Hawisher and Selfe note that, "People can exert their own powerful agency in, around, and through digital literacies. In particular cultural ecologies, some individuals may even confound society's expectations regarding race, class, age, and gender" ("Becoming Literate" 3–4). A particularly revealing example of self-sponsorship is shared in Hawisher's and Selfe's work. Their participant, Melissa, "lied" to get a manual to teach herself. This adds and fits into the personal, psychological barriers participants create and are confronted with:

My interest now in computer literacy affords me access both socially and professionally. I'm INCLUDED in communities, rather than being on the margins doing what an African American woman might stereotypically do, which is often nothing related to technology if she is in Education or Liberal Arts. Reflecting on my earlier experiences, I'm certain that had I not lied, and then obtained the manual, and had I not been self-motivated in acquiring a computer of my own, my employability and mobility would have been drastically different. ("Becoming" 28)

Melissa's experience, consistent with *Los Puentes'* data and stories, highlights that self-sponsorship is significant throughout the United States. Despite even self-sponsorship, participants have run up against forces that they had to manipulate in order to learn desirable literacies. *Generación* 1 self-sponsored 221 times, while the younger *Generación* 2 indicated a decrease to 124. This noticeable decrease occurs after the explosion of the home computer, so while participants continued to self-sponsor, the numbers showed a decrease of almost one half.

Family and Friends

Family and friends took on an important role in teaching participants new electronic literacies. Participants indicated that family taught them 171 times, and friends 128. These two groups, again, are outside the realm of teachers' influence, yet obviously are influential. Similarly, Hawisher and Selfe document Brittney's learning experiences at her friend's home: "A huge amount of credit goes to the Barra's (Mitzi and her father) for my technological progression—they taught me everything. I would go over to Mitzi's house and together we would try (and try) to create the things necessary for my homework" (Hawisher and Selfe "Becoming" 16–17). As *Los Puentes'* data and stories corroborate, key sponsors for participants are family and friends, which often can mean they must seek out the individuals in places other than their own home or school.

Teachers

Teachers played an important role in participants' lives on the border. At some point participants indicated teachers had taught them an electronic literacy 245 times from the 13 categories. Also, of note is that *Generación* 1 and *Generación* 2 saw a growth in teacher influence, from 111 for 1920–1985, to 134 for 1986–2001. I assume and suggest here that the increase, albeit minimal, is due to the increased availability and the increased use of technology for pedagogical purposes by teachers. I had originally thought the numbers would be higher, yet I speculate that more affluent school districts would see measurable increases over the same time span.[10]

Though Brandt focused on traditional literacy, her take on the impact and influence of teachers teaching electronic literacies is higher than my own: "At our most worthy, perhaps, we show the sellers how to beware and try to make sure these exchanges will be a little fairer, maybe, potentially, a little more mutually rewarding" ("Sponsors" 183). Through traditional writing approaches taught in schools, a fair number of students would agree that we writing teachers do not teach them to write any better. Most likely they would not see our writing classes in the same beneficial light that we do. In regard to electronic literacy, I suspect participants do not learn from teachers because they simply do not offer such trainings. Teachers have become used to assuming students already know when they come to their classes, that they will learn, or that they will sink (*Generaciones*). While Brandt found "outside" sponsors to be significant, that is with overt motives, the results from the participants in this study do not directly agree. Yet I believe the results *do agree* in a more ominous way. Brandt saw traditional literacy sponsorship as economically motivated in the twentieth century. I believe the sponsorship of electronic literacies in the twenty-first century is ever-more economically motivated and rife with rhetorical motives, so much so that it requires employees to have the skills *before* they ever apply for a job, much like what teachers require about their students. The sponsor pool of data and stories suggests participants are learning electronic literacies any way they can. The next section examines *where* participants said they learned electronic literacies.

Gateways

Gateways are about both awareness and access to technology in order to learn and create using electronic literacies. If we are not in an appropriate place, the odds are high that we will not have an awareness of the technology needed to create electronic literacies, and most obviously access would not be an issue. I begin this section with a story participant Gabriela Valdez (b. 1982 Juárez) shared with me about her parents' move from a remote area of Mexico to Juárez, Mexico, which has a population of one and a half million:

> My parents come from south Mexico, to people from those places, technology has not been something transcendental in their lives. In those places few people move themselves in cars as most of them use horses for these purposes. These are towns where technology is poor, and their styles of life do not require technologic innovations as more urbanized areas do.
>
> My parents were first introduced to technology once they left their birth places in search of a better life. But computers still didn't come into their life until I went trough Middle School where I began to get involved with computer technology. When asked about technology, my mom always says, *"Si no fuera porque mis hijas están envueltas en la tecnología por sus estudios, jamás hubiera aprendido a utilizarla ya que de donde yo vengo todo es muy antiguo, y la poca tecnología que existe pocas personas pueden costearla o disfrutarla."*[11] On the contrary, my dad was reluctant to change his ways, even thought he does assert that *"La tecnología es algo que se ha convertido en parte esscencial en la vida y es algo importantísimo para aprender para las nuevas generaciones, sin embargo soy ajeno al uso de ella."*[12] (Gabriela Valdez)

Gateway awareness and access, then, come to exist because of personal choice and economic mobility, especially the locations where participants can, under the right circumstances, access technology and learn the types of literacy they desire.

Once in a place, awareness of a gateway takes on a multitude of meanings. For example, many in the El Paso and Juárez community are aware that computer labs exist on the UTEP campus. Unless they are students they cannot use the technologies available within the UTEP labs. Or, like participant Enrique Loaeza (b. 1983 El Paso), he was aware of the technology gateway his father had created in his home, but he was ostensibly not allowed to use, yet he managed to use it despite his parents' restriction about this:

> I first learned how to use computers by myself. My father was always too busy to teach me and the computer was just there in the

house. I would turn it on and see where the buttons would take me. I was always discouraged by my mother to get off the computer only because she did not want me to break it and then they would have to pay for it. She would always tell me to wait for my father so that he could teach me. (Enrique Loaeza)

If we have awareness and access to such sites, this research suggests our traditional and electronic literacies have a much better opportunity to experience varying levels of sponsorship, as the last section on sponsorship revealed.

Next, I discuss notions of what gateway has meant in the literature. This is followed by thirteen gateway questions asked of my participants that parallel the thirteen sponsor questions, that is, instead of asking *who* taught them e-mail, for example, they were asked *where* they learned e-mail. The aim of the gateway questions was to discover the specific locations where participants learned an electronic literacy.

Gateway Meanings

A gateway is a place such as a home or school that has technology that can be used to communicate visually, textually, and aurally. The very definition is a tautology, that is, gateway implies in its very name what it has available, yet for many gateway could just as easily be called "locked iron gate." The reason often cited for not having technology at home or school is due to low socioeconomic standing. Kenneth Burke argued that we need a place to "stellen," or stand, in order to "vorstellen," understand.[13] In terms of electronic literacies, not having a gateway to stand in means you are displaced, you are other, you are outside, and you are not in a position to learn to understand. Being outside of a gateway is common enough on the U.S.-Mexico border, where laws, money, and race keep thousands standing where they cannot understand.

The literature on having or not having a technological place to stand came to be called the digital divide, not, of course, the locked irongate. According to Light,

Periodical indices show 1996 as the first year the digital divide leapt into the spotlight as a focus of public attention and action, although the origins of the term are unknown. Thus, the Clinton administration's National Telecommunications and Information

Administration (NTIA) issued a report in 1995 calling attention to information "haves" and "have nots," without mention of a digital divide (NTIA, 1995). A second NTIA report in 1998 and its accompanying publicity helped to popularize the term. (3–4)

Any discussion of gateways needs to consider the metaphor of the digital divide, because embedded within it is the notion that socio-economic standing either grants people access (and allows them a place to stand), or it keeps them locked out. Yes, there are gateways that we all are aware of, but there are also borders with locked iron gates that keep us outside of the gateways. The *El Paso Times* reported that according to Border Patrol statistics "a mind-boggling 1.1 million people were apprehended trying to cross illegally," and that for "every person caught trying to illegally cross the border, five to eight others make it" (11B). The number of those who "make it" across suggests they have found a way through the gateway. The issue for the estimated "five to eight others [who] make it" becomes issues of awareness and access. It is not as if the illegals make it across and society delivers an open gateway of any type they wish. However, this research did not focus on the experiences of illegal immigrants to this country. I am certain, however, that the results of such a study would open up even more questions about the roles of sponsors and gateways. If we use gateway as a term, it would, perhaps, be more socially revealing and accurate to create tiered notions of gateway and consequently "the divide."

The locations where participants from *Los Puentes'* research have access or are aware of technology are important to distinguish. Participants listed a diverse array of technology gateways, such as schools, homes, and the workplace, which also tend to offer resources such as software, and Internet access.

An additional concept came to light from the participant responses that I coined *cubbyhole gateway*; it fits partially in the overarching category of gateway, yet it stretches the boundaries in significant ways and will be discussed next.

Cubbyhole Gateway

Several participants viewed their jobs early in their lives or careers as dead-ended, yet the jobs created, often inadvertently, electronic literacy opportunities. From the self-confidence they learned more electronic literacies and strived for more challenging jobs. From these experiences my concept of cubbyhole gateway took on major importance. Selfe and Hawisher characterize what I have coined cubbyhole gateways as unskilled, surplus labor: "These latter individuals provide the unskilled, low-paid labor necessary to sustain the system I have described—their work generates the surplus labor that must be continually re-invested in capital projects to produce more sophisticated technologies" ("Technology and Literacy" 18).

It is, however, the surplus labor jobs at establishments such as McDonald's as a cashier that create participants' self-confidence that they can learn and do more than they had thought they were able. Cubbyhole gateway is an effective example of a zone of proximal development (Vygotsky) in that participant employees who work these jobs may not initially have the literate skills to do a job like a computerized cashier, but with the right training (aka sponsor as more competent peer) participants can do tomorrow alone what they were only able to do with competent peer assistance today. These surplus jobs create opportunities for participants by allowing them to see that they can master the literacy necessary for a specific job and from that they create continual opportunities. I will illustrate this with three stories.

The first is Melissa's, from Selfe's and Hawisher's work (*Literate Lives*). The second is Villanueva's personal account from *Bootstraps*. The last is of Laura Schuster from *Los Puentes'* research. Melissa begins, "A computer for me was something to be used by skilled people. And it was so far out of my grasp. It probably was not until I was well out of high school—I'm even thinking that it was after the army—yeah, it was when I worked in a bank. All I knew was how to flip it on, put my little password in, and do my own work." But once Melissa started working with computers, she seemed to have no fear of plunging right in: "It wasn't until I wanted this temporary job and it required that I have data processing skills on a certain kind of computer. I lied....I had them convinced that I knew what I was doing on the computer. So that catapulted me into other jobs that required computer skill and I just, that's what I remember doing, getting the book. It all came with the book" ("Becoming Literate" 10–11).

Victor Villanueva's cubbyhole story began when he dropped out of school:

Like many of those who are young and uneducated, his first jobs are with the fast food industry—hamburgers and kraut dogs and chili dogs and tacos and burritos at the local Bun 'n' Run....Moving up, he becomes a short-order cook. Mom gets him an interview where she works as a keypunch operator for a computerized accounting firm. He maxes a math test and carries himself well with the interviewer, is hired as a checker, looking for keypunch errors when journal balances don't balance. One of the company's computer operators joins the Navy. Victor is sent to Honeywell computer operations school in Los Angeles, where he learns to operate a Honeywell H-200, a massive machine that holds 16K of memory. And again there is hope for the future. (43)

Villanueva's experience is more common than we think. At times individuals, who in one context or another have been pushed aside, find that in another setting they develop new literacies. In this form of cubbyhole gateway experience, I believe Villanueva also fits the top-down sponsorship that Brandt observed among her participants. However, this experience reflects the importance that we need to give to cubbyhole gateways, viewing them as bootstrap opportunities for those without boots or those with frayed or broken straps.

Los Puentes' participant, Laura Schuster (B: 1960 El Paso), began work in the 1980s and had work experiences similar to Melissa's. Her family moved to Juárez when she was an infant, but she now lives in El Paso. Her work life gives us glimpses into the impact that the technology boom of the 1980s had at this time. Laura's first job in El Paso was in a chain store's electronics department, where she said, "I first came in to contact with computers in 1988 at work. Very minimal use-no use of Internet. We were only trained on what we needed to know for work." This "surplus job" made her aware that she could learn new electronic literacies. The job itself she saw as fun because she was able to "play-learn" many of the new electronics to hit the market at the time. This prepared her for her next position at another ostensibly surplus job in a medium-sized office managing apartments. She began learning "to post rent at an apartment complex," and advanced to management because of her work ethic and her ability to learn and even seek out sponsors to help her learn some of the necessary electronic literacies for her to continue advancing in this job.

Cubbyhole jobs such as those of Melissa, Victor, and Laura started off in—and many others like it such as a chain store clerk who uses a computerized cash register, a stocker who uses a handheld inventory computer, a delivery person who uses a handheld tracking computer, a car wash operator who uses a keypad to set the wash to fit the car, and so on—alert many participants of literacy to the fact that they can

learn to work with technology, learn the necessary electronic literacies, and potentially grow into more expanded roles because of their
newfound confidence. Because of stories like Laura's that I heard in
my research and from other similar accounts reported in the literature
like Melissa's and Victor's, cubbyhole gateways have the potential to
serve as crucial sites for research and for creating more in situ literacy
pedagogies.

Summary Data of Gateways on the Border

In Hawisher's and Selfe's research they indicate, in terms of gateways, that schools are the primary gateway where participants learn
electronic literacies, the workplace second, community centers and
libraries third, and home fourth ("Becoming" 31). Of 773 responses
to questions about gateways, *Los Puentes'* research is quantifiably consistent with their findings: schools are a significant gateway at 347.
An important difference occurs in that Selfe and Hawisher list home
as a lower-tiered gateway. In this research, 326 responses indicated
they had learned some form of electronic literacy at home. The other
categories listed in the Summary Data of Gateways on the Border
Table suggest that the other gateways, while important, do not compare with schools and home.

Selfe et al. conclude that "This project has reminded us that people
often acquire and develop the literacies they need in places other than
the classroom where, often, instructors tend to limit literacy activities
to the narrow bandwidth of conventional written English" ("Stasis" in
"Becoming Literate" 29). As my participant Susana Romero (b. 1980
Juárez) explained to me, she learned with help from friends and in several of their homes: "Playing video games became one of the things my
friends and I did all the time. We would have constant competition to
see who would get further along but at the same time we all were able
to learn from each other" (Susana Romero). Moreover, Susana's point
that she and her friends all taught each other highlights the sociali-
zation of the zone of proximal development in developing electronic
literacies in the twenty-first century on the border, though I believe
this experience is akin to many learners of this century regardless of
geographic location.

Several studies indicate that Latinos are less likely to have access
to technology such as the Internet at home. Though published a
decade ago, the report "Getting America's Students Ready for the

21st Century" found that 86 percent of parents view the home as gateway because they felt that a computer at home would significantly improve children's education and social mobility (10). According to a National Center for Education Statistics study in 2003, based on nursery school through twelfth grade, Hispanics were the least likely to use the Internet, and "limited access at home can erode a student's ability to research assignments, explore college scholarships or just get comfortable going online" (Feller 5A).

Homes were an important location for participants in this research, and many had indicated that their family had pushed to purchase technology. Nevertheless, several other *Los Puentes'* participants indicated that cost and access were important. On the U.S. side Alicia Rodriguez (b. 1949 Tornillo, Texas) said, "It was very hard here in the U.S. We really didn't have access to computers near by." In Mexico Elisa Alvarado (b. 1982 Juárez) believed

> that in Mexico it is a lot harder to obtain electronic literacy because of economic circumstances. People that work from paycheck to paycheck will not purchase a computer if they have no use for it. Here in the United States we have computer stores that will give you a computer based on credit that you can pay on a month to month basis in Mexico I don't believe this program exists.

Cynthia Smith (b.1963 Durango, Mexico), who lived in Juárez and El Paso, saw it as difficult everywhere: "Computers were very expensive and only rich people could afford having one. Here in the U.S. they were also expensive when they came out. Our parents never purchased one. I would have to come to school to use the computers here. In U.S. economic factors make it hard to access computers outside of the school."

However, Alexa Cardenas (b. 1976, El Paso) saw it as difficult in Mexico and easy in the United States: "Access to computers in Nazas, Durango, is not very easy; we have limited access to them. I believe that the social, political, educational, religious, and economic factors make it difficult to develop electronic literacy in Nazas, Durango. In the U.S. the access to computers at school, public libraries, and at home is very easy."

According to participants, access is an issue. Another nuance to this is revealed in research published by the *Digest of Education Statistics*, which indicates that "It is a fact, for instance, that Black employees or

Hispanic employees are *much* less likely than white employees to use a range of computer applications in their workplace environments" (458). Only 39/762 Latino/a participants' responses indicated that they had learned any electronic literacies at work!

Hawisher and Selfe elaborate on the technology border that permits and separates:

> The specific conditions of access have a substantial effect on people's acquisition and development of digital literacy. Thus, access to computers—and to the literacies of technology—cannot be accurately represented as an isolated or monodimensional formation. Rather, access is best understood as part of a larger cultural ecology. Physical access to computers is necessary but insufficient for the acquisition and development of digital literacies. ("Becoming" 3–4)

In other words, once you are through the gate, you still must find a way, and inevitably there are many more gates to gain access to.

Finding the means once in, is what the *Los Puentes'* data and stories helped me see as a potential area needing further research. How do participants become electronically literate once in? To begin the process, I believe it is necessary to consider the dynamic among sponsor, participant, and gateway, or what I have coined the Dynamic Zone of Sponsor-Gateway-Participant (DZSGP).[14] The DZSGP helps to reveal the fragility of the cultural ecology with actual participant and sponsor interaction experiences.

The combination of variables of the DZSGP is succinctly observed by K. H. Au who stresses that "the idea that tools for communication are human creations that arise out of the 'hybrid culture' of interactions among people" (Florio-Ruane and McVee "Ethnographic" 82). Brandt similarly observed this with her participant, Dwayne Lowery. In his example "workplaces, schools, families bring together multiple strands of the history of literacy in complex and influential forms. We need models of literacy that more astutely account for these kinds of multiple contacts, both in and out of school and across a lifetime" (Brandt "Sponsors of Literacy" 179). The DZSGP helps us to ask important questions about the specifics of present Sponsor-Gateway-Participant dynamics and the "Hybrid Zones" that result from their interactions. In the DZSGP diagram I have added hybrid zones to represent the new, evolving nature that results from all these variables interacting. Light further characterizes the complexity of such interactions:

> Technologies are not independent of the society in which they are created or of the context in which they are used (Bijker, Hughes, & Pinch, 1987; Cuban, 1986; MacKenzie & Wajcman, 1985). Their array of interactions with different people, organizations, institutions, and cultures—such as individual teachers, schools, or academic subjects—makes it difficult for any particular technology to have uniform or even entirely predictable effects (Fischer, 1992; Wajcman, 1991). (6)

The DZSGP asks us to consider the influences that individuals have in society, that others have on them, and they on others, the locations of the technology, if they have access or not, how they gain access, as well as the outcome of the interactions. From this lens we see that the synergy caused by all these variables at one time and place also changes as the individual moves about, outside or within his/her overarching ecosystem.

Conclusion

Several points can be drawn from this examination of sponsors and gateways. First, *Los Puentes'* data suggests that participants are learning on-the-job electronic literacies in cubbyhole gateways. These sites of learning are important in the twenty-first century because workers in these positions most likely will not attend academic institutions for personal, social, or economic reasons. Instead of characterizing cubbyhole gateways as dead-end or surplus jobs, we need to view them as stepping-stones, as potentialities, to growth in self-esteem and as economic motivators in the best and worst sense of the word. Cubbyhole gateways follow Lankshear's and O'Connor's observation that on-the-job training is needed:

> Sociocultural research generally, and investigations of literacy in situ more specifically, strongly support the proposition that we should be integrating literacy work into site-based activity, recruiting and training literacy educators from among people "on the job" and directing more professional development about literacy toward *them*. (35)

Los Puentes reveals that in situ training and learning *already* takes place as cubbyhole gateways. On the one hand, this informal business literacy training has been taking place since the time of the guilds and more recently as Brandt has observed in post World War II, yet Lankshear and O'Connor seem to be calling for a more formalized system to achieve this. I agree with them, with the exception that formally trained educators (teachers) not be excluded in the process. Even with cubbyhole gateways in place, Light found several potential social and economic challenges:

> Digital divide initiatives can help low-income Americans who are segregated in poor neighborhoods gain new job skills. Yet, simultaneously, transportation constraints may not allow them practical access to existing employment opportunities. We have seen early versions of this dilemma already, in difficulties with good-spirited initiatives aimed at encouraging Silicon Valley companies to hire and train more African Americans from Oakland, California. The success of these programs presumes the ownership of a car, an improved public transportation system, or housing prices low enough so people can afford to live relatively close to work. Telecommuting and remote work may mitigate some of these constraints, yet they simultaneously present new forms of segregation. (15)

The findings suggest that while cubbyhole gateways work, that is, in situ training works, the literacy divide in essence is misnamed and ill-conceived, as I suggested earlier. Once again, it appears to be a socio-economic divide above all else. At this point the most we can push for are more *puentes* to create more opportunities for participants, sponsors, and gateways to intermix in the ever-evolving hybrid zones as characterized in the DZSGP Illustration.

Perhaps the most urgent place to focus attention is in the mirror and ask: What can I, teacher-citizen, realistically change today? An important part of the *puentes* mix is teachers. While I would like to suggest significant changes that affect us at the national, state, and local levels, I understand that essential changes at these levels will not happen. We need to think more localized: The person in the mirror. What the sponsor and the gateway data reveal is that we teachers can affect change in potent ways, one participant and one moment at a time. While the impact is not on a grand scale, it is, nevertheless, noteworthy. We are able to effect important life and literacy changes one-by-one that have a generational impact.

However, because teachers appear to have less effect on participants' learning electronic literacies than I had thought, my suggestion is to begin first by paying more attention to teacher electronic pedagogical literacies, and trainings in the classroom. This would begin with an investment in teachers. They would need trainings in developing technologies, software, and regular support, all of which we know are rare. Teachers' actual use and ability, while they have increased, are still quite low. Teachers who have technology should have more influence in software development; this would ensure better content specific software that content teachers could actually use in their electronically enhanced classrooms.

Moreover, we teachers need more and better instruction in critical reflection on the impact that technology has in our lives. This is in line with Selfe's and Hawisher's plea that, "Computer-using teachers instruct students in how to *use* technology—but, all too often, they neglect to teach students how *to pay critical attention* to the issues generated by technology use" ("Technology and Literacy" 20). Nevertheless, I believe their recommendation suggests that teachers *do not* need computer labs, or even technology for that matter. Critical awareness can take place by using traditional classroom pedagogies.

With or without technology rich classrooms, teachers may want to consider what Au looked at: "the point of contact between teachers and young readers and writers. These encounters are viewed as not only points of contact among people whose prior cultural experiences may differ, but as occasions that are cultural in their own right—places of learning and transformation" (Florio-Ruane and McVee 82). Au's advice establishes teachers, students, and location into the pedagogical picture as an important site in and of itself. Our students spend twelve to thirteen years in these settings (not counting college), so as teachers we need to begin treating them as special and magical (our Disneyland of the intellect). We need to make participants' experiences as special and memorable as Disneyland. The big difference, however, is that our gaze is not specific to student or teacher. Instead it is on the place and on the dynamics of the instruction that unfolds. The unfolding becomes a cultural experience when we view technology instruction as an unfolding cultural experience, one energized by generational differences of teachers and students, of the technology available, how it is taught, used, and studied, and how these further modify the cultural experience that is the classroom. By increasing our role as educators of technological literacies, that is, by expanding our direct sponsorship, we increase the impact we have on our students developing literacies and their critical awareness of the impact technology has in their lives. If technology rich classes are not available, students need to understand why, and become educated to the unequal distribution of school funding at the national, state, and local levels.

Last, the twenty-six technology sponsor and gateway results illuminate that participants' "awareness" that gateways are out there was important. The happy scenario is that being aware may lead to discovering a means to access these technological gateways. However, the issue of the digital divide appears again as socioeconomic. In many ways awareness of where technology is located is akin to trying to cross from Mexico to the United States and only separated by a river, the Border Patrol, canals, fences, and documentation. Light argues the technological point of this:

> While reports on the digital divide often mention race or income, they do so in the service of an argument that focuses on access to computers and not on other causes of inequality. Yet rhetorical claims about the social, economic, and educational consequences that follow from access to computing remain broad (Biggers, 2000; Hafner 2000; Henderson, cited in Cha, 1999). (Light 13)

Los Puentes Stories helps us to begin to understand the rhetorical nature of sponsors and participants, based on their specific responses. As I indicated at the start of this chapter, I view the admixture of stories gathered from participants and the presentation of the quantifiable data in the tables and charts as a hybrid approach for this examination of sponsors and gateways, one intended to maintain the closeness of story enveloping a larger number of quantifiable responses.

Notes

1. Participants used Mexican if they were born or lived in Mexico. If they were from El Paso, a few used Mexican-American. The majority used Hispanic. I use Latino/a. Arcelo Suárez-Orozco and Mariela Páez in *Latinos: Remaking America* (2002) argue that they prefer the term because it is "generous" and "*Latino* is a new and ambiguous invention," (3) capturing all sorts of people and cultures. My own reasoning, and I have had too many discussions about this, which means there is no one answer or fixed agreement, for using Latino/a is because the term is *not* ambiguous. I view Latino/a with a root that stands out, Latin. The Spanish language comes primarily from Latin, mixed with Arab, Greek, and other languages as well. Of course, we all know we are speaking of peoples who speak some form of Spanish, or perhaps none, but whose parents or upbringing in some way made them feel Latino/a. This could be in type of music, dress, food, and so on. In this open way Latino/a allows for

racial and ethnic variety in the broadest ways. Speaking from a U.S. perspective, the term also embraces other speakers and cultures with a Latin root, such as Portuguese, French, and Italian. The U.S. Census Bureau uses Hispanic: "1/Hispanic refers to people whose origin are Mexican, Puerto Rican, Cuban, Central or South American, or other Hispanic/ Latino, regardless of race" (U.S. Census Bureau). Gloria Anzaldua wavers between favoring "Chicano/a" in *Borderlands/La Frontera* in the chapter titled "La Conciencia de la Mestiza." Susan Romano, "Tlaltelolco: The Grammatical-Rhetorical *Indios* of Colonial Mexico" points out that "latino" in the New World meant "trilingual proficiency in Latin, Spanish, and at least one vernacular, such as Nahuatl, and which later would qualify the educated Tlaltelolco indio for coauthorship of bi- and tringual catechetical texts" (262).

2. I adapted and revised Selfe's and Hawisher's survey of electronic literacies as a model for my survey.

3. Data and stories for the first part of this research, examining participants born between 1920 and 1985 are reported in *Generaciones*' Narratives: The Pursuit and Practice of Traditional and Electronic Literacies on the U.S.-Mexico Borderlands (forthcoming, Computers and Composition Digital Press, 2009).

4. I use *generación* in Spanish instead of "generation" in English to be consistent with my use in *Generaciones*, where definitions of *generación*/generation derive from the *Oxford English Dictionary* and the *Real Academia Española*.

5. Author's Trans.: I am neither from here, nor there, by singer songwriter Facundo Cabral. Similarly, Puerto Rican poet, Tato Laviera, expresses this:

> Tengo venas aculturadas [Author's Trans.: My veins are adapted]
> escribo en spanglish [Trans: I write in Spanish]
> abraham in español
> abraham in english
> tato in Spanish
> "taro" in English
> Tonto in both languages [Author's Trans.: A fool in both languages]
> —Villanueva, *Bootstraps* 28, from
> Flores et al. 214.

6. For discussions on ecologies see Cooper; Barton; Florio-Ruane and McVee.

7. Elsewhere she similarly describes and further teases out sponsors as, "a concept that I came to call 'sponsors' of literacy. Sponsors are any agents, local or distant, concrete or abstract, who provide, enhance, or deny opportunities for literacy learning and gain advantage by it in some way. Sponsors appeared all over people's memories of how they learned to write and read, in their memories of people, commercial products, public facilities, religious organizations, and other institutional and work settings." (Brandt "Literacy Learning" 4).

8. A twist to Brandt's view is what Hull et al. discovered in their investigation of workplace literacy practice. They discovered that if top-down sponsorship does not consider their employees' social roles and identities, in this case the literacy initiative failed.

9. Discussed in depth in *Generaciones Narratives*.

10. Selfe and Hawisher have similar data from their survey, yet have not compiled it to my knowledge. I would be interested in undertaking such a project to compare some of the regional differences that may exist.

11. Author's Trans: If it wasn't for the fact that my daughters were into technology because of their studies, I would never have learned to use it, since I come from where everything is really old, and the little technology there is very few people can afford it or enjoy it.

12. Author's Trans: Technology has become an essential part of life and it's very important for the new generations to learn. For me, however, I am far away from using it.

13. In Spanish: *Estar de pie* (stand) in order to *entender* (understand).

14. Selfe and Hawisher use Lemke's notion of "patch" to describe this idea, which is similar to what I propose here with the Dynamic Zone of Sponsor-Gateway-Participant. They

write, "In using the term *patch,* we are indebted to the work of Jay L. Lemke.... When we use the term *patch,* we refer to the smaller eco-units of families, peer groups, institutions, professions, etc" ("Becoming Literate" 39). I found this concept useful in characterizing the interactive dynamics of literacy meaning-making, yet I find it wanting in two ways. First, the concept of a patch suggests it is fixing something broken, or literally popped. Second, I see the process as dynamic and evolutionary, illuminating both predictable and unpredictable change caused especially by human intervention; in this sense the DZSGP is more indicative of hybrid unities that are in themselves also undergoing constant changes.

Bibliography

Berthoff, Ann E. "I. A. Richards and the Concept of Literacy." In *The Sense of Learning,* 136–49. Portsmouth: Boynton, 1990.

Bizzell, Patricia. *Academic Discourse and Critical Consciousness.* Pittsburgh: University of Pittsburgh Press, 1992.

———. "Arguing about Literacy." *College English* 50 (1988): 141–53.

Brandt, Deborah. "Accumulating Literacy: Writing and Learning to Write in the Twentieth Century." *College English* 57 (1995): 649–68.

———. "Literacy." In *Encyclopedia of Rhetoric and Composition,* edited by Theresa Enos, 392–94. New York: Garland, 1996.

Brey-Casiano, Carol. "Literacy Problems Affect Every Segment of American Society." *El Paso Times.* January 8, 2006, 7B.

Brodkey, Linda. "On the Subject of Class and Gender in 'The Literacy Letters.'" *College English* 51 (1989): 125–41.

Daniell, Beth. "Against the Great Leap Theory of Literacy." *Pre/Text* 7 (1986): 181–93.

———. "Composing (as) Power." *College Composition Communication* 45 (1994): 238–46.

Donehower, Kim. "The Power of Literacy: How Ordinary People Understand Literacy as a Means for Social Change." CCCC, Phoenix, March 1997.

Feller, Ben. "Less Access to Internet Still Working against Minorities." *El Paso Times.* September 6, 2006, 5A.

Fonce-Olivas, Tammy. "El Pasoans Emphasize 'Reading is Essential.'" *El Paso Times.* September 9, 2006, 3B.

Gere, Anne Ruggles. *Intimate Practices: Literacy and Cultural Work in U.S. Women's Clubs, 1880–1920.* Urbana: University of Illinois Press, 1997.

Goody, Jack. Introduction. In *Literacy in Traditional Societies,* edited by Jack Goody, 1–26. Cambridge: Cambridge University Press, 1968.

Goody, Jack and Ian Watt. "The Consequences of Literacy." *Comparative Studies in Society and History* 5 (1963): 304–45.

Graff, Harvey J. *The Legacies of Literacy: Continuities and Contradictions in Western Culture and Society.* Bloomington: Indiana University Press, 1987.

Hawisher, Gail E. and Cynthia L. Selfe with Brittney Moraski and Melissa Pearson. "Becoming Literate in the Information Age: Cultural Ecologies and the Literacies of Technology." *College Composition and Communication* 55, no. 4 (2004): 642–92.

Heath, Shirley Brice. "Protean Shapes in Literacy Events: Ever-Shifting Oral and Literate Traditions." In *Spoken and Written Language: Exploring Orality and Literacy,* edited by Deborah Tannen, 91–117. Norwood: Ablex, 1982.

Hilton, Terry. "Border Statistics Are Staggering." Letters to the Editor. *El Paso Times.* November 1, 2006, 11B.

Hirsch, E. D., Jr. *Cultural Literacy: What Every American Needs to Know.* Boston: Houghton, 1987.

Holzman, Michael. "A Post-Freirean Model for Adult Literacy Education." *College English* 50 (1988): 177–89.

Killingsworth, Jimmie. "Product and Process, Literacy and Orality: An Essay on Composition and Culture." *College Composition Communication* 44 (1993): 26–39.

Lunsford, Andrea A., Helene Moglen, and James Slevin, eds. *The Right to Literacy.* New York: MLA, 1990.

Mortensen, Peter and Gesa E. Kirsch. *Ethics and Representation in Qualitative Studies of Literacy.* Urbana: NCTE, 1996.

Moss, Beverly J., "Creating a Community: Literacy in African-American Churches." In *Literacy Across Communities,* edited by Beverly J. Moss, 147–78. Creskill: Hampton Press, 1994.

Ong, Walter J., Jr., "Literacy and Orality." *ADE Bulletin* 58 (1978): 1–7.

———. *Orality and Literacy: The Technologizing of the Word.* London: Methuen, 1982.

Radway, Janice A. *Reading the Romance: Women, Patriarchy, and Popular Literature.* Chapel Hill: University of North Carolina Press, 1984.

Resnick, Daniel P., and Lauren B. Resnick. "The Nature of Literacy: An Historical Exploration." *Harvard Educational Review* 47 (1977): 370–85.

Scenters-Zapico, John T. *Generaciones' Narratives: The Pursuit and Practice of Traditional and Electronic Literacies on the U.S.-Mexico Borderlands* (forthcoming, Computers and Composition Digital Press 2009).

Scribner, Sylvia, and Michael Cole. *The Psychology of Literacy.* Cambridge, MA: Harvard University Press, 1981.

Selfe, Cynthia L., and Susan Hilligoss. *Literacy and Computers: The Complications of Teaching and Learning with Technology.* New York: MLA, 1994.

Sreberny-Mohammadi, Annabelle. "Media Integration in the Third World: An Ongian Perspective." In *Media, Consciousness, and Culture,* edited by Bruce E. Gronbeck, Thomas J. Farrell, and Paul A. Soukup, 133–46. Newbury Park: Sage, 1991.

Street, Brian V. *Literacy in Theory and Practice.* New York: Cambridge University Press, 1984.

Stuckey, J. Elspeth. *The Violence of Literacy.* Portsmouth, NH: Boynton/Cook P, 1991.

Swearingen, C. Jan, ed. *The Literacy/Orality Wars.* Special Issue. *Pre/Text* 7 (1986): 115–218.

Tannen, Deborah, ed. *Spoken and Written Language: Exploring Orality and Literacy.* Norwood: Ablex, 1982.

———. *Ways With Words.* New York: Cambridge University Press, 1983.

Taylor, Denny, and Catherine Dorsey-Gaines. *Growing Up Literate: Learning from Inner-City Families.* Portsmouth: Heinemann, 1988.

Villanueva, Victor. *Bootstraps: From an American Academic of Color.* Urbana, IL: NCTE, 1993.

Walters, Keith. "Language, Logic, and Literacy." In *The Right to Literacy,* edited by Andrea A. Lunsford, Helene Moglen, and James Slevin, 173–88. New York: MLA, 1990.

CHAPTER THIRTEEN

Las Cobijas/The Blankets

RAFAEL JESÚS GONZÁLEZ

a Carmen González Prieto de González

Son olas las cobijas que me tejió mi madre;
sus manos las ondean,
manos jóvenes, uñas color, olor, forma de almendras;
manos maduras, fuertes, decisivas;
manos ancianas como arañas ciegas y precisas.
Cuenta y cuenta puntadas el gancho de la aguja,
cuentos de nunca acabar;
parece que crecen las cobijas,
se alargan
y amenazan inundar la casa.
Son una mezcla de sarapes de Saltillo
y tablas huicholas suaves y flexibles
con franjas coloridas anchas y ondulantes.
En sus pliegues y dobleces
parecen desplegarse las leyendas de los soles,
los cuentos de las creaciones,
las historias de los mundos y los dioses.
Son telas, redes de mil colores
para atrapar los sueños como peces
en los mares obscuros de las noches.
Hechizos de mi madre, adivinanzas,
misteriosos criptogramas de sus pensares;

¿Qué penas amenguaban, que temores?
¿Qué sueños, qué recuerdos, qué emociones
guiaban sus dedos veloces y precisos
contando puntadas, produciendo estas mareas
de estambres pavo-reales?
Ya muerta, sus manos quietas bajo tierra,
en mis sueños siguen creciendo las cobijas
y en las noches de invierno
cuando la lluvia gris asota las ventanas,
aun me abriga con arcos iris
mi madre.

The blankets my mother knit for me are waves;
her hands stir them,
young hands, nails the color, smell, shape of almonds;
mature hands, strong & decisive;
old hands like spiders blind & precise.
The hook of the needle counts & counts stitches,
stories without end;
it seems the blankets grow,
stretch,
& threaten to flood the house.
They are a cross between sarapes of Saltillo
& Huichol yarn paintings, pliant & soft
with wide & undulating colored bands.
In their pleats & folds
there seem to unfold the legends of the suns,
the creation stories,
the histories of the worlds & of the gods.
They are weavings, nets of a thousand colors
to trap dreams like fishes
in the dark seas of the nights.
Spells of my mother, riddles,
mysterious cryptograms of her thoughts;
what pains did they comfort, what fears?
What dreams, what memories, what feelings
guided her fingers fast & precise
counting stitches, producing these tides
of peacock yarns?
Now dead, her hands still beneath the earth,

in my dreams the blankets still grow
& in the winter nights
when the gray rain whips the windows,
my mother still covers me
with rainbows.

CONTRIBUTORS

Erika Gisela Abad Merced is a doctoral candidate in American Studies at Washington State University. She is co-editor of Washington State University's Women's Studies Department zine, *Outside the Box.* Her dissertation examines the limitations of Christian-centered Puerto Rican nationalist rhetoric. She is a poet, activist, and scholar, with poems as well as an article appearing in *Dialogo.* She has also published poems on immigration, Puerto Rican community organizing, and Puerto Rican nationalism.

Damián Baca is an assistant professor of English and Mexican American studies at the University of Arizona, where he teaches comparative technologies of writing, American Indian rhetoric, Chicana/o and Latina/o literature, rhetoric in Mesoamerica and colonial México, U.S./Mexico borders, globalization, and ancestral literacy. He is the author of *Mestiz@ Scripts, Digital Migrations, and the Territories of Writing* with Palgrave Macmillan, 2008. His work has also appeared in *College English, Authorship in Composition Studies,* and *Dialogue: A Journal for Writing Specialists.* As a recipient of NCTE's Cultivating New Voices among Scholars of Color Research Foundation and the Ronald E. McNair post-Baccalaureate Achievement Program, Baca is committed to mentoring students of underrepresented populations as they prepare to enter the professoriate.

Tracy Brandenburg is an assistant professor of Spanish at Wells College, New York. Her work has appeared in the *Revista Canadiense de Estudios Hispánicos* and in *Semiotics 2000: Sebeok's Century.* She received the Kevelson Memorial award from the Semiotic Society of America for her article "Rap and the Semiotically Real." She is currently working on *Beyond the Black Palace,* a book that traces the life of the great living Zapotec painter Nicéforo Urbieta from his time as a prisoner during Mexico's dirty war to his return to his village in search of what remains of pre-Hispanic culture. Brandenburg is particularly interested in questions related to writing, especially in the context of pre-Hispanic Mesoamerican cultures that many still consider to have been without writing. The primary subject of her investigation is the contemporary practice of pre-Hispanic writing/painting. She is indebted to her friends and colleagues, the artists and campesinos of Santa Ana de Zegache, Ocotlán, Oaxaca, who first showed her the many ways they continue to write without words.

Rafael Jesús González, Professor Emeritus of Creative Writing and Literature, has studied and taught at numerous institutions, including Universidad Nacional Autónoma de México, University of Texas at El Paso, University of Oregon, Western State College of Colorado, Central Washington State University, and Laney College. His bilingual poetry and scholarly articles are widely published in reviews and anthologies in the United States, Mexico, and abroad. Also a visual artist, his work has been exhibited at the Oakland Museum, the Mexican Museum of San Francisco, and others. He was Poet in Residence at the Oakland Museum of California and the Oakland Public Library under the Poets and Writers "Writers on Site Program" in 1996. In 2002 he received the annual Dragonfly Press Award for Literary Achievement and was honored in 2003 by the National Council of Teachers of English and Annenberg/CPB for his writing.

Laurie Gries is a doctoral candidate in Composition and Cultural Rhetoric at Syracuse University. Her research interests include theories and philosophies of the visual, material rhetoric, rhetorical theory, and historiography. Her dissertation, "Still Live with Rhetoric," forwards a methodology for tracing the circulation of material objects as they move in and out of rhetoricity across time and space. In the classroom, Gries teaches visual research methods to explore the ways in which material and visual rhetorics play an active role in shaping the collectivities in which they circulate.

Dylan A. T. Miner is an assistant professor of Transcultural Studies in the Residential College in the Arts and Humanities at Michigan State University, where he holds appointments in American Indian and Chicano/Latino studies. His recent work has appeared in *Aztlán: The Journal of Chicano Studies, Realizing the Impossible: Art against Authority,* and *Third Text.* His intellectual projects include the cultural expressions of Indigenous and working-class struggle, while his visual production functions as an anticolonial narrative device. He has exhibited work throughout the United States, Canada, Europe, South Africa, and Australia, including the Institute for American Indian Arts, the National Museum of Mexican Art, Native American Rights Fund, La Galería de la Raza, and the Cherokee Heritage Center in Oklahoma. He is currently working on a book analyzing the role of Aztlán in Chicana/o art and visual culture.

Georganne Nordstrom is an assistant professor of English at the University of Hawai'i, Manoa. Her publications include "Embracing the Other: Illusions of Agency." *International Journal of Diversity in Organisations, Communities and Nations* 5.1 (2006), "Mauna Kea: Temple under Siege." Rev. of *Mauna Kea: Temple under Siege*. Dir. Puhipau, Joan Landers *The Contemporary Pacific*. Ed. Vilsoni Hereniko. 18.1 (Spring, 2006): 207–210, "Finding Their Way to the Writing Center: Language Perception of Pidgin Speakers and Non-Native Speakers from Asian Countries" *Proceedings from The Seventh College-Wide Conference for Students in Languages, Linguistics, and Literature* (National Foreign Language Resource Center: Honolulu, 2004) 55–59, "Nainoa Thompson: In Search of History." *Horizons: A Journal of International Writings and Art* (Kapiolani Community College: Honolulu, 1999). Her research examines the literature of Hawai'i as rhetorical action, literacy and ethnography, and writing with new media.

Laura E. Pérez is an associate professor of Ethnic studies, Spanish and Portuguese, and Chicano studies at the University of California, Berkeley. Her teaching and research areas are in contemporary U.S. Latina and Latin American women's writing, Chicana/o literature and visual arts, and contemporary cultural theory. Some of her publications include "Reconfiguring Nation and Identity: U.S. Latin and Latin American Women's Oppositional Writings," "Reflections and Confessions on the 'Minority' and Post-Colonial Immigrant ID Tour," "For Love and Theory: An Ofrenda," and "El desorden, Nationalism, and Chicana/o Aesthetics," and *Chicana Art: The Politics of Spiritual and Aesthetic Altarities* with Duke University Press, 2007.

Rocío Quispe-Agnoli is an associate professor of Spanish and Portuguese, American Indian studies, and Director of the Center for Integrative Studies in the Arts & Humanities at Michigan State University. Her publications include *La fe indígena en la escritura: identidad y resistencia en la obra de Guamán Poma de Ayala* (Fondo Editorial de la Universidad Nacional Mayor de San Marcos 2006), "Más allá del convento/Beyond the Convent Walls: Studies on Colonial Spanish American Women" *Cuadernos de Estudios Humanísticos y Literatura*, Universidad de Puerto Rico-Humacao Vol. 5 (2006), "*Y ancí por la carta nos veremos*: textos coloniales visuales y la construcción de la diferencia" Ed. Stephanie Kirk *Desplazamientos y disyunciones: Nuevos itinerarios de los estudios coloniales* (UAP 2007), "Explorando los espacios peruanos en los años '40: José Ferrando y *Panorama hacia el alba*. Ed. Luis Dapelo. (Fondo Editorial de la Pontificia Universidad Católica del Perú 2007). Her research areas include global indigeneity, postcolonial studies, Latin American and Caribbean studies, colonial Spanish American literature, Spanish, Portuguese, and Quechua.

Cristián Roa de la Carrera is an associate professor of Spanish and Latin American and Latino Studies at the University of Illinois, Chicago. He has focused his research on historical narratives about Spanish imperial expansion and the negotiation of cultural differences within Spanish colonialism. He is the author of *Histories of Infamy: Francisco López de Gómara and the Ethics of Spanish Imperialism* (UP Colorado, 2005), co-curator of the renowned exhibit "The Aztecs and the Making of Colonial Mexico" at the Newberry Library 2006–2007, and co-editor and co-translator of *Chimalpahin's Conquest: A Nahua Historian's Rewriting of Francisco López de Gómara's Conquista de México* with Stanford University Press. In addition, he has published multiple articles in journals such as *Hispanic Review, Revista Chilena de Literatura,* and *Colonial Latin American Review.*

John Scenters-Zapico is an associate professor of Rhetoric and Writing Studies (RWS) at the University of Texas at El Paso, and Co-Director of the Professional Bilingual Writing Certificate. He has published in journals such as *Rhetoric Society Quarterly, Rhetoric Review, American Indian Quarterly,* and *Computers and Composition* (online and hard copy). His electronic book, *Generaciones' Narratives: The Pursuit and Practice of Traditional and Electronic Literacies on the U.S.-Mexico Borderlands,* is forthcoming with Computers and Composition Digital Press, 2009.

Victor Villanueva is Regents Professor of English at Washington State University. He is the recipient of numerous awards, including the Edward R. Meyer Distinguished Professorship in Liberal Arts, "Rhetorician of the Year" for 1999, the 1995 NCTE David H. Russell Award for Distinguished Research and Scholarship in English, and the Richard A. Meade Award for Distinguished Research in English Education. He is editor of *Cross-Talk in Comp Theory: A Reader* (in its second edition), and co-editor of *Latino/a Discourses* (2004), *Language Diversity in the Classroom* (2003), and *Included in English Studies* (2002). He has other books, articles, book chapters, and reviews, many of which have been anthologized, and he has delivered more than 100 speeches in campuses and other venues throughout the nation.

INDEX

CPSIA information can be obtained at www.ICGtesting.com
Printed in the USA
LVOW11*1802210715

447067LV00005B/40/P

9 780230 619036